thick as
thieves

thick as thieves

A BROTHER, A SISTER—
A TRUE STORY OF TWO TURBULENT LIVES

Steve Geng

Henry Holt and Company
New York

Henry Holt and Company, LLC
Publishers since 1866
175 Fifth Avenue
New York, New York 10010
www.henryholt.com

Henry Holt® and 🏛® are registered trademarks of
Henry Holt and Company, LLC.

The excerpt from "The Current Cinema" by Veronica Geng
is reprinted by permission of the *New York Review of Books.*

Lines from "Mistah Kurtz—He Dead" by Veronica Geng, originally published
in the *New Yorker,* reprinted with permission of the Wylie Agency, New York.

Sections from "Talk of the Town PAAF" by Veronica Geng, originally published
in the *New Yorker,* reprinted with permission of the Wylie Agency, New York.
Courtesy of Conde Nast Publications.

Excerpts from *Love Trouble: New and Collected Work* by Veronica Geng,
copyright © 1999 by the Estate of Veronica Geng, are reprinted
by permission of the Houghton Mifflin Company. All rights reserved.

Distributed in Canada by H. B. Fenn and Company Ltd.

Library of Congress Cataloging-in-Publication Data

Geng, Steve
 Thick as thieves : a brother, a sister—a true story of two turbulent lives / Steve Geng.—1st ed.
 p. cm.
 ISBN-13: 978-0-8050-8056-8
 ISBN-10: 0-8050-8056-2
 1. Geng, Steve.   2. Geng, Veronica.   3. Brothers and sisters—New York (State)—New
York—Biography.   4. Thieves—New York (State)—New York—Biography.   5. Drug
addicts—New York (State)—New York—Biography.   6. Authors, American—New York
(State)—New York—Biography.   7. New York (N.Y.)—Biography.   I. Title.
 CT275.G356A3 2007
 974.7'043092—dc22
 [B]   2006047173

First Edition 2007

Designed by Meryl Sussman Levavi

Printed in the United States of America
1 2 3 4 5 6 7 8 9 10

A certain man went down from Jerusalem to Jericho, and fell among thieves, which stripped him of his raiment, and wounded him, and departed, leaving him half dead.

—LUKE 10:30

thick as thieves

Prologue
The Big Rift

One of these days that kid's gonna get his tit in a wringer. It was the voice of an old, familiar ghost, and it spoke to me as I stumbled through waist-high drifts in the blizzard of '96. According to newscasters, this was the worst snowstorm to hit New York in decades. Parked cars on Tenth Avenue were visible only as little bumps on the white, silent landscape. And still it came down, big wind-whipped flakes that nipped my cheeks and scrambled my senses. I wasn't exactly homeless, but some instinct had been driving me through the streets, hunched into the storm. There was little refuge back where I'd come from.

Kid's gonna get his tit in a wringer.

The ghost, of course, was my father. He'd loved that expression, and I could still picture the baleful look in his eye as he snapped it at my mother whenever I pissed him off. Dad had been a career army guy with a hard-knocks take on life and a sideways rap on everybody, especially his kids. My sister and I rarely took anything he said seriously. I'd even enjoyed his rants, anticipating him like I did the guy on *The Honeymooners* with his zoom-right-to-the-moon routine.

Suddenly a sign loomed up out of the whiteness: EMERGENCY ROOM.

Don't know why I hadn't thought of it weeks ago. I stepped into St. Luke's-Roosevelt Hospital, glad for a timely reprieve.

In the warm ER waiting room I found a place to sit down and a dog-eared copy of yesterday's *Daily News*. The pain in my thawing hands suggested frostbite and my wheezing was probably a bad case of pneumonia. There was an unexplained gash on my forehead and my face was cross-hatched with shaving nicks that refused to heal. I looked like I'd been in a street brawl. Booze and drugs, once my greatest comforts, had been sending me into seizures, and I couldn't remember the last time I'd eaten a meal.

Don't get me wrong. I'm not the type to sit around and boohoo. It was a damned good run I'd had at life on the edge. I'd savored my legit days as an actor with the same relish I'd got from a good score, or singing in a jailhouse doo-wop group. But as the bookies say, I'd lost my good looks. Lady Luck had jumped ship many moons ago.

After an hour or so (I was in no hurry) a nurse came by with a clipboard and asked me what the trouble was. The butts in the ashtray were just starting to look good when she came back and told me I was getting admitted. They put me in a ninth-floor room with a view of the snow-laden ramparts of John Jay College. Laid out on a bed of crispy-fresh linen were clean pajamas and one of those little robes that go on ass-backward. In the bathroom were brand-new toilet articles wrapped in sterile plastic. Food was delivered right to my bedside! I mumbled my thanks to Jesus, Mary, and Rudy Giuliani and passed out.

It might've been hours or days later, as I drifted in and out of consciousness, when a doctor in a white coat and necktie came in followed by two female backups. His eyes were riveted on a clipboard.

"So what's the skinny, Doc?"

"Mr. *Gang*?"

"Geng, as in Genghis Khan."

"Chinese?"

"Alsatian."

The two backups started fidgeting and the doctor scribbled something on his clipboard: *responses vague, evasive.* I couldn't actually *see* what he was writing, but a certain number of institutional interviews will sensitize your radar.

"According to the tests, Mr. Geng, you've developed thrombocytopenia. What that means is that you have practically no platelets."

"Christ, what the hell are those?"

"Platelets," he said, "are cells that make your blood clot. Your body's inability to produce them explains why those cuts on your face won't heal. You also have chronic pneumonia, are severely dehydrated and malnourished, so you'll have to remain here until we . . ."

He rambled on, but I stopped listening after I heard *you'll have to remain here.* Fine with me—anything to put off the rumble with Jack Frost. Just before the doctor and his flunkies filed out he asked, "Do you have any family that you'd like me to notify?"

Mom and Dad were long gone, and Ronnie had been having her own troubles since losing her job at the *New Yorker*. She was always supportive whenever I cleaned up and went legit, but seeing me once again in dubious condition was the last thing she needed. "I got a sister. I'll call her myself, later."

"Give me her name and number anyway. Standard procedure."

After they were gone I lay there for hours, staring out at snow flurries blowing off rooftops. Finally I made the call, got my sister's answering machine, and left a message about being in the hospital with some kind of a thrombo thing. Feeling suddenly expansive, I placed another call to my main gazain Smitty, told him to bring me some smokes and a little taste on the down low.

Next day they arrived almost simultaneously, Veronica hard on the heels of Smitty, who wasn't the sort you want to introduce your sister to. Smitty had done a bid in Sing Sing for a homicide when he was still in his teens, or as he put it, he'd "gone upstate with a body." He and I had blundered into the middle of a gang fight once and I saw him shank a guy—stuck homeboy in the chest and strolled off cool as you please. Smitty had a little sailor's roll when he walked, and when he blew into my room that day in an army field jacket and his perpetual jailhouse fade, I was delighted to see him.

"Smitty."

"Hey, cuz."

"You straight?"

He patted the cargo pocket on his field jacket, sat down, and immediately began helping himself to my lunch.

Before I had a chance to see what Smitty had brought I looked up and there was my sister, wearing an old tweed topcoat I gave her once when I was flush. She was standing in the doorway, her brown hair limp from the snow, reluctant to cross the threshold. I looked for that jaunty smile of hers, but her delicate features were etched with deep worry lines, and her chin was tucked into the turned-up coat collar.

Ron's reaction to sickness and tragedy had always been unpredictable, so bedside manner was not her strong point. Still, she was my big sis, and though her literary life was mostly a mystery to me, I'd always found in her eyes the same girl who'd watched over me since the cradle. Her face never seemed to age at all; beneath the surface there was a tug-of-war going on, ever since we were kids, that gave her features an air of gleeful devilishness. At that moment, though, she looked more frail and downhearted than I'd ever seen her. Her face was drawn with exhaustion, and her expression hardened as she took in Smitty.

"Ronnie, jeez. My friend here showed up two minutes before you did."

Smitty had commandeered the only chair, but with something strangely approaching chivalry he stood up, cheeks bulging with my macaroni and cheese, and offered the seat to my sister.

Veronica nodded icily, waving off the chair. "Thanks," she said, "but I really can't stay. I just popped by to see if you're alright." There was a terrible weariness in her voice.

"I'm fine, Ron. Really. They got great doctors." Suddenly I wanted to cheer *her* up. "I should be outta here in a couple days. But it's great to see you. Nobody ever comes to visit in here."

Ronnie raised her eyebrows and tilted her head to indicate Smitty, standing over my lunch tray, reeking of booze and examining a plastic bowl of Jell-O with unfeigned interest. Our eyes met for a moment and her expression seemed to say, *Well, you chose your life so don't blame me.* And then her gaze drifted away.

I'd seen that faraway look a million times—a wry half smile with her eyes focused on some remote, inner landscape. It was her knee-jerk reaction to pointless anecdotes, belligerent fathers, and the harebrained dilemmas of her younger brother. That distant, dreamy look of hers brought uncomfortable discussions to screeching halts, signaling her retreat into a private place where it was safe, and probably lonely too.

I fumbled for my robe on the back of the chair and knocked over the IV drip. When I finally got it straightened out I looked back up and Ronnie was gone.

"That's a cryin' shame," said Smitty, wagging his head philosophically.

"Sis just rounded on you like a jailhouse con. By the way, cuz, you want this Jell-O or what?"

I should've told Smitty to scram when Ronnie showed up. Maybe there was something she was hiding that she might have confided if he hadn't been there. Later, that scene kept looping through my head. I couldn't believe I'd sat there and let her walk out on me, my sister, perhaps the only person in the universe I really cared about.

You have to understand: Ronnie and I had survived growing up together as army brats, with friends and schools left in the lurch each time we moved to a new locale. Mundane questions like, "Where are you from?" tripped us up, sent our minds reeling back through army bases and foreign cities glimpsed only briefly as our father's military career shuttled us about the globe like gypsies. It was a blessing and a curse growing up that way, but it forged a bond between us that I'd always deemed unbreakable, no matter how divergent our lives became.

She was my hero, full of endearing contradictions—so fragile that she seemed to go through life teetering on the brink of tears, yet she remained the most resourceful and self-reliant person I'd ever known. I watched her go from playing fag hag at The Hip Bagel and the Bleecker St. Tavern, to writing stories for every rag from *Ms.* and *Cosmo* to the *New Republic*, until she finally found a home in the fiction department of the *New Yorker*. I saw her get her heart broken in one ill-advised romance after another, then recycle them into funny stories and become one of the best humorists and editors of her day.

She, in turn, saw me get flattened by an endless string of calamities, starting with my first broken arm (at age seven) right up through the time some girlfriend slipped a Mickey into my coffee and torched me with lighter fluid. I had such a penchant for trouble that at one point my parents told me I wasn't welcome in their home anymore. But my sister remained a steady beacon, showing me where the real world was whenever I drifted too far astray. All our lives we drove each other into fits of laughter with our takes on people and the universe around us.

But after all those years of Ron and me against the world, I'd begun to take her for granted. When push came to shove, for the umpteenth time, I turned my head for an instant and bam—she rounded on me. It's not like I'd meant to betray her. It's just the way the deal went down. Shortly after that visit to St. Luke's, she cut off all communication with me.

From the hospital I moved into a residence in Chelsea that provided subsidized housing for people on disability. Six months went by and no Ronnie. She wouldn't answer my calls, letters, or pick up the phone.

One day I went over and rang her doorbell for five minutes. When nobody answered I sat on the stoop next door for hours hoping to catch sight of her. Probably a good thing I missed her, though. I looked like hell and was still holding on to the booze and drugs. Lurking outside those elegant brownstones on the Upper East Side I felt like an alien. The neighbors were giving me nervous looks, and when a cop strolled up I decided it was time to split.

She must be alright, I told myself, or I would've heard *some*thing.

Six months turned into nine, then a year. Sometimes I called her number just to hear her voice on her answering machine, but I soon gave that up. Hearing her message over and over hurt too much. I searched my room for phone numbers of people she was close to, tried 411 but couldn't remember last names or spellings and had ended up barking curses into the phone. Many of her friends were famous writers and critics. Not only was I baffled about how to get in touch with those people, but I dreaded the idea of approaching them. What would I say—that my sister wouldn't return my calls? She'd worked at the *New Yorker* for almost twenty years. When she lost her job it seemed like she'd lost her family, her friends, and her only home. In the end I figured she was overwhelmed by her own problems and just couldn't deal with mine anymore. I certainly had other distractions as my health continued to plummet.

Before I knew it, it was Christmas Eve 1997, a year and several months after the hospital. I found myself slumped in an armchair in the common room of the residence, absentmindedly watching a rerun of a football game. Next to the television was an artificial tree with lights, tinsel, and Christmas balls sprayed with frosting. I had five bucks for cigarettes, and in five days my disability check would arrive. I was grateful for these amenities. Far as I knew, there weren't any good retirement plans for thieves.

The holidays always made me think of my family, and images of them flickered at the edge of my peripheral vision. . . . Dad in his favorite armchair, hair slicked back with Vitalis, complaining about the goddamned commies taking over the unions . . . Mom doggedly going about her household chores with a cigarette stuck in her jowly face. My sister once quipped that she looked like a Raymond Chandler character on the way to a homicide. A happy moment with Veronica came into focus. As the muted play-by-play from the football game faded into the background, my sister's face and voice came to the fore.

"Hey, Steve," Ronnie said as I opened the door to her apartment. "C'mon in. You came at just the right time."

It must've been somewhere around 1991, during my thespian days, and we were very close. I flopped down on her studio couch and studied her. Ronnie was two years older than me, but she kept getting better looking with age. Her brown hair had a touch of gray that softened her intensity and a few enduring freckles fell across the bridge of her nose.

"Can I get you an orange juice or something?" She knew I'd stopped drinking then and was totally supportive—the whole planet was supportive of that decision.

"Listen," she said, "I need your help with a bit of dialogue for this story, okay?"

My sister had built a career for herself not only as a writer but also as a brilliant editor—guys like Philip Roth faithfully sought her advice—and I remembered how flattered I always felt when she asked for my help. Every bit of wall space in her apartment was covered with shelves crammed full of books, her coffee table stacked with magazines and journals, testaments to the one true passion in her life—writing. People didn't always work out, but a sentence you could usually get straight.

She came out of the kitchen, handed me a jelly glass full of orange juice, and made a beeline for a pack of True Blues next to her typewriter.

"Okay," she said, "here's the deal. This guy is conducting an orchestra, see, and I need an expression, just a sentence or something that somebody says that is totally inappropriate."

Her face screwed up in concentration as she lit a cigarette, but the amusement in her eyes gave her away. Her proposal was typically illogical since she didn't specify *who* makes the remark. But I knew her only too well. It was a MacGuffin, and she wanted an equally illogical response.

"Alright," I said. "How 'bout this. Remember when Jake is the emcee in a sleazy strip club?" It was our favorite movie, *Raging Bull*, with De Niro. "He turns to the half-drunk, deadbeat hecklers in the audience and he goes, 'Yez sound like a buncha junkies inna pay toilet.' "

Ronnie choked on her cigarette and almost fell out of her chair. "God, I don't believe it. That is absolutely divine."

I remembered the rush of pleasure, hers and mine.

The uncomfortable feeling of being scrutinized snapped me out of the daydream, and when I opened my eyes I noticed that a few other residents had drifted into the TV room—a guy in a Triple Fat Goose snorkel jacket and a famished-looking woman in a housecoat and bunny slippers. I wondered how long they'd been watching me, and I turned my head away when I realized that tears were running down my face.

"Hey, Steve," said Bunny Slippers. "My carfare check got held up in the mail 'cause, you know, the holidays and all? Let me get two dollars till the mailman shows, okay poppy?"

"What do I look like, Santa Claus over here?"

"Yo, Steve," said Goose. "These peoples got me stressed out up in here."

I pulled a quarter out of my pocket and handed it to him.

"What's this for?"

"So's you can call somebody who gives a shit."

They both laughed. We were all bone tired and running on empty but felt lucky to be inside on a cold night. Bunny Slippers's remark about the mailman reminded me that I hadn't checked my box for days, maybe a week. Trouble always arrived via the postal system—bills, bounced checks, bench warrants, threats from collection agencies, letters from the hospital. But then, there might be a Christmas card or a letter from my sister, or a reply from one of her friends I'd written to for news about her—the Denbys, the Schjeldahls. But Ron wasn't writing and her friends lived in another world. Looking for mail from them was a chump move.

I forked over a couple of crumpled bills to the woman, knowing damn well what she needed it for but hoping to buy myself a little more privacy. Sure enough, she sent Goose out to the deli for a forty-ounce Bud and retreated to her room. I shut my eyes and tried to crawl back into the memory of my sister, longing to hear her voice, or to see her face light up when she spotted me on the street. But the connection was broken.

Anger abruptly swept aside the wistfulness as I recalled her pal James Hamilton's glib remarks when I'd called him several months before. "No, I haven't seen Veronica around for a while. I'm not sure what she's up to, but, sure, I'll tell her you're looking for her if I see her."

She never got in touch, nor did he. I admit, I was jealous of her friends and never liked Hamilton, a photographer for the *Village Voice* and her intermittent boyfriend for years. But what possible reason could he have for lying to me?

Famished for details about her, I tried to remember the stories she'd written. A line from one of my favorites, "My Mao," came to mind: *The Chairman despised loose talk. Each time we parted, he would seal my lips together with spirit gum and whisper, "Mum for Mao."* It was one of the pieces in her first book, *Partners,* and I smiled as I recalled the dedication page:

To my brother, Steve.

Ron never told me, when that book came out, that she'd dedicated it to me and I'd almost forgotten. But there it was, unshakable proof in black-and-white—she loved me. She hadn't dedicated the book to her famous editor in chief, William Shawn, whom she'd adored, or to her editor, Roger Angell, or to any of her writer friends like Philip Roth or Ian Frazier. She'd dedicated it to me, her little brother. Knowing her disdain for sentiment, the fact that she hadn't told me about it seemed to make it that much more personal and true.

And so the night before Christmas slipped away, the lights winked unnoticed on the tree, and no one came by to bother me for hours, a lifetime when you got one foot in the grave and the other on a banana peel.

Where did you go, Ron, with your dreamy little smile?

part one
philly

chapter 1

Winter in Philadelphia, 1946. I climbed out of bed, tiptoed across the bare wooden floor, and stood by the door to my sister's room. I was three and she was six.

"Sssst. Hey, Ron."

The inner door connecting our bedrooms was sealed shut, but moonlight exposed a knothole in the panel. I pressed my ear against it, tapped code with a knuckle—*shave and a haircut*—and waited for the two-bits response. No dice.

"Ronnie. You awake?"

The radiator hissed and clunked. I got down on my hands and knees and whispered under the crack at the bottom.

"Hey, Ron?"

"Shhhh." Bedclothes rustled and footsteps padded lightly on the floorboards.

I slipped on my Buster Browns, crept silently out of my room, and crouched by her door that opened onto the second-story hallway, right at the top of the stairs.

It was a two-story row house in a neighborhood called Olney. We'd moved there from an army base in Virginia when Dad got himself transferred to the Navy Yard in South Philly. The house next door, occupied by a grim, elderly German couple named Eisman, smelled like beef gravy, pipe tobacco, and something unidentifiable that raised my hackles and made me shy away from their front door. When I once queried Ronnie about the odor, she'd sniffed, smiled, and said, "Mustard gas."

World War II had drawn to a dramatic close but nobody took the time to explain that to us. My sister and I continued on with our own patrols and missions.

Veronica opened her door and stepped out into the hallway. Her freckled face was a mask of grave seriousness, her pigtails stuck out at right angles like antennae, and her eyes radiated wariness as she surveyed the terrain. She was two and half years older than me, but without my tenacity this mission wouldn't get past the top step.

"Take your shoes off," she whispered. "They'll hear us."

"The floor's cold."

"Shhhhh."

That stairway was steep and treacherous, with white struts supporting a shaky mahogany banister on one side. I usually flew up two at a time to show off my agility, or trudged up sullenly under the lash of punishment: *Go to your room!* Veronica ascended and descended each and every time with the careful deliberation and poise of a Hollywood diva—eager or troubled, she could always climb the hell out of a flight of stairs.

Night missions called for stealth, so we caterpillared down, butts inching slowly to catch up with feet on the next step. Leaning forward and peeking through the banister struts, we had a great view of the couch on the far side of the living room where our parents sat smoking, talking, or listening to the news or Jack Benny on the radio—*Oh, Raaaaaachester! Yowza, Mistah Benny.* Sounds of studio applause and canned laughter crackled like static.

Charles Emil Geng, or Charlie as Mom always called him, sat at one end of the couch with his khaki shirt open, his belt unnotched, and the waistband on his gabardine army trousers unbuttoned for comfort. His nose, ears, and belly were slightly too big for the rest of him, and his dark gray hair was always slicked back with hair oil. As an officer he maintained an erect, military posture, but at five foot five he looked more like a tailor than a soldier.

Mom, née Rosina Butter (pronounced *Boo*-ter after her Austrian father), sat at the other end of the couch with her feet propped up on a has-
sock, massaging her insteps through her stockings. Rosina had once been
a looker. Her early portrait photos captured the dark, flashing eyes of a
born romantic, but by the time we moved to Philly in 1946 her skin had
lost some luster and she'd gotten a bit thick in the hips.

My ideas of romance were hazy then, but there sure wasn't anything
sexy or even affectionate happening on that couch—just two middle-aged
hooples rubbing their feet and airing out their paunches after dinner and
a hard day's work. Mom took out the comb that held her hair up and let
the dark, auburn folds fall down the back of her housedress, signaling the
end of another long day.

"Christ," Dad mumbled as he flipped through the bills, "we're all
gonna end up in the poorhouse."

He'd been in his midforties when Ronnie and I were born, a bit late
to have kids, and when World War II started he'd been too old to ship out
and leave his family. War babies by default, Ron arrived eleven months
before Pearl Harbor and I showed up eleven months before D-day, just in
time for wartime rationing, and thus marking the origin of Dad's all-time
favorite expression, "Christ, I haven't seen one of those since forty-
three."

As we hunkered on the stairs I nudged her with my elbow—So, *now*
what? She flashed me the sign for silence.

The radio said, *Use Ajax, bum-bum, the foaming cleanser, bubba-
bubba-bum-bum-bum* . . .

Ronnie eavesdropped with a wide-eyed, rabid intensity, her nose
twitching with curiosity, but I just got antsy sitting there. Once the initial
thrill of daring passed, spying on Mom and Dad was about as riveting as
watching paint dry. But I loved mimicking the radio jingles. "Wash the
dirrrrt right down the drain . . ."

"Be quiet!"

". . . bubba-bubba-bubba-bum."

Dad lurched up off the couch and glared at us. "What the hell are you
two doing up there? Christ, it's the middle of the goddamned night. Now
go to bed, the pair a yez!"

Sometimes I'd leave Ron sitting there, retreat to the top of the
stairs, and hide in the hallway shadows. Then I'd spring out as she

reached for the door to her little sanctuary. I had what my mother called a rubber face, and at times like this I twisted it into horrible contortions.

"Raaahhhgg!"

Ronnie would have an instant of terror, yank her door open, and slam it in my face—but not before she shot me a withering look of betrayal. I had no idea why I loved to devil her like that. She was my goombah, my ace boon coon, my main piece o' change.

"Hey, Ron. You okay in there?"

Silence.

"C'mon, Ron. I was only kiddin' around."

Her silences were huge. She looked so fragile at times that it seemed like a harsh word would shatter her into pieces.

Our house was a drafty affair with red clay roof tiles, creaky wooden floors, and a musty, spiderwebbed cellar full of Dad's arcane military junk. After living on army bases in the south, it was the closest thing to a real home I'd known (and, as it turned out, would ever know). On holidays, when the place filled with noise, company, and smoke, my parents occasionally sequestered me in a playpen, out of the way of guests trudging from the front door to the kitchen, while my older sister was allowed to traipse around like a big shot. It seemed monstrously unfair, and I harbored vengeful fantasies as relatives and neighbors passed by, men in uniform smelling of Bay Rum and women with spiky brooches, goofy flapper hats, and glistening lipstick. Leaning over, they pinched my cheeks and blew boozy kisses while I studied the world through the wooden bars.

As I got bolder I started prowling in our parents' bedroom, stealing coins and rubbers out of Dad's dresser. Sometimes I'd sneak Mom's fur coat, rich with the aroma of perfume and mothballs, out of the closet to curl up on. But there was something sacrosanct about my sister's room, and she lorded over it with protective secrecy. I'd knock on her door and peek inside.

"Hey, Ron. Can I come in?"

"No." She started to shut the door but I stuck my foot in the jamb.

"I'm coming in there."

"Mom! Steve won't let me close my door!"

"Alright now. Leave your sister alone."

What the hell was she doing in there? Piqued, I'd sneak in whenever the opportunity presented itself, and as time went by I saw the posters on her walls go from Brer Rabbit to characters like Elvis and James Dean. Later, back in my own room, I'd hear her whining. "Mother, somebody's been in my room messing with my things."

I hunkered behind my door, snickering. She couldn't prove jack. What did she expect Mom to do—dust for prints?

In my room I had a window with an angled view of the rosebushes and wrought-iron fence that separated our backyard from that of the neighbors. A complicated electrical junction hung between the houses, right above my lookout, and I'd stare out enchanted as robins and crows perched there to rest, preening their feathers and defying the deadly voltage that coursed under their claws. A bird would catch me looking, cock its head, and glare back with a fierce eye, transfixing me like small prey.

I spent hours scanning the alley that ran behind our house where huge holes in the concrete stayed filled with water after it rained and old men with pushcarts navigated around the muddy pools. One guy sold blocks of ice stacked under a canvas tarp. Another guy had a grinding wheel to sharpen our mother's scissors and kitchen knives. It was a shady universe out there and it beckoned with the promise of adventure. Boys pitched pennies and puffed cigarettes in the shadows behind the drugstore. Stray dogs rooted in garbage cans. Across the alley a tall hedge hid the backyard of a boy who was crazy. Down the block the alleyway disappeared from sight, but I could still pick out the top branches of a weeping willow tree where Dickie Downs shot sparrows with his BB gun.

At night the moon shone through my window, sometimes with a glare so near and bright I felt I could reach out and touch it, and at other times with a remote, milky face whose expression changed from dour to benevolent with distant, passing clouds. I loved the moon. My favorite childhood poem was "The Owl and the Pussycat." When Mom read that to me I was overjoyed as they sailed off with a stash of money and plenty of honey and "danced by the light of the moon, the moon . . ."

I had no idea what Ronnie thought about as she lay in her own bed and observed the same landscape. She had a bookshelf full of books, something our parents never thought to install in my quarters. Our rooms were lonely places and my imagination filled in the mystery of my sister's private moments—maybe reading her favorite book, *Alice in Wonderland*, studying the encyclopedia, or shooting telepathic signals to Brer Rabbit and Elvis.

On moonless nights, shut in my room in a house where nobody communicated much, misty, insubstantial things lurked in the gloom. Once I woke and saw a birdlike creature watching me from behind the radiator, standing dead still, its talons disappearing into the floorboards, sharp beaked and radiating menace in its every aspect. Thinking that a hawk or some other predatory bird had flown in through my open window, a thrill of delight ran up my spine, but when I got up and turned the light on there was nothing, not even a dust bunny.

Morning daylight chased the shadows, and when we came downstairs, Ron and I usually scarfed our porridge at the big cherry-finished wooden table in the dining room. Dad didn't eat breakfast with us on weekdays. It was a long commute by streetcar and subway to the Navy Yard in South Philly, so he was up and out very early, dressed in his green gabardine or summer khaki uniform. We never saw him leave or kiss Mom good-bye, if they even did such a thing.

One morning I was sitting at the dining room table with Ron. In front of us were steaming bowls of oatmeal seasoned with cinnamon, butter, and Pet evaporated milk. She'd just started elementary school and was so self-conscious about a missing front tooth that she'd stopped smiling altogether. I only got to see the gap if I could make her laugh. Ron's eyes darted around, and when she was sure Mom was busy in the kitchen, she rubbed her hands in her hair and whispered, "Hey, Stevie. Shampoo!"

I was no dummy. I scooped up handfuls of porridge and plopped them on my head, gobs of oatmeal running down my neck and forehead as I basked in warm, gooey shampoo thoughts. Ron pinched her nose to cut off her laughter, exposing the space in her teeth, and ducked under the table. Mom came in, yanked me out of the chair, and jammed my head under the kitchen faucet, but the scolding was a small price to pay for such a wealth of my sister's laughter. I've been told that my own smile and laugh were as infectious as my sister's, but I gave them away cheap, exuding an ingratiating charm in the never-ending struggle for sympathy and attention. Ron was much more illusive. Relatives and neighbors would go to absurd contortions to make her laugh. She knew something that we didn't, and if we could just get her to laugh, then maybe she'd clue us in, allow us to draw a little closer.

But to me, her laugh was the clearest manifestation of love, and I learned early how to get it. When the struggles of childhood seemed too frustrating, too difficult to endure, I'd just seek out my sister and dump a consecrated bowl of oatmeal on my head.

Dad, though, didn't buy into Ron's mirth. "She looks like a good meal of corned beef and cabbage would put her on her feet."

"Look at this kid, she turns sideways, you can't even see her."

"Listen to miss hoity-toity over there. She can't even tell you what time the balloon goes up."

Ronnie'd get dressed up for Easter Sunday and Dad would point at her new shoes and say, "Christ, you could land a plane on those skis."

If Mom said to stop picking on her, he'd retort, "Aw, I'm only kiddin' around." But his "kidding around" would reduce Ron to tears and she'd run to her room and slam the door shut, *bam!*

If he did make Ron laugh, she was laughing at him, not with him. He didn't care. He'd walk down the street with us and all of a sudden he'd fart real loud—*bbrraaaaap!* Then he'd look all around and go, "What— who the hell said that? Did somebody say something?"

Chick, as he was called in his youth, liked to say that he "came up the hard way." He ran away from a poor home in Providence, Rhode Island, at fifteen, lied about his age to join the navy, and then sailed around the Philippines on a mine destroyer during World War I. Sometime later as World War II approached, he went to work in the army reserves. He'd grown up in a time when children were seen and not heard, and his reply to any request from Ron and me usually began with "Awferchris-sakes . . ." or was met with a peremptory, "No!"

"Hey, Dad. Can we go bowling?"

"Christ, do you kids have any idea how heavy a goddamn bowling ball is? Look at yez. You're lucky you can lift a piece a toast."

One day we were headed out to the backyard with a ball and some gloves and Dad said, "*Now* what the hell're you two up to? You can't play ball out there. You're both gonna get your ass in a sling."

"I'm only gonna show Ronnie how to pitch."

"Oh, *you're* gonna show Ronnie, huh? *You're* gonna . . . ? Jesus Christ, what the hell do *you* know about baseball?"

Dad followed us out to the backyard, sat on the wooden steps by the back door, and commented on Ron's progress.

"Christ, that kid couldn't hit the backside of a barn if her life depended on it."

"C'mon, Ron. Don't listen to Daddy. Pitch it in there."

"I don't know, Steve. Maybe we should forget it."

"Just relax and let it rip, Ron. You had some zip on that last one."

I was highly invested in getting my sister to throw like a boy, which may have been as unnerving to her as Dad's relentless nagging. Ron reared back and heaved the ball, which sailed over into the Eismans' yard.

"Ho-ho!" Dad bleated triumphantly. "Now what're you gonna use for a baseball? I don't know why you kids can't listen to reason."

"Don't worry, Ron. I saw where it went."

"Not so fast, bub," Dad snapped. "You climb in there you'll really get your tit in a wringer."

Ron burst into tears and ran into the house.

My sister once confessed to me a theory that, since there was *no way* we could be our father's children, we must be the offspring of our mother's first marriage. (Rosina had been briefly married to a man named Pitman who died of tuberculosis shortly afterward.) Ron had an old photograph that she enjoyed showing me in support of this theory. The photo showed our mother and a dashing young man, both dressed very fashionably, sitting in a Stutz Bearcat convertible on some scenic mountain road. Mom looks like a twenties flapper in the shot.

"Yeah," I said to her, "but don't our birth certificates say we were born to Charles and Rosina Geng?" Ron just got this look on her face and shrugged her shoulders in such a way that I immediately thought, *Birth certificates can be forged!*

The only evidence I ever saw that gave weight to Ron's suspicions came one Saturday afternoon when Mom and Dad took us to meet our godfather, Daddy Pitman, the father of Mom's first husband.

Pitman lived in a stately old hotel downtown. After sitting around in beautiful leather armchairs in the lobby, while Mom fidgeted at the desk and Dad took the bellhop through his routine of flashing his ID cards, a tall, elderly gentleman in an elegant three-piece suit and a camel's hair topcoat came down the wide marble staircase. He stepped with a dashing style reminiscent of those older leading men like David Niven and Fred Astaire. Ronnie was riveted, unable to speak, and I couldn't help but notice the striking resemblance in their brown eyes and chiseled noses. I can't remember if he actually spoke to us, or shook our hands and kissed us, or gave us his blessing. I remember only a sense of sadness that came over him as he stood there looking at Ronnie and me.

In the taxi on the way home my sister burst into tears, like Little Orphan Annie snatched out of the arms of Daddy Warbucks. Meanwhile Dad was sitting up front flashing his ID cards and trying to ingratiate himself with the cabby. No wonder my sister cherished the image of a Gatsby sort of lifestyle, just on the other side of the Looking Glass. It was a vision she would pursue with every fiber of her being throughout the rest of her days.

I took Ron's antagonism toward Dad with a grain of salt. He did have a good strong nose, which I inherited, and his ears stuck out from his head in the exact way that Sinatra's did as a young crooner. I loved the cavalier look of his gabardine uniform and saucer hat, his old leather briefcase, and the aroma of Vitalis and cigarette smoke wafting off him when he'd come striding through the front door after work. He could move around a dance floor (*Lay down some iron* as he called it) with a certain grace and I suppose there was a romantic appeal to a guy who had traveled around the world in the navy. In spite of his foibles I craved his love and approval, often standing by the sink in the morning to watch him shave.

"Hey, Dad, when can I start shaving?"

"Tuesday."

Dad would snap that at us when he didn't want to be bothered, Tuesday being the vague day that never came. But his impatience and ill humor only drew attention to his faults as he stood there in his blown-out Jockey shorts, rinsing his safety razor, approaching fifty and unable to conceal the potbelly and sagging pectorals from years of office work. I envied other boys their younger fathers, men with flat stomachs who showed them how to spiral a football, or how to put your hip into a left hook. My father couldn't even get his small, typist's hands *around* a football.

Of course, once Dad had a few drinks in him he'd forget his age and diminutive size and one day at a street fair I saw him get pushed around by a bigger and even more obnoxious brute. Dad had started the fight with a nasty wisecrack, but he didn't have the ass to back up his mouth. I wanted to rush to his aid but fear froze me in my tracks—not fear for me but for what the man might do to Dad if I went off. Secretly, I suffered mightily for my father and yearned for the day when I'd grow up big and strong enough to take his back in battle—or to wrap my hands around his neck and throttle him.

Ron, totally baffled about what Mom found appealing enough in our father to marry him, telegraphed her feelings by snorting, rolling her eyes, and subjecting us to her favorite weapon—the silent treatment. The contention between her and Dad could be ignited by anything, even the dog, a mutt we named Stubby. Part beagle and part wirehaired terrier, Stubby had the droopy ears of the former and short tail of the latter, and was named after the part that went over the fence last, as our father liked to say. Dad always talked to Stubby in baby talk, like he did with any dog that passed within his range. At dinner he'd feed scraps to the dog under the table and whenever Stubby missed one, Dad would point at the piece of food excitedly and lapse into baby talk.

"*Deah* wit *is*! Deah wit is wite *deah*!"

"Mother!" Ron said. "Daddy's feeding the dog again."

"Aw wuzzy talkin. Dat piece fell off my plate."

Dad spoke that way to dogs in the street on their owner's leash, "Wuzzy doin' deah? Aw, wuzza widdle woozy woo woo," the owner shooting us queer looks and Dad going on and on until the dog rolled over and peed on itself in a desperate attempt to ingratiate. I found this vaguely embarrassing, like bad comedy, but it infuriated my sister. Ron would roll her eyes then turn on her heel and go home in a huff. She needed a father she could look up to, not a buffoon who competed with us for the attention of dogs.

Dad's antics didn't seem to bother Stubby one way or another. He was a game little pooch, always up for mischief. I'd take him out for a walk, point at the hedges by the front lawn, and go, "There's a *pussy*cat in there!" Incensed, he'd hurl himself into the thick bushes, growling and snarling in frenzy until I had to drag him out by his leash. Stubby never cut pussycats any slack, whether real or imagined.

One night Ronnie and I were sitting with Stubby in front of the latched screen door that opened onto our porch. The front door of our house was left open for ventilation on summer nights with only the screen door shut to keep out the insects, and it was magical to sit there in front of it, peering through the screen as the night darkened with an approaching storm. Lightning bugs winked out beyond the porch as the air grew cool and heavy with moisture, and at the first crack of lightning, wind-whipped trees were backlit in stark relief. Great titans of light and darkness seemed to battle across the sky. I sat behind the screen door scoffing at them and daring them to strike nearby, while Stubby whimpered and Ron looked on, entranced.

"Hey, Ron," I said. "Watch this." I pointed out at the lawn and whispered urgently to Stubby, "There's a *pussy*cat out there!"

True to form, Stubby snarled deep in his throat and shot through the door like he was fired from a cannon, leaving behind a cartoonlike, dog-shaped hole in the screen. Dad was furious and made Ron cry, yelling at us that we'd ruined his house and probably killed the goddamned dog. Stubby came back, though, and later I tried to get Ron to laugh about it, but she was still too sore at Dad.

One day I was told that Stubby was "found under the couch." I took this to mean dead, or deceased, although nobody ever uttered those words. Stubby's death was passed over like a detail in the daily tabloids— "Man found behind Dumpster." I never really saw Stubby when he was dead (other than in my imagination, stretched out on his side, little crosses for his canceled eyes like Jughead in the *Archie* comics). I can't remember him being buried or anything, and had no idea what people did with a dead dog.

After Stubby died Ron walked silently through the house like Greta Garbo with a wistful, preoccupied expression on her face and spent most of her time behind the closed door to her room. One day when we were napping on our parents' beds, I turned to her to see if I could pierce her mood.

"Hey, Ron," I whispered "Are we ever gonna grow up?" Seemed like a pertinent question since our parents were unable to discern the point at which we'd outgrown things like naps, playpens, and baby talk.

"What?"

"You know, like Mom and Daddy."

"Like *Dad*dy? Jeez, I hope not."

"Why's that?"

"What Daddy did is more like, I don't know, like photosynthesis or something."

"Photo what?"

"What plants do. We just had that in school. Now go to sleep."

Daddy's a plant? Where did she get this stuff? I lay there for a while watching the worry lines between her eyes smooth out as she slipped into sleep, lips lightly parted next to the pillow, the collar of her flannel nightgown framing the delicate skin of her face. I listened to her breathing, hoping that she'd wake up and talk to me some more. But when sleep finally came, I was dizzy with watching tomb beetles morphing out of the fleur-de-lis patterns on the wallpaper.

chapter 2

"**H**ey, Ron. Wanna go to the publics?"

"I'm reading."

Bad news. Ronnie loved shutting the door to her room and escaping into a book.

"Aw c'mon, Ron. We could get water ices and play on the swings."

Children often develop a direction or goal early in life. Mine was simple—get out of the house. I wasn't allowed to roam unsupervised yet, but sometimes I could finagle my sister to take me to the school yard at Lowell School where the Protestant kids went, the publics, and where life no longer remained cramped and static but was imbued with danger and movement.

"Okay, Steve, but you have to promise not to disappear again."

"Cross my heart and hope to die." Secretly, I loved that she worried like hell when I eluded her watchful eye and vanished.

Once we got outdoors our moods lightened, like the feeling you'd get if you crossed over the border into Mexico and left the cops behind. We passed by a Johnny Smoker tree (catalpa) and I picked up one of the cigar-shaped pods and stuck it in the side of my mouth.

"Hey, Ron, gotta light?"

She stifled a laugh. "Steve, don't. They'll make you really sick."

The public school yard at Lowell was a choice hangout for neighborhood kids. A sturdy iron fence that was spiked on top surrounded Lowell's several square blocks of concrete, with school buildings on one end, a row of oak trees on one side of the buildings, and a huge sturdy set of swings on the other side. The open spaces were used for men's softball games that lasted from late afternoon until it was too dark to see anymore. These games were not for kids. They were hard-hitting, fast-pitch games played by strapping guys with tattoos and DA (duck's ass) haircuts who smoked cigarettes and could wallop the ball clear across two blocks of concrete and out onto the trolley tracks.

Ron went immediately to the swings where the girls hung out. "Steve, give me a push, will you?"

I could usually get in a stickball game in the shady niche between the school buildings where a single, double, triple, or home run was scored by which floor your ball bounced off.

There were always three or four young publics lounging around on the marble steps that led up to the padlocked doors of the school. Some of the boys were only slightly older than I, but they were already doing a good imitation of the big guys playing softball—hair slicked back in a DA with gobs of Dixie Peach pomade, a cigarette dangling from the corner of a sneering lip, and some seriously high-waisted pegged pants with dragnet pockets that bloused over box-toed shoes. (My favorite box-toed shoes had external tongues with a zippered latch—Flagg Flyers.)

I watched the publics with fascination and was jealous of their easygoing sexuality. One day I observed with envy while a boy asked a girl for her lipstick, then sat down on the school steps, pulled out his cock, and, much to the girl's delight, used the lipstick to write (apparently) her name on it.

Ron would wave at me as she kicked back and forth on the swings, a happy and dreamy look on her face as she rose up above the sunny vista of baseball game and trolley cars rumbling down Fifth Street, but she showed little interest in the goings-on that drew my furtive attention. When we left the school yard and headed for home, Ron's steps grew more deliberate. Next thing she was back in her room reading.

* * *

Getting out of the house wasn't always fun and games. Every few months we'd go pay our respects to Mom's parents, Granma and Granpa Butter, who'd emigrated from Vienna, Austria, in the late nineteenth century and lived across Philly in Germantown. It was the late forties, early fifties, and all around us America was evolving into a strange, postwar–art deco era of prefab housing, televisions and toasters that resembled rocket ships, and cars with fins, vinyl interiors, and suicide knobs. I was desperate for a car and a television, so the trek to our grandparents' was like being dragged backward in time.

The neighborhood boys in Germantown looked like The Dead End Kids, with baggy britches, corduroy knickers, and tweed newsboy caps. I'd see them in the street outside Granpa's playing skelly, or bottle caps, a game like shuffleboard with chalk-drawn squares where you launched your bottle cap across the asphalt with a flick of your finger. Dad once cracked, "Christ, these kids look like they just got off the goddamn pickle boat."

On the brick wall of a nearby building was scrawled a familiar bit of graffiti—*Kilroy Was Here!*

Granpa had been a butcher in the old country, but he lost his shop in Philly when the Depression came along and he went to work in a brewery. He had an old-world look with his tweed suits and heavy mustache, and when we arrived at their apartment he always took Ronnie and me one at a time on his knees while he sat in his favorite armchair and did the old riding-the-horsy routine, bouncing us up and down on his knees while he prattled on in German.

"And now comes the farmer (*die Bauer*)," he'd say, "riding his horse down the road," and his right knee came up while the left one was going down, so we lurched crazily from side to side. Then the farmer tried to gallop and we're all over the place until the farmer fell off his horse, Granpa abruptly straightened his legs out, and we slid down his legs to his shoes. We always shrieked when he did that, but I felt way too old for such nonsense and was happy to escape Granpa's beery breath and hairy paws.

Ronnie, on the other hand, could barely repress her glee, and always gave herself up to this childishness with a relish that I found amazing, even when she was an eight-year-old in the third grade. She loved the old guy, and I'd catch her doing a Sid Caesar version of his horsy bit—

"Comes now dee bower, clip clop inza shtrazza." She'd trail behind him mimicking the way he walked, with a little Charlie Chaplin shuffle, but impatient, leaning forward like Groucho as though he walked against a strong wind. When Ron loved someone she transformed their failings into endearing quirks. Dad's failings, though, were just failings.

The one stellar moment at Granpa's arrived after dinner when we all gathered in the living room, darkness descended on the house, and Granpa turned on their old Philco radio—a huge, wooden floor model that stood taller than me. It had a little green light that shone in the dark when it was turned on and was the only light in the house as we listened to *The Lone Ranger* and *The Shadow*. I'd lie on the cool linoleum tiles in the dining room, thrilling as the opening notes of "The William Tell Overture" sliced through the night.

Later when the fights came on live from Madison Square Garden, Granpa and our father settled into some serious beer drinking, cigarette smoking, and spitting into coffee cans. Here were the simple, productive skills of men, and I'd sit on the floor nearby and watch, an apt and eager pupil.

"Christ," said Dad, scowling at his beer, "they should pour this stuff back into the horse."

Meanwhile, the announcer called the blow-by-blow as Kid Gavilan bolo-punched Danny "Bang Bang" Womber into retirement.

Radio was magic and I prayed to have one of my own.

Sure enough, one night I discovered a General Electric plug-in on my bedside table. I have no recollection of how or why that radio got into my room, whether it had been a birthday or Christmas present, or if the table in my room was simply a convenient spot in an otherwise cluttered house. But somewhere during my first years in school I was fiddling with the dial and chanced on a station that hooked me solid. All night I laid there listening to hipster disc jockeys like Jocko Henderson spin rhythm and blues. *Time for the weather, baby, as Jocko scans the skies with his big brown eyes.* Hours of doo-wops by those bird groups, The Crows, The Ravens, The Flamingos, doing "the blows" in four-part harmony— *whooooo, wha-ah-ah oooooo*—punctuated by Chuck Berry and Earl Bostic tunes that made me want to jump up, dance around, maybe get a tattoo.

After Jocko, Fat Harvey Shelton came on with *Jazz at One*, right through the midfifties, spinning tunes by Lester Young, Sonny Stitt, and

Coleman Hawkins, although the names meant nothing to me then. I kept it turned down real low so my sister wouldn't get a bug up her ass and attract our parents' attention.

When I turned six I joined my sister at St. Helena, a traditional Catholic elementary school with nuns in habits and classes on catechism and the Golden Rule. I ambled around those classrooms in an awkward, self-conscious daze, paralyzed by the sudden, close proximity to other strange boys and girls, desperate to elude the harsh, probing scrutiny of the nuns. I was so terrified and confused I couldn't remember a thing from class after the pledge of allegiance. Loud buzzers and bells would suddenly go off signaling atomic bomb drills and we'd cower under our little desks ("Stick your head between your knees and kiss your ass goodbye!" as Dad liked to say) until the nun rang the all-clear bell.

Ron was three grades ahead of me so I rarely saw her there, and being a straight-A student she was up and out earlier than me, so we didn't walk to school together either. Then every term Mom and Dad would compare her report cards to mine: "Why can't you be more like your sister?" It wasn't like Ron flaunted her good grades, but even the way she *under*played it really burned my ass. My first few years in school were strung out on a paranoid, unnerving tightrope. I couldn't wait to get back home and night to fall so I could go to my room and tune in rhythm and blues or *Jazz at One* on my best friend, the radio.

One night the broadcast came live from an R & B show at the Municipal Auditorium and the scenario played out in my head in vivid detail: four pallbearers carried a coffin onstage, horns and piano doing a marching vamp, the coffin popped open, and Screamin' Jay Hawkins leaped out in a white tuxedo and shrieked "I put a *spell* on you!"

Who knows what fate or instinct guided my hand that first night I scrolled across the AM dial, but once I found rhythm and blues I was spellbound. Though only a child I was entranced by the heartbreak and sadness in that music and felt a woozy joy in the sweet texture of the voices and the huskiness in those tenor saxophones. I couldn't put a color to it—I was still too sheltered at that point—but some part of me recognized the blues, like an old friend from a previous life, exotic and far removed from our middle-class existence. I could taste that music in the back of my throat and feel it in my bones like a toothache, thrilling me and making me feel alive. While visions of sugar plums or plunging down the Rabbit Hole danced in my sister's head, while she dreamed of being a missionary, a nurse, an actress, a veterinarian, or maybe even a writer, my mind was choreographing childlike images of getting my heart broken, going mad with torment, and pacing the floor to the strains of Ivory Joe Hunter doing "Since I Left You Baby (I Almost Lost My Mind)."

My sister, though indifferent to that music, perked up one day when she passed my room and heard me doing the chorus to Little Willie John's "All Around the World," where Little Willie says if he don't love his woman, then *grits ain't grocery, eggs ain't poultry, and Mona Lisa was a man.*

Ron leaned in the doorway. "Steve, what was that?"

When I repeated it for her she bent over laughing.

I asked her what grits were and who was Mona Lisa? She just laughed and said, "God, Steve, who cares? I mean, *grits* ain't *grocery*? That's got to be the greatest thing I ever heard." Maybe she didn't get the blues at that age, but the lingo definitely struck a nerve.

At Catholic school we were graded on other things besides academics. We were given grades on our moral character—things like Self-Control, Discipline, and Obedience. My sister, little brownnoser that she was, always got straight As on those too, while I got Ds and Fs. I began developing clever skills of my own: I started stealing money from our parents. I'd take my little cronies to the drugstore, walk in, and slap a five-spot on the counter.

"Okay, sir. I'll have, uh, six Tootsie Rolls, ten caramel creams, five Bazooka Bubble Gums, a box of Black Crows, and, uh, a pack of cigarettes, please. You know, for my dad." I tapped the fiver and asked, "Do I still have enough money there?"

"Oh *my*, yes. But what brand does your dad smoke, son?"

I scanned the packs on display under the glass case, my forefinger drawn to the red bull's-eye. "Oh yeah, those right there."

"LSMFT," said Dickie Downs. "Lucky Strike means fine tobacco."

"Your dad smokes Lucky Strikes?"

"Yeah. That's it. What he smokes. And don't forget some matches." Big shot. An hour later we came staggering out of the alley behind the drugstore, all green at the gills.

But sometimes I stole for no reason other than the exquisite thrill of getting away with it. I once took a twenty-dollar bill from Mom's purse, a lot of money in the fifties, and was so intoxicated with that much dough that I got scared and jammed the bill in the corner mailbox—no candy bars, no backslapping from fair-weather friends, just the subversive power and unknown repercussions that were left to my wild imaginings.

And then there was arson. I'd steal from our kitchen those huge, wooden matches that burst into flames if we hurled them at the ground, or bounced them off one another's jackets in a match fight shoot-em-up. Creeping around the neighborhood after the Christmas holidays, I'd jam dried-up Christmas trees left out for the trash collectors under parked cars and light them. Once I set fire to a canvas tarp slung over a huge truck. I never hung around to witness the results, but lying in bed that night my imagination conjured up hellish scenes that jolted my whole body with surges of excitement and terror. Those feelings would morph into remorse and I'd cringe and weep at what a monster I was becoming. Finally I'd fall asleep exhausted and wake up the next day feeling refreshed, and with no memory of the incident. I never walked back by one of my arson attempts to observe the results, and couldn't remember their locations anyway. Luckily for the neighbors, that phase in my development was short-lived.

Aside from my radio, being cooped up at home was suffocating, and school was drudgery, but there was one family event that I loved. Mom's sister, Elinore, and her husband, Bill Graff, lived across town on Cottman Avenue with their two daughters, Lori and Judy, both about Ronnie's and my ages, and once a year when New Year's Eve rolled around they'd come pick us up in their car to go dancing at an old German dance hall downtown called the Gewerbe. (Guh-*vair*-bee means "trade" in German, so it was probably a local union hall.)

We'd all pile into Uncle Bill's shiny new Ford, me in the back with Mom, Ron, and our two cousins, while Dad sat up front with Bill and Ellie.

"So, Cholly," Bill said as he started up the car. "How's Uncle Sam treating you?" Bill Graff was a bearish guy who refereed football games and had the broadest Philadelphia accent of anybody I ever heard. Ron was nuts about him. He also smoked a pipe that gave the interior of his car a delicious aroma.

"Christ," Dad said, already half lit before we'd started, "they got commies runnin' the goddamn labor unions and Truman don't even know what time the balloon goes up."

"We just had that in school," Ron said. "Three branches of government. Judicial, legislative, and balloon branch."

Ellie turned and shot Ron a look.

Ron loved our two cousins and the chance to mingle with other girls, and as soon as we headed across town they'd start those lamebrain car games like Twenty Questions—Is it animal, vegetable, or mineral? Lori and Judy, though, in their matching little sailor suits, dimpled cheeks, and jet black hair, were so cute that wedged in next to them on the backseat I'd get a boner.

Cars, like radio, were magic. Compressed in a moving capsule, the combined patter of two families became screwball comedy that contrasted nicely with the world flickering by like a movie. Hurtling through Philly's lamplit streets in Uncle Bill's car, we skidded along trolley tracks where sparks from the overhead electrical connections showered down like a fireworks display when the trolleys lumbered through intersections. We cruised down spooky streets like Erie Avenue, past dingy ramshackle stoops in poor neighborhoods with gaudy Cadillacs parked at the curb, and kids playing in the street scuttled out of the way as our headlights bore down on them.

"Hey, Mom," I said, "how come we don't get a car like Uncle Bill?"

"Your father had a bad accident driving a jeep in the Philippines when he was in the navy," Mom said, "and swore he'd never drive again."

Ron sneered. "In the *na*vy? When was that, the Spanish-American War? They didn't even *have* jeeps back then."

Aunt Ellie turned completely around in the front seat, laughing, "That's pretty quick, honey. You learn that in school too? The only thing your mother and I learned in school was to keep our legs closed when we sat down. You're not in a barn, dear, they'd say."

Mom, under a black velvet hat secured with pearl hatpin, blushed and smiled hesitantly, her heavy Austrian features lapsing into all-purpose mode that expressed amused disdain (after all the years of Dad's crudeness), resolute pride in her family, and acute embarrassment in the eyes of her children.

We zoomed by guys hawking hot pretzels from the grassy divider of a huge boulevard lined with sycamore trees, and cruised past wealthy colonial-type houses where, behind frosty windows, soft lights revealed families at dinner tables, all glimpsed in a passing moment, or savored whenever we stopped at a traffic light, and Bill would fire up his terrific-smelling pipe while Dad went on, "And then this Kefauver sonofabitch . . ."

"Is it bigger than a breadbox?" Lori asked.

Ellie was the real ham in the crowd and looked like a flapper with her jet black bobbed hair and slinky cocktail dresses. She considered herself something of a comic and would not be outdone by my sister. "Did I tell you kids the one about the harelip who goes into the diner for a sandwich? The counter guy is a hunchback, see—"

"Oh for God's sake, El," Mom said.

When we finally arrived I reluctantly got out of the car and we all filed into the Gewerbe, a huge building with marble staircases and an enormous dance floor that was covered with salt or sand to facilitate dancing and sliding your feet. At one end of the auditorium was a bandstand with a live band in lederhosen that played a lot of oompah-pah polkas. It was schmaltzy cornball compared to the blues, but after the nuns at St. Helena's I was happy to have family members around me and I found the Gewerbe to be a great good time.

While the grown-ups waltzed or polkaed, all us kids would go sliding across the slick, sandy floor, playing tag and seeing how fast and far we could slide. Ronnie had lots of girls to play with and I was in seventh heaven showing off my sliding abilities. There were plenty of other boys to roughhouse with, but even the girls got into roaming around and causing mischief, sticking hairpins into all the balloons, knocking things over, and crashing into the dancers in a game of tag, playing hide-and-seek in the cloakroom (duck in there, try to cop a feel off Lori and Judy), or stealing beers off the deserted tables. I saw Ron in her plaid jumper and frilly blouse doing the polka with Uncle Bill, oompah-pah, blushing as she tried to hide her amusement and awkwardness with the goofy dance. There was an atmosphere of wild abandon at the Gewerbe and most of the grownups got good and soused.

At one point Uncle Bill and my father took me by the hand after they'd had a few too many and dragged me over to the bar to get me a beer of my own, Dad wanting to show off what a gutsy eight-year-old he'd raised. They didn't know that all of us kids had been swiping beers off the tables and were already half lit.

I don't think I've ever seen a bar since that could compare to the Gewerbe's for sheer magnificence. It was almost half a block long of dark, polished wood with a shiny, brass foot rail. On the other side of the bar, behind the mirrored shelves that were stacked with murky bottles of liquor, there was a bowling alley made of real grass and you could hear the ball banging into the pins.

We found Granpa knocking them back with a small crowd of his cronies and a substantial pile of empty shot glasses lined up in front of him. He maintained an aura of tremendous dignity, and as we approached he grabbed me under the arms, hoisted me up to sit on the bar, and gave me a beery kiss on the cheek. I was, after all, his namesake and the son of his favorite daughter. Then he gave me my first beer (at least he thought it was my first) in a small soda glass. I tossed it off amid the guffaws of all his old drinking buddies, who were probably making wisecracks about how the apple don't fall too far from the tree and such.

Suddenly a terrific scuffle broke out as Uncle Bill and my father tried to wrestle Granpa away from the bar. They were unsuccessful and we had to leave him behind to fend for himself.

Once the simple joy of roaming our neighborhood got into my blood, I became as reluctant to come home as Granpa was to leave the bar, or Ronnie to leave a good book. I'd be out on Nedro Avenue when darkness fell, bending over to tighten roller skates to my shoes with a skate key, preparing for one more thrill ride down the hill past Dickie Downs's house. I could just make out Ronnie's face in the front window, looking out for me, and hear Dad's strident whistling from our porch, signaling time for dinner. But I was well hidden behind the Woodcocks' Chevy sedan. From open windows came the homey smells of dinner cooking, roast pork and sauerkraut, the sounds of The Ink Spots, or the flickering images and crackle of canned laughter as families sat down to their favorite TV shows.

I pushed off, ignoring the rumbling in my stomach, and hurtled down the street, cloaked in shadow, the wind cool on my face, the sound of skates-on-asphalt hissing in my ears. Lightning bugs winked against the inky silhouette of a tree. At the end of the block I shot into a circle of lamplight, through the intersection, and off again into darkness. People say the moon doesn't cast shadows—don't believe it.

I paid for my footloose shenanigans, though, especially if I missed dinner—got hollered at, smacked around, and sent to my room without eating. At least Ron never took any pleasure in seeing me get punished, I'll say that for her. She just retreated to her own room with a puzzled look on her face like, *What did I ever do to get born into this madness?* I'd go to bed with my head ringing from the smacks and weep bitterly, which was okay in itself. I reveled in drama, and like the blues, weeping heightened the sense of being alive, a feeling hard to come by in a saccharine Cold War era of *I Like Ike*, and tunes like "How Much Is That Doggie in the Window?" and "Eh, Cumpari" dominating the Lucky Strike *Hit Parade*. Thank God for Joe Turner and Screamin' Jay Hawkins.

And so life moved along with the carefree feeling of skating downhill with a blues tune in my head, and thoughtless of the stop-and-crash consequences. There were great snowy days in winter when Ronnie and I dragged our sled over to Fisher Park and went sledding down this big hill that attracted kids from all over Olney. Halfway down the hill was a ledge where the hill flattened out for a few yards, and the abrupt transition made your sled hurtle through the air before coming down on the bottom part of the slope.

"C'mon, Ron. Sit in front of me. Stick your feet onto the crossbar and hold on." This was my world—the physical world of thrills and daring.

"Don't go too fast, Steve. And slow down at the ledge, okay?"

"Okay."

I never slowed at the ledge. That was the whole point, to shoot off into space like Wile E. Coyote. We tore down the hill with her hair blowing in my face. I could see her confused expression, glimpsed at an angle from behind, torn between joy and terror, then screaming as the sled hurtled briefly through the air. At the bottom she pelted me with snowballs and stormed up the hill in a huff, furious that I'd scared her. Whenever she went down the hill solo she'd drag her feet as she approached the ridge that sent you off into space, but she was always proud of herself at the solo attempt. Prudence was always a great virtue of hers, a virtue that would help her avoid pitfalls that I'd dive into like a gopher down a hole.

Our last few years in Philly flashed by in a blur as Dad got promoted to lieutenant colonel, and Mom, puzzled at how to deal with her quirky kids, belatedly started reading Doctor Spock. Ron had tacked up a poster of Brando to her wall, and I was happily frittering away my lunch allowance at the local hoagie joint punching up Chuck Berry tunes on the jukebox. Somewhere in the early fifties we finally acquired a television, and I'd race my sister home from school so I could tune in to Tom Mix Westerns and those deliciously violent cartoons, like *Farmer Gray versus the Mice.* But if Ron beat me to it I'd have to suffer through *Kukla, Fran and Ollie* or those corny *Merrie Melodies* cartoons where flowers, farmyard animals, and inanimate objects burst into song in broad, stereotyped caricatures— squeaky, squint-eyed Orientals or big-lipped darkies, rolling their huge white eyeballs and rubber-legging around de ole plantation. Racial naïveté seemed rampant in the fifties, at least in our neighborhood and the land of the boob tube.

At night our parents preempted the television for a mishmash of variety shows featuring Lawrence Welk and Milton Berle, and Ron would campaign relentlessly to stay up for her all-time favorite, *Your Show of Shows* with Sid Caesar, Imogene Coca, and Carl Reiner. The thing that struck her was how seriously the characters in the skits took themselves; they weren't trying to be funny. They were confused, or even deranged, but they were deadly earnest in their attempts to communicate and get what they wanted. My sister would be in stitches.

Though violence turned my sister off, we both delighted in anything that smacked of the subversive, and our whole family was glued to the television through the McCarthy Senate hearings. Dad would curse and sneer, Mom would murmur, cluck, and wag her head, and Ronnie and I would have a ball mimicking the delightful speech patterns of bombastic accusation and evasive insinuation.

Sunday mornings offered a brief respite from drama when we all attended Mass. Our whole family seemed awed by the old pre–Vatican II pageantry, the Latin liturgy intoned by the priest in his embroidered robes, and the smell of incense as the sun shone down through those magnificent stained-glass windows. Ron, looking angelic in her Sunday dress, was particularly taken with church and even enjoyed the self-sacrificing discipline of fasting before Mass. But once we got home the wonder evaporated and conflict picked up again over the simple ritual of reading the Sunday newspaper, the *Philadelphia Inquirer.* Ronnie and I fought over first dibs on the comics, Dad sneered over the headlines and the sports pages, and Mom worshipped the advertisements.

"Charlie, did you see this beautiful new vacuum cleaner, the Hoover?"

"The *Hoover*? We got commies taking over the railroads and you're telling me about a goddamned vacuum cleaner?"

"We should definitely get the vacuum," Ron said, "before commies take over the Hoover."

"Where the hell do you kids get this crap?"

"We refuse to answer that question, Senator," I said, "on the grounds of the abracadabra."

"You better stick to your funny papers, the pair a yez."

My sister and I would spend hours lying on the living room rug, her nose quivering eagerly as we poured over the panels of *Pogo* and the Sunday comics. Ron adored *Pogo*, and every Christmas she'd stand on a chair and proudly sing or recite the entire lyrics of "Deck the Halls" as misconstrued but enthusiastically performed by Albert Alligator and Pogo Possum: "Deck us all with Boston Charlie, wallah wallah wash and Kalamazoo . . ." It was clear to me, even at that early age, that my sister was infatuated with language, and the colorful vernacular of the denizens of the Okefenokee Swamp no doubt appealed to her mischievous wit. I was still too young, though, to appreciate the political satire.

My early creative impulses erupted in physicality and mimicry. I was all over the place, a real ham right from jump street, and much of my love of performing sprang from the desire to entertain my sister. The bit she liked most was my imitation of Johnnie Ray singing "Cry." Ray, a pop singer in the fifties with a blond pompadour, was deaf in one ear and wore a hearing aid when he sang. He'd get so carried away during performances that he would tear his clothes off, and Ron would egg me on to perform this routine whenever she caught me in a loony mood on our front porch.

When your sweetheart, sends a letter, of good-byyyyyyyyyye (rip, tear, buttons popping)

Ronnie howled with laughter at each shirt that I tore to shreds in a blind frenzy, falling to my knees weeping and sobbing. I knew that Johnnie Ray was deaf in one ear, but I played him as if he was blind. I figured if deaf was compelling, blind would be *more* so.

Cruising through adolescence I had to pause at another intersection—sex, and the heady touch of romance and first kisses, although none of that happened around our house. Ron made the mistake of having some friends over for a party in our backyard one year and Dad came lurching out half lit and made cracks like, "Christ, where the hell did you find these monkeys?" When Ron asked if she and her friends could make sandwiches, Dad said, "*Sand*wiches? What, for all these wisenheimers? You kids must think food grows on trees." And then, of course, there was the balloon thing and his ever-popular baby carriage gag—How does it go? On wheels, har-har, you get it?

So my sister and I went to other kids' houses to play those sexy kissing games like Post Office or Spin the Bottle. I'll never forget kissing Mary Sykes in a game of Post Office, and soon after I took to following her home from school. Mary was thin, dark, with huge brown eyes and wore braces on her teeth (come to think of it, she looked much like my sister, although prettier to me), and I'd tag along offering to carry her books, desperate for a smile from that bow-shaped mouth that flashed with metal when she opened it. Smitten, and heartsick with her rebuffs, I stood on the sidewalk in front of her house one day, and when she failed to appear, I lobbed water balloons onto her porch until her mother came out swinging a broom and chased me.

Ronnie, years ahead of me, wouldn't be caught dead at a game of Spin the Bottle with her younger brother, and since I was incapable of empathizing with a girl about sex at that age I can't speculate on her reactions. The only ideas I had about sex were fantasies that sprang from a calendar poster of Marilyn Monroe that Dickie Downs and I once found in an abandoned sewer pipe—and that we ritually peed on.

Mom and Dad were a total loss at explaining the birds and the bees. Once when I was about nine I asked our mother, as she passed by the open door to my bedroom with a laundry basket, why I kept getting erections.

"Hey, Mom," I said, indicating my cock that had sprung up to my belly button with a life of its own. "What's this all about?"

She halted in front of my door and her mouth flew open like a character in a horror movie. She almost dropped the pile of laundry. "Well, uh, I think that means you need to go to the bathroom, Steve." Off she went and that was that.

Later I overheard two publics bragging about how they'd taken a girl into the woods, had her lie down on the ground, and then "fucked" her. It was not a word that was bandied about so much back then and that was the first time I'd heard it. Confused further by Mom's remark, I pictured the publics performing something not unlike Dickie's and my ritual with the M. M. poster. Lord knows what Mom passed along to Ronnie.

All our father ever did was make wisecracks about Ronnie's physical shyness, which only increased her doubts about herself. For me, our father had only ominous (and, as it turned out, prophetic) warnings: "You better wise up, bud, or you're gonna get your tit in a wringer."

That was the sum total of my sex education.

Skating into my double-digit years (and Ron into her teens), another memorable intersection loomed into my sights: the Fern Rock movie theater, on Fifth Street across from Fisher Park. It was six blocks from where we lived and cost only a quarter for the matinee, so we were trusted and even encouraged to go unsupervised. I went there on Saturday afternoons with my neighborhood pals, Robbie Woodcock and Tommy DePaolo. This was the arena where I fell in love with the pulp serials of the fifties, *Flash Gordon* and *Tarzan*, starring Buster Crabbe. They'd have live demonstrations onstage during an intermission between the serial and the feature—the national yo-yo champions doing a promotion for Duncan yo-yos, slick-looking guys with huge pompadours, zoot suits, and two-tone wingtips, whirling their yo-yos in blurring arcs and making them Loop the Loop, Walk the Dog, or Rock the Baby in the Cradle.

If we were lucky, we had enough money for some Good & Plentys or a box of popcorn and a Coke. Once darkness descended and the screen lit up with the first terrifying scenes from *The Thing from Another World*, we were completely transported.

The best time I ever had at the Fern Rock was the day Ronnie and I went to see *Rebel Without a Cause* with James Dean. We went to the early matinee and didn't come out until it was dark out. When it ended for the second time, I turned to my sister. "Hey, Ron. Don't you think we should get back home? Daddy's gonna be furious if we stay any longer and miss dinner." Attendance at dinner was like a sacred rite to Dad.

"It's alright, Steve," she said with a sly smile, her eyes still moist from the final scene. "You're with me, so Daddy can hardly blame you. Let's just stay until the guy in the leather jacket drives off the cliff one more time, okay?" We agreed that this was our favorite part.

As much as I loved the camaraderie of clowning with my buddies during the movies, there was nothing like watching a movie with my sister. I'd never seen anything like Dean's performance and was much taken with him, but Ronnie's favorite character was Buzz, played by Corey Allen, who goes over the cliff in the game of Chicken. I was acutely aware of every scene that produced the slightest reaction in her. We had such an ability to empathize that I was able to see the movie through her eyes, and thereby raise my own level of perception. It was a real gift and I never lost it. I've always been able to watch movies with a little bit of my sister watching with me even when she wasn't there.

But Dad was as unforgiving about us missing dinner (James Dean or no) as Ron was about his relentless nagging, and one night at the Olney Diner he figured he'd teach us a lesson—not an easy stunt to pull on Ron, who was always on the lookout. The Olney Diner was where we went several times a year to give Mom a well-earned break from cooking (and all of us a break from Spam and macaroni and cheese). It was one of those art deco joints that resembled a Pullman car, wrapped in stainless steel with vinyl booths, each booth with its own miniature jukebox hanging over the windowsill. It was 1955, Dick Clark's *American Bandstand* was all the rage, but I found more of my beloved rhythm and blues on the jukeboxes at the Olney Diner. If it was me who got the first quarter into the box, then you were going to get Little Richard. Ron preferred early Elvis, like "That's All Right, Mamma." Mom dug Sinatra, but Dad seemed as content to listen to Little Richard as he was to the drumming of his own fingertips on the tabletop, which probably reminded him of an army marching band.

"Okay," Dad said after he looked at the menu and decided on his own choice. "What do you two want?"

Ronnie and I, happy to finally be able to choose what we wanted to eat, announced our favorites, the hot turkey or hot roast beef sandwiches with mounds of mashed potatoes and gravy. I could've gone through life eating nothing else.

"Well," Dad said with relish, "that's terrific. But what are you kids gonna use for money?"

Ron and I looked at each other helplessly. The waitress started fidgeting.

"C'mon, Charlie," Mom said. "Don't tease them. They look starved."

"Aw, what're you talking, Rose," he said. "These kids got no idea what it means to starve."

When the waitress asked my sister what she wanted, Veronica deadpanned in a clear, grown-up voice, "I'll just have a glass of water and a toothpick, thank you, please."

There was a terse silence, lines drawn in the sand.

"Oh, come on, hon," the waitress coaxed. "How about a nice hot turkey sandwich and some of those yummy mashed potatoes?"

Ronnie wasn't having any of it, and I just went on and ordered what I wanted, glancing around the table warily, waiting for the explosion.

As soon as the waitress left, Dad smacked the table with his hand, causing the silverware to jump and heads to turn in our direction. "Where the hell do you get off? You goddamn well better have something to eat, smartass, or a good wind's gonna blow you off your feet."

He looked desperate, but all his eye-bulging fury could not make her budge. Ron had one-upped him and we all knew it.

Dad mumbled to the waitress when she came back, "These kids are getting too big for their goddamn britches."

He was right. It seemed like a small thing, just another tiff, but the effect was subtle and profound—my sister had demonstrated quite clearly that our parents were no longer entirely in control. Dad never pulled that gag on us again. I was glad for Ron and impressed with her ability to turn our father's own game around on him. But I felt for Dad too, knowing that once again his cornball remarks had provoked everybody's ire. I occasionally found myself in the role of middleman.

"Hey, Ron," I said to her once, "you know how Daddy just doesn't seem to know how to express himself real good? Well, maybe that's why he always makes with the wisecracks, don'tcha think?"

For an instant her eyes flashed dark with anger and betrayal, then she threw her head back and guffawed like a horse braying. "Steve," she said, "if Daddy was any better at expressing himself, believe me, we might not have survived this long."

Life hit a bump in the road when I turned eleven and briefly lost my sister—Ron got shipped off to a Catholic girls' high school in Philly called Melrose Academy. (Dad was campaigning to ship me off to Valley Forge Military Academy, but I got a reprieve when we moved again.) Off she went with her suitcase and her hockey stick.

Ronnie thrived on whatever was happening at Melrose and seemed transformed. Her face got brighter, her smile wider, and her brown hair smoothed out to a dark, rich, medium length. As she began to dress in fashionable school blazers and pleated wool skirts, she looked terrific and her confidence soared. I was happy to find her in such good spirits, but I harbored a wistful kind of envy, especially as Mom and Dad swelled with pride and bragged about her to our neighbors and relatives. I watched jealously as she practiced field hockey in the backyard. Well, I thought, it's only a prep-school sport for girls. Her knees and elbows stuck out in that coltish quality that certain girls exhibit, but she attacked the ball with such tenacious ferocity that I had to give her a grudging respect, comforting myself with the fact that she still couldn't throw a baseball.

After Ron shipped out I got a consolation prize in the form of a trumpet Dad bought me, and I started taking lessons from a bleary-eyed, chain-smoking musician at Pfaffs Music Store on Fifth and Olney. This may have been instigated as a result of Mom's Spock readings, I don't know, but I got only as far as the opening riff in Pérez Prado's "Cherry Pink and Apple Blossom White." I played it over and over hundreds of times, slurring the note on *Pinnnnnnk* the exact way Prado did. But without his wonderful salsa band to back me up (to say nothing of his gorgeous tone) it became unendurable. Dad would say stuff like, "Why don't you play 'Far Far Away'?" The opening bars of "Cherry Pink" have set my teeth on edge ever since. After several months I put the shiny, golden horn back in its felt-lined case for good. Too bad. With my ear for music, who knows, I might've been the next Chet Baker. Instead I would end up only with Chet's bad habits.

One weekend when Ronnie was back home, we were sitting around the living room floor with the Sunday papers and we overheard our parents discussing moving to Europe, where Dad would be stationed for the next six years. I exchanged looks with Ron over the panels of *Pogo*, hoping to read in her face some clue as to how this new development would affect us. Surely she'd be heartbroken to leave Melrose. But she just flipped the page and started in on *Blondie* or *Beetle Bailey*. Her feelings, as usual, remained guarded and a mystery to me, and I suspected that she'd picked up some purposeful direction in high school that yet eluded me.

The only semblance of direction I'd acquired by the age of twelve had to do with getting out of the house, the Path of Least Resistance, and a certain affinity for style, romance, and footloose thrills. When I heard we were leaving Philly, all I could think was—Europe? Where the hell was that? Would they have Chuck Berry and *Mad* magazine over there, and could I wear my hip, new black chinos with the belt in the back?

part two

army brats abroad

chapter 3

aris, 1960. I was seventeen, standing on the quai St. Michel overlooking the Seine with my new GI buddies—Augie, a dark-eyed Mexican Italian, and Wilfred, a sandy-haired James Dean type, both hipsters from California. We leaned over the ancient stone abutment, flipped our cigarettes into the water, and watched them float toward Ile de la Cité, where the elegant spires of Notre Dame were all lit up with spotlights.

"Whoa," I said. "No wonder they call this the City of Lights."

"That's for the rubes, Kid," said Augie. He'd spent his youth prowling around Los Angeles and had his own take on dramatic lighting. He lit up another Lucky Strike and added, "Sometimes I get the suspicion that if I suddenly ran behind one of those buildings I'd catch a couple of teamsters on a smoke break. C'mon, I'll show you where the action is."

We walked back up rue de la Huchette—a dark, narrow street on the Left Bank where mist from the nearby river made the cobblestones glisten, hinting at mystery and furtive goings-on—and ducked into a little jazz club called Au Chat Qui Pêche (at the cat who fishes).

Dad, after three years of duty in Heidelberg, Germany, had gotten himself transferred to Orléans, France, only sixty miles south of Paris, an hour's drive or a dollar on the train. Some of the best musicians of the era, like Coltrane and Miles, were performing there on a semiregular basis and I got up to Paris every weekend I could. Ron was winding up her first year at the University of Pennsylvania back in Philly. I was envious, and missed her when I got left behind in high school in Heidelberg, but that passed quickly when I hit Paris—this was where the fun really began. The first night I stepped into Au Chat Qui Pêche, it was like falling in love.

Augie and I hung by the door, letting our eyes adjust to the dim lighting, while Wilfred went to the bar for a couple Heinekens. From speakers suspended in the corners came Coltrane's tasty tenor solo on Miles's arrangement of "Bye Bye Blackbird" and it washed over me like a cool wave. I scoped out the long bar littered with smudged glasses, smoldering ashtrays, and faces full of feigned nonchalance. The nuances in style and stance were fascinating—all chiaroscuros, with black knit ties and white spread collars, black blazers, and sweaters draped over shoulders with studied carelessness, bodies and legs jackknifed and scissored in world-weary postures. Paris was in the fashion forefront of the slightly Edwardian look of the later sixties, the students added a touch of Mao, and on the Left Bank it was all boiled down to a fine art. I doubted if Ron was picking up on anything like this at Penn.

I was so busy ogling some guy's threads who was sitting cross-legged at the bar—black corduroy tunic with tarnished silver buttons and stitched, square-toed wingtips—that I barely noticed Wilfred return with the beers.

Augie said, "Why don't you just ask him if you can suck his dick?"

"Hey, look at these guys," I protested. "Where the hell do you buy clothes like this?" These guys were way outta my league, standing there in my London Fog raincoat and PX corduroys.

"Aug's right," Wilfred said. "You gotta watch these shoes. They're all kinda *comme ci, comme ça.*" He splayed out his hand, palm down, and waggled it sideways. "You catch my drift?"

Wilfred was fond of calling French people "shoes" for reasons I never quite understood. We'd met at the Enlisted Men's Club at Coligny Caserne, the military headquarters base where Dad worked. There were some great musicians doing their army tour in the base bands, guys like Albert Ayler, and a piano player named Vincent Falcone who later became Sinatra's band leader. They'd practice and jam in the music rooms in the EM Club, which drew the attention of jazz buffs like Augie and Wilfred.

These guys were a few years older than me, and when they shed their uniforms for civvies they looked like characters out of a new wave flick—sunglasses, continental suits, and dark pullovers, racing around in sports cars with a trunkful of black-market cigarettes. They referred to me as "the Kid," and Au Chat Qui Pêche was their favorite spot in the Quarter.

"Look at this one," Wifred said, gesturing at an African guy in a T-shirt, a suede blazer sans lapels, and some really wide, pin-striped bell-bottoms that belled over shoes so quaint they looked like clown shoes. This character had the new look down pat, but he had an old look too that set him off from the American blacks I knew—chiseled features, ebony skin, and tufts of hair that lacked only the ivory bones of some ancient tribe. He had a gray canvas bag full of newspapers over his shoulder with *Herald Tribune* stenciled on it as he worked his way down the bar toward the door.

Wilfred bought a paper off him and tucked it under his arm. "Tomorrow's early edition. No self-respecting shoe in Paris should be caught without one."

"How does a newsboy afford clothes like that?" I wanted to know.

Aug said, "He sells other shit besides newspapers."

Before I could ask him what other shit, a girl at the other end of the bar caught our attention. She was doing a little dance as she stood there, moving slowly against the beat like a cobra swaying to a pipe. She was a hophead named Odile whose game was to ingratiate herself with the musicians who headlined downstairs in the jazz cave. There were some thoroughbreds down there that night, Jackie McLean and Freddie Redd, jazz giants in their own right who were in town doing a Jack Gelber play, *The Connection*, a story about junkies waiting for the Man. Odile was wearing a short fur jacket and way too much eye makeup for the occasion. Wilfred said she looked like a raccoon on a bad day, standing on its hind legs sniffing the air for a free meal. After years of schoolgirls in varsity sweaters and bobby socks, I thought she was the sexiest thing I'd ever seen.

As we curlicued down the tiny winding staircase that led to the jazz cave below, Jackie McLean bumped into me, hurriedly coming up the other way.

"Sorry," he mumbled. "I need a fix."

Maybe it was a line from the Gelber play, or he thought I didn't speak English, or more likely he just didn't care. American musicians enjoyed a loose freedom in Paris back then that wasn't available to them in the

States. With Algerian terrorists blowing up cafés, right-wing militants from the OAS trying to assassinate de Gaulle, and riotous student protests fanning the flames on both sides, the gendarmes had bigger fish to fry. There was a little bit of the Wild West about Paris in those days, and on jukeboxes or PA systems in joints all over town, Miles laid down a moody, fragile soundtrack through the Harmon mute on his trumpet.

In Orléans our family lived "on the French economy," the term for living off base. Our first apartment there was in a modern high-rise on the boulevard Alexandre Martin, an elegant old thoroughfare split down the middle with a tree-lined park, where carnies set up rinky-dink fairs in the summer. There was a butcher shop with a horse-head sign and a bakery across the boulevard from us. Several blocks from our building the boulevard ran into a traffic circle, Place Gambetta, with two huge, busy saloons, Le Tavern and Le Berrys. Guys in dusty work clothes drank shots of wine early in the morning, growling over the tabloids with a Gauloise smoldering in the corner of their mouths. At night surly waiters served up heaping plates full of steamed mussels in wine sauce with loaves of fresh-baked bread. Across the plaza from the saloons was an ancient train station, Gare d'Orléans, where we'd catch the shuttle to Paris. Out my bedroom window I could look down behind our building at the red-clay tennis courts and row after row of colorful flowers in the manicured gardens of le parc Louis Pasteur. Our building seemed out-of-place in that setting, almost an eyesore, like something out of a Jacques Tati movie where the hero is always in conflict with his ultramodern, baffling surroundings.

At first I had to ride a school bus to get to the high school out at the army base, Forêt d'Orléans. Forêt looked like two square miles of parking lot, sprinkled with Quonset hut buildings like small airplane hangars. These were the barracks and offices of the Army Special Services companies, where the base band was quartered, as well as a motor pool and an MP detachment. The school was much smaller than the huge one in Heidelberg. I found the same textures of ponytails, white bucks, and crew-cut rah-rah, but Orléans High was more intimate, and it didn't take me long to pick up on the rebels. I'd spot them when they smoked, drank in the local cafés, or boogied into the school cafeteria with a copy of *Waiting for Godot* hanging out of a back pocket—the beatnik wannabes. They wore boatneck sweaters, shades, and had that laid-back slouch over their cheeseburgers.

They were a refreshing change from the juvenile delinquents I'd hung with in Germany, drinking like hooligans and going on "kraut hunts."

After three years of army-based bowling alleys and teen clubs, I was waking up to the fact that I was in Europe. Dad bought me an old Citroën *traction avant* (front-wheel drive) to get to school in: a black sedan that resembled a thirties gangster car, with running boards, a gear shift that stuck out of the dashboard, doors that opened ass-backward, and little illuminated arms that flipped out of the door panels when you hit the directional signals. The well-worn leather seats and upholstered interior gave off a wondrous odor of crankcase oil, dried leaves, and Gauloise tobacco, and having a car put me in striking distance of all kinds of thrills. In a single day's driving I could hit the bullrings of Spain, go south to the Riviera, or go east to Italy. In an hour I could be in Paris, Left Bank jazz clubs or Pigalle, where hookers with pink hair would stick their fingers in your bum. Whole new cultures, languages, architecture, and approaches to personal hygiene (Pigalle whores usually washed your balls in the sink and themselves in the douche bowl) were all within reach.

One week it was Levi's, varsity jackets, basketball games, high school dances, and dizzy crushes. There was a girl named Barbara Rynerson I was mad about who always slow-danced with her belly pushing into my erection until I was literally creaming in my pants, while "I'm Mister Blue, wa-oo-wa-oooo" crooned out of the PA system. They were sweet moments, but I was unsure how to take it to the next level and found teenage romance frustrating. No problem, because the next week it was bell-bottoms, black corduroy tunics, coiffed hair, Left Bank jazz caves, and Pigalle *poules*. There was a thriving black market for everything from cigarettes, Levi's, and Johnnie Walker Scotch, to gas coupons and cases full of gas masks. Algeria was fighting for her independence from France and surplus ordnance from the bases brought in a high price. I'll never forget the first time Augie and Wilfred introduced me to Tar, the old Algerian fence for black market goods and our main connection for kif and hash.

I navigated my vintage Citroën through busy weekend traffic along the boulevard de Clichy, the car radio tuned to a jazz station, something like Radio Luxembourg and Charlie Mingus doing "Better Git It in Your Soul." We drove past Place Blanche and the Moulin Rouge, past juke joints and tattoo parlors and the cafés that sold *biftek* (steak) sandwiches. At rue Germain Pilon I pulled over and parked by the brasserie on the corner. I loved the boulevard de Clichy. It had the atmosphere of a carnival midway. Two street boys came over to the car and flashed porn photos, but Wilfred waved them off.

Augie was quick to take charge. "Wilfred, wait five minutes. Let me and the Kid go in, get Tar outta bed, know what I mean?"

Wilfred laughed in that lazy, southern California way he had that was more like an ironic goof on laughter.

Augie turned to me. "Alright, how much gas you got?" As company clerk for Special Services, Augie had access to forms that allowed us to circumvent the ration limit.

I reached into the glove compartment and extracted a stack of stamp books held together with a rubber band. "I only got thirty-six hundred liters, Aug. Had to pick up my old man after school so I couldn't make the PX at Olivet."

"That's good, Kid. That'll give you a couple hundred to fool around with after expenses."

Actually, my take should have been more like five or six hundred, but innocence and a stiff prick have always been a costly combination.

The doorways all along Germain Pilon were now crowded with luscious-looking hookers. Some sported huge bouffant hairdos in a wide range of colors—chartreuse, violet, teal. Others were laced up in leather and one carried a riding crop that twitched against her thighs. They all showed enormous cleavage as they click-clacked back and forth on high heels, balanced precariously on the tiny strip of sidewalk afforded by the narrow, cobblestone street. They pursed their lips and hissed at the passersby.

"Hé, cheri! Vien. Je t'enmene." Come. I take you.

We crossed the street to the Hotel Central and ducked into a musty hallway that led to the foyer of the hotel. Augie fired off more instructions. "Take a seat at the bar. Couple a minutes Tar'll lay some grass on the bar. Maybe some hash if he's got. Just sit tight. Roll up a jay. You know, be cool. We divvy up back in the short. Got it?"

In the dimly lit foyer, an ageless old man in a corduroy shirt and khakis lay curled up around a flea-bitten dog on a couch covered with an army blanket. They appeared to be asleep, but the old man bounced up spryly when we walked in and showed us a grin full of tobacco-stained teeth in a smoky brown face.

"Ey, my fren. Wachoo got me, Augie? Levi's? Johnnie Walker?"

While Tar led Augie through a beaded curtain into a back room, I stepped through an archway over to a tiny zinc-topped bar, perched myself on a stool, and slowly took inventory of the joint. Although I'd made this trip a few times before, this was the first time I'd been invited into the hotel where business was transacted.

Surprisingly, the room that held the bar extended all the way back to the street, providing space for half a dozen small tables and chairs, like the space in a saloon for dining, although I couldn't imagine eating anything that Tar cooked in this hovel. Then I noticed that I wasn't alone.

All the way in the back of the dining area, four somber Africans sat silently at one of the tables. They were all dressed alike—black suits of some shiny fabric like sharkskin, with high, white celluloid collars and black knit ties. They all had their forearms braced on the table showing several inches of snow white cuff, and their eyes gleamed white out of round, ebony faces. They sat so still I first thought it was a painting or some sort of freestanding sculpture. Spooky.

A green drink in a liqueur glass appeared on the bar, next to several oily, cone-shaped packets of kif wrapped in brown paper. I could just barely hear a jukebox or a radio playing a popular tune of the time—some French–Arabic thing with a tinny rhythm and monotonous lyrics. I pulled a pack of Zig-Zag papers from a hip pocket, opened one of the packets of kif, and rolled up a joint. Might as well show my cool now that I was allowed into the inner sanctum. I noticed Wilfred stagger past with the footlocker full of cigarettes.

Half a joint later I detected another rhythmic sound coming from the table in the back. The Africans were mumbling in some guttural lingo that reminded me of bop-talk, that old hipster version of pig latin where you put *eez* after the first consonant or before the first vowel of every word. But these guys exuded a power way beyond that of the street hipster. They looked like they'd taken root and grown right up through the floor, so perfectly did they merge with their surroundings. To me they personified the cosmopolitan Parisian; the idea that they were political never occurred to me. I was a blooming hedonist, and the aristocratic bearing of these four guys could only make them princes in the world that I aspired to—fast money, jazz music, and sex. Their posture appealed mightily to the mimic in me and I longed to run over and sit with them and get down with their mumbo jumbo.

My head began to spin from the kif and a pungent odor made my mouth fill with saliva. Augie and Wilfred had joined me, and I noticed Tar was cooking peppers in a frying pan over a small stove behind the bar. Tar picked up a pepper with a fork, smeared a bit of green and red speckled paste on it, and offered it to me.

The Africans were all looking our way.

Augie nodded his head. Reluctantly, I accepted the offering from Tar. I took a bite and chewed as delicately as I could. It was red hot and perspiration broke out on my forehead. I grabbed the green drink in the liqueur glass and tossed it off.

When I set the glass down and looked around, Augie and Wilfred were laughing and Tar was beaming his gap-toothed grin. My head suddenly stopped spinning from the kif and I never felt more sober in my life. I smiled back at Tar who put three more glasses on the bar.

"Ça marche?"

Augie nudged me. "He wants to know if you like his shit."

Wilfred countered, "Tell him to go fuck himself, Kid. They pulled that routine on me first time I was here. Probably what he poisons his fucking dog with."

Then we were all laughing and being studiously ignored by the silent Africans, a montage of white eyeballs, white collars, and white cuffs against ebony skin, like the keys on a piano. Strange winds blew out of the Paris night; adjusting sails, I tacked eagerly into the fray.

I was sitting in school back in Orléans one day when two men from the Criminal Investigation Department of the army came in and pulled me out of class. They wanted to know who my GI friends were. It scared the hell out of me, and when I got evasive, one of them pulled out a packet of Tar's kif and asked me where I got it. The lie came easily. I told them some hooker in Pigalle had offered it to me and that I'd been too embarrassed to turn it down. Apparently Dad had found some of Tar's reefer in a coat pocket of mine one night when he was snooping, and without saying a word to me he took it to the CID.

I'd never quite forgiven Dad the time he roughed me up back in Germany. I'd come home drunk after midnight, and he'd lurched wild-eyed out of his chair, drunker than I was, and attacked me in the kitchen, crowing, "You're killing your mother." He pushed me so hard into a kitchen counter I almost cracked my skull on a can opener fastened to the wall. Then he sly-rapped me with a roundhouse punch and I grabbed his arms to keep him from hitting me again. I don't know where my sister was at the time—she'd become increasingly elusive in high school as she'd begun to pursue a scholastic career like other juniors and seniors—but Mom came careening out of the bedroom and started yelling, "How dare you lay hands on your father!" Finally I skulked into my room as Dad grumbled, "That kid's a bum and he's always gonna be a bum!" I'd forgiven him many of his cracks, but not that one, suspecting there was a grain of truth in it.

So now I knew what he really thought of me. His warning that one day I'd get my tit in a wringer was evolving into, "Christ, that kid's gonna cause an international incident and get us all sent back to the States." I sneered at him, thinking him now a stool pigeon and disappointed that he'd been too cowardly to ask me about the grass himself. Although resentment isn't quite the same thing as having a direction in life, it revved me up and gave me some torque.

Ron came home from college for a few weeks that summer, and I recall finding her sitting on the couch in our living room in Orléans, smoking a cigarette and perusing a *Paris Match* magazine. She was wearing her hair cut short à la new wave French flicks (Jean Seberg in *Breathless*) and looked trim and hip in her flannel pajamas with the pants rolled up over her shapely calves. This was the same kid who'd smuggled gin in perfume bottles on Girl Scout trips back in Heidelberg ("We could still taste the Evening in Paris," her friend Carolyn Thune once told me), and got into boy-crazy, "making-out" marathons with her high school classmates, but Penn had given her a new image. I'd always been fond of her delicate features. Now there was a sharper arch to her eyebrows and a wry downward tug at the corners of her mouth, a new haughtiness that pushed out at the space around her and made for a protective cocoon.

Our father came out of the bathroom and stood by the couch, drying his hands on a towel. His hair had a silver sheen to it now and his paunch had grown a few inches, all of which made him look like a provincial European with his new thin mustache and tweed jackets. He stared at Ron's unpacked luggage next to the couch and fumbled in the pockets of his gabardine trousers, like he was searching for the proper phrase.

"Christ, Ron. What're you gonna do? Sit around all day in your pee-jays? Dinner's almost ready."

"Gee, I didn't know we were dressing for dinner. I'll just go slip into my combat boots and web gear."

"Aw, don't be silly. You got two suitcases full of clothes right there, and your mother will take you shopping tomorrow if you . . ."

"Stop it, Charlie." Like an actor appearing on cue, Mom stuck her head out of the kitchen. "Leave her alone. She's on vacation and she can wear her pajamas all summer if she wants to."

"Christ, Rose. She hasn't unpacked anything but her toothbrush for two days, sitting around all day in her pajamas and now it's getting dark out."

Ronnie choked on her cigarette smoke as she laughed. "It's getting *dark* out? Well, why the hell didn't anybody tell me? That's a horse of a different color. I better go unpack my night-vision goggles." She got up from the couch and headed for the bathroom to wash up for dinner.

"You better unpack more than a toothbrush, you want to go running around France, smarty-pants. You're not in Philadelphia anymore."

These squabbles barely registered with me anymore. My head was filled with the sounds of Coltrane, my olfactory sense tuned to the aromas of Pigalle—Gauloise tobacco, North African kif, fried saturated fat, cheap cologne, evaporating bodily fluids, and limestone dust. I was spending whole weekends in Paris and ignoring my studies. The only class in school that even vaguely interested me was English. My cronies and I would bring in book reports and read aloud from the writings of Henry Miller, William Burroughs, and even the Marquis de Sade. We wanted to see if we could titillate the cheerleaders or make the English teacher, Miss Rich, squirm. Miss Rich had the biggest breasts of any woman I'd seen, but she was so passionate about literature that we could've brought in *Mein Kampf* or the *Kama Sutra* and she would've been just as delighted and tolerant of our lustful looks.

But no matter how amusing the classes at school, they could not compete with the romance of what was going on in Paris. The Algerian crisis had made the term *plastique* (plastic explosives) part of everyday conversation, I was making fast money on the black market, and Bud Powell, one of the greatest bebop pianists of all time, was having his last stand at the Blue Note. Why waste time sitting at home reading Henry Miller or the *Kama Sutra* when a well-rounded sex education could be had with my GI buddies and the hookers in Paris?

The whores on rue Pigalle were a few levels up from the leather and war paint *poules* over on rue Germain Pilon. The pecking order went even further downhill as you explored side streets around Place Pigalle, where the chicks had dicks, or farther north in Saint-Denis, where they were big, buxom, and black. There was a clearly defined hierarchy and it didn't bode well for girls who wandered onto somebody else's turf. The girls along rue Pigalle had a more reserved, satiny come-on in their well-cut short skirts and Brigitte Bardot hairdos.

According to Wilfred, Augie preferred the black ones in Saint-Denis and bragged that he even let them sit on his face. The image of a voluptuous woman squatting over me made my dick hard, but Wilfred warned me against it.

"You know what they say don't you?"

"No, Wilfred. What do they say?"

"Now I'm not saying anything about Augie here, you follow me?"

"Yeah yeah, so what do they say?"

"They say that if you go down on a bush, you'll go out on a limb."

I had no idea what that was supposed to mean. The vernacular I was picking up wasn't mature enough to keep pace with the experience, and Wilfred and Augie got such a bang out of parodying GI crudeness that their patter sounded like porno routines. Which is how my early sex life remained in my memory—exhilarating but tinged with sleaze, savoring every new sexual twist and turn yet always longing for a more enduring and romantic ideal.

Rue Pigalle was a GI strip. Everybody smoked Marlboros and the jukeboxes were stacked with current 45s from *American Bandstand*'s latest hit parade—everything from The Coasters' "Searchin" and Chuck Berry's "Johnny B. Goode," to white-bread pop like Paul Anka's "Diana" and whichever asshole did "Itsy Bitsy Teenie Weenie Yellow Polka-Dot Bikini." The whores had the final say about what went on the jukebox and I preferred the Madison Bar where Ray Charles tunes dominated.

I found Monique with her bleached-blond hair and pink orlon sweater leaning against the jukebox, chewing bubble gum and miming the words to "Hit the Road Jack." She smiled when she saw me, blew a bubble and popped it with her little white teeth, but didn't move a muscle in my direction. She exuded a certain confidence now that I was a repeat customer. It was as close as I'd come at that point to having my own girlfriend, and a warm glow started to flow up through my belly. Wilfred had gone down the street to Dirty Dicks to look for something strange, but for the past several weeks I'd been coming back to Monique at the Madison, passing up propositions from more exotic and voluptuous types in order to pursue a deeper, more meaningful relationship. Besides, there were too many drunks in uniform at Dirty Dicks.

I took a stool at the little service bar and ordered a Heineken. Before I even had a chance to drink it, I felt Monique's hand on my thigh and the next thing I knew we were upstairs in one of the tiny rooms and she was washing my cock in the sink. I could scarcely believe how smooth and supple her body was, like a teenager's, and I was fascinated with the soft, curly hair that obscured her pink vagina. She always smelled clean and freshly bathed, so I didn't hesitate to ask her if she would sit on my face. She laughed and pretended like she didn't know what I was talking about.

"You know," I said, lying on my back on the bed. "Sixty-nine. *Soixant neuf, tu comprende?*"

"Oo la la!" She touched my lips with her fingertips. "You want I should sit here?"

As she maneuvered herself over me on the bed, on all fours and facing my feet, I was afforded a worm's-eye view of one of nature's biggest mysteries—the female sex organs. My mouth salivated and excitement drove me to the verge of orgasm before she'd even touched me. Slowly she lowered herself until she was touching my lips and her pubic hair circled my mouth like a Vandyke goatee. It was an upside-down embrace, but still a kiss nonetheless, from mouth to pussy, but still lips to lips. The strangest feeling of intimacy raced through me at the idea that I was communing directly with her sex.

"Like this?" she asked, smiling at me upside down between her legs.

"Mmmmmmm."

As soon as she took my cock in her mouth and stuck her finger in my ass it was all over.

As if to punctuate my orgasm, the entire building shook with the impact of a nearby explosion. The walls and the floor lurched and I heard glass breaking in the distance as I squirted onto the sheets. I started laughing, but Monique immediately got up and stood by the door in a listening posture. I wanted to ask her what it was, but she put her finger to her lips and cracked the door so she could listen out into the hallway. First there was only a strange silence, in great contrast to the noise of the explosion, then the sound of footfalls as someone descended the stairs in a hurry and Monique closed the door.

"What was that?"

"The crazy Algerians. They blow up the city piece by piece. Last week I go to the cinema, boom, no more cinema. Big smoky hole. *Merde!*"

The wail of sirens drifted to my ears, and as she padded across the room I could see that she was rapidly losing her good humor. Once again I was reminded, if only for a fleeting moment, what a terrible influence sexual desire was—so powerful that it could populate a planet, and so cunning that I was projecting fantasies of taking Monique to dinner and the movies. But once I'd "shot my load" the illusion evaporated. I looked around at the shabby room and couldn't wait to get the hell out of there.

"Okay, baby," Monique said, "time to hit the road unless you give me more money, *tu comprends?*" She went and squatted over the douche bowl while I hurriedly pulled on my clothes.

My sister's pursuits were of a more intellectual nature—she was fast becoming an honor student at Penn—but she was not without an ear for music, and the next time she came back to Orléans for a summer visit she brought me a Chet Baker and Gerry Mulligan record. I was highly uncomfortable with her in those days. I'd developed all kinds of complexes about how I should be acting and dressing and was so self-conscious around her that it probably wasn't much fun for her either.

"Hey, Ron. What are the guys at Penn like?"

"What do you mean?"

"Well, what do they wear and all?"

"There's this one crowd, they ride Indian motorcycles and wear corduroy suits."

Her eyes were shining with some memory, so I tried to get more detail. "You mean corduroy suits like Anthony Perkins in *Psycho?*"

"Hell, I don't know, Steve. I'm trying to read, alright?"

She always got very touchy when I asked her about the guys she was interested in, although, come to think of it, I wasn't real forthcoming about girlfriends. What was I gonna do—tell her about Monique at the Madison?

Later we were sitting on the couch after Mom and Dad had gone to bed. I'd put the Baker–Mulligan record on our old Telefunken hi-fi and Ron showed me some short stories that she'd written, which I thought were terrific. One was about a girl in a play and a guy who's helping her get made up, and only when the girl is totally transformed by the makeup does he finally kiss her. Another one was about a guy and a girl sitting in a jazz club. The girl is tapping her foot on the wrong beat, which drives the guy up the wall. That one riveted me.

Ron watched me as I read that story. She was sitting very close to me on the couch, peering over my shoulder at the page and then at my face, and when I smiled she laughed, knowing that I'd recognized in it an anecdote I'd once told her. When I finished reading I looked up at her and for a moment felt that connection, an almost unbearable closeness with her—blood close, us against the world—that I would never know with another human being. She laughed and smoked some more as she went on about how she'd always loved the idea and wanted to write about it because it made her think of me, and when her eyes teared up I thought for a moment that she was going to cry, but she crushed out her cigarette and waved her hand like it was the smoke.

A hundred things flashed through my head that I wanted to say to her, but the sudden intimacy had made us both very uncomfortable. I sat there stupidly rereading the damned story, hoping she wouldn't see in me the terrible mixture of pride and longing I felt for her as I read it again and compared her life with mine.

Baker and Mulligan had started in on their signature arrangement of "But Not For Me" for the second or third time when Dad appeared, all bleary-eyed in his blown-out Jockey shorts, snooping really, but trying to cover it by asking if we wanted a snack. Ron said, "A *snack*? Christ, do you have any idea what time it is?" We laughed and Dad mumbled something unintelligible. But we were all sleepy by that point and we went to bed and the moment was gone.

She was reading Ayn Rand that summer. When I asked her about it she said that I probably wouldn't like it. I'd been reading Sartre, Camus, Kerouac, Burroughs. It angered me when she said that. What am I—too stupid to read a goddamned book? So I read *Atlas Shrugged* and told myself that I liked it. I can't remember anything about it, though, other than "Who's John Galt?" or maybe it was

"Where's John Galt?" But I could quote passages from *Naked Lunch* almost verbatim.

This whole business of recommending books to read was something Veronica took way too seriously for me to comprehend. She'd been very taken with J. D. Salinger's stories about the Glass family, the *Nine Stories* and *Franny and Zooey*. The theme of oversensitivity and spiritual arrogance was a mystical thread that fascinated her in her last year at the University of Pennsylvania, and she even wrote her honor thesis about the Glass family and how Seymour was, in fact, a banana fish.

Truth be told, any influence my sister might have made at that time in my life could have only been for the good, because the books that I was reading as I followed my own thread (Jean Genet is another that comes to mind) were romanticizing lives of crime and self-indulgence.

The last summer we were in Orléans, several of Ron's friends from Penn stopped by our apartment driving a rented Renault. They were all going to the running of the bulls in Pamplona. My sister was waiting for space-available flights that were free to military dependents and could not catch up with her friends, so they asked me if I wanted to join them. They had to depart immediately to make the fiesta when it started on July 7. Dad figured I'd be less likely to cause an international incident with Ronnie's friends than with my GI buddies, so he gave me a couple hundred bucks and let me go, happy to be rid of me for a few weeks.

It turned out to be two of the most memorable weeks of my life. I developed a mad crush on Ronnie's college roommate, Suzanne, which peaked when we shared a room in a pension in San Sebastián on the way to Pamplona.

The guys dropped Suzanne and me off in San Sebastián to spend a day strolling around the romantic beaches, while they drove down to Madrid to pick up another friend. Suzanne was a big, handsome Irish girl, with dirty blond hair down below her shoulders, a faint scar on her nose suggesting a childhood break, and clear blue eyes. Later that day, after taking a shower to rinse off the saltwater, she donned a simple cotton peasant's dress. Then she took me to a little clothing store and encouraged me to buy several striped, boatnecked French sailor shirts with three-quarter-length sleeves that she promised would be the envy of all the guys at the running of the bulls.

At dinner Suzanne was totally engrossed in a book, and by the time coffee was served, along with a fruit and cheese platter, I was miserable. She must have felt my eyes on her, and every once in a while she'd smile at me, take a sip of coffee, glance politely around the dining room, and then go back to her reading. I noticed several other travelers who were eating alone and doing the same.

"Suzanne?"

"Hmmm?"

I couldn't see the cover of the book, so I asked her what it was that she found so engrossing.

"Some novel by this woman that everyone at Penn's reading—*Atlas Shrugged*. Something to do with personal empowerment. Kind of refreshing after all that existential crap I was into, like Sartre and Camus. I doubt if you'd like it."

It was similar to the conversation I'd had with my sister the summer before—same book, same snooty attitude, and now that I'd read it I could see the connection—but I was willing to forgo comments if it improved my chances to get in her pants. "You didn't like Camus?"

She shrugged again and glanced around the dining room, catching the eye of a guy with a neatly trimmed beard who was also reading. He saluted with his glass of wine and she smiled back.

"I loved *L'etranger*," I said a little desperately. "It was so simply written I even read it in French."

"Look, Steve. I'm really bushed. I think I'll turn in early tonight."

"You sure you don't want me to leave you alone so you can flirt with the professor over there?"

"Tell you what. Why don't we have a couple brandies? I think you drank too much coffee and I don't want you keeping me up all night. Deal?"

"Okay, deal."

"Besides, the professor isn't my type."

"Oh yeah? Well, what is your type?"

She drummed her fingers on the table for a moment. "Don't tell anybody, but you're probably more my type than anyone I've met in a long time." She let that sink in and then leaned forward. "Unfortunately, you're about five years too young besides being my best friend's younger brother, so don't push your luck."

The brandy didn't help much. I tried hard that night not to toss and turn, but sleep wouldn't come. I lay there on my back in the dark in my Jockey shorts and tried to think of things a more mature guy would do or say. Suzanne, lying on her side with her back to me, wasn't having much success with sleeping either. At one point I heard her chuckle softly to herself and felt the vibrations in the mattress.

"You awake?"

"I was just thinking about your sister, how funny she is. Did you know you both have the same smile?"

I wasn't sure if this information increased or decreased my chances for sex. "What do you mean, funny?"

"Oh, God, I don't know. She . . . well, she's on the dean's list at Penn, which is a really big thing there, I shit you not. I mean, she might be the most brilliant person I ever met, but then she flat out refused to put her head under water." She started giggling again. "So they, they told her they were going to flunk her in phys ed, can you believe it? I mean all she had to do was dive into the goddamned swimming pool. I don't know. Maybe it's not all that funny. You had to be there."

Yeah, I thought a little enviously, you had to be there.

"I hope she's alright," I said for lack of anything better.

"Here." Suzanne sat up and turned her back to me. "Help me with this." As I unhooked the clasps of her bra, she laughed again.

"This seems terribly incestuous."

She let me fondle her bare breasts for a while, but nothing more. Finally I went into the bathroom and did the *puñeta*, wondering miserably if I'd go blind before I was ever mature enough to have a woman like Suzanne.

The next day we hitched a ride to Pamplona with a couple of wild-haired, sunburned, expatriate American students in their Citroën Deux Chevaux, one of those goofy cars you see all over France with a top that rolls back like a sardine can and bounces around on skinny wheels and elongated springs like a Tin Lizzy. We drove through the Pyrenees with the pedal to the metal, hurtled through quaint little villages with horse-drawn carts, and the driver kept taking his eyes off the road, rubbernecking to point out local color and guzzle wine out of a bota.

"See those guys with the rifles and shiny three-pointed hats? They're the Guardia Civil, Franco's bully boys, so stay as far away from them as you can get."

A Deux Chevaux (two horses) has a top end of about fifty klicks per hour, but sailing down those two-lane mountain roads, gravity compensated for horsepower. Suzanne whooped with pleasure each time we leaned way out over a cliff on a hairpin curve, while I cringed and prayed that the driver would keep his eyes on the damned road.

Not having read *The Sun Also Rises*, I was overwhelmed with the all-night drinking, carousing, and endless dancing in the streets at Pamplona, with the heads of huge puppets bobbing above the noisy throng, reminding me of the Mummers parade in Philly. The sidewalk cafés surrounding the main square were overflowing from sunup to sundown. A band of singers, dancing and holding hands in a circle, would catch me walking alone through the square and surround me and not let me out of the circle until I'd joined in the incomprehensible song, something like *No veeno le goosta, beep bitty beep beep beep,* and drag me, hands still locked, into somebody's house off the main square for free food and wine. Loose women of all nationalities traipsed around pie-eyed, but I couldn't seem to make headway with them, so I'd go searching for Suzanne. She wasn't having any trouble in that area—all the guys were hitting on her.

On opening day of the Fiesta of San Fermin, Antonio Ordonez went mano a mano with Louis Miguel Dominguin. In the first fight the bull was so huge and fierce that he shook the whole stadium when he crashed into the *barrera*. The crowd rose to its feet and cheered the bull. Ordonez then stepped out into the ring and made a breathtaking series of opening passes with the cape that had the entire crowd back on its feet—moments of hushed silence were followed by delirious cheering. Suzanne told me that those passes were called Veronicas, after the woman who wiped the face of Jesus on his way to Calvary with the cross.

Seamlessly, Ordonez took the bull out of the final pass and enticed it to hurtle around him in a tight circle, searching with its horns for the cape that flared out about the fighter's still, graceful figure. For a moment it was like sculpture, a ton of muscle and horn wrapped around the delicate man. Finally he snapped the cape out from under the bull's nose and left the bull standing there heaving and stunned. Everybody was on their feet screaming, Olé! He turned his back to the bull and walked slowly over to the crowd. He must have made some movement that was too quick, because just as he was bowing and dedicating the bull to the people, the beast snapped alert and hurtled across the ring right into his backside. I'd gone to the fights anticipating rooting for the bull, but it was a horrifying moment when it happened and I doubt if a soul in that arena wanted to see it. Ordonez shot out of the ring and up into the crowd like he was fired from a cannon. The bull followed right after him, over the *barrera* and up into the stands.

Somehow they coaxed the bull back into the ring and carried Ordonez off to the infirmary. It was such a magnificent bull that when Dominguin and his crew came out to kill it, everybody threw seat cushions and bottles into the ring and they let the bull live.

Luckily the horns had passed on either side of him, and the next day Ordonez was back in the ring with his chest all taped up and making passes at the bulls. Though he was never quite as good again, that amazing series of Veronicas he made on opening day had afforded me a glimpse into the brutal but elegant pageantry of bygone days. I never saw anything at a bullfight worth mentioning after that. Hemingway didn't make the running that year, and rumors about him gave the fiesta a heightened texture of danger and expectation. When we all heard later that he'd blown his brains out, it seemed the final curtain on that era. Other writers and friends of Hemingway said that maybe he couldn't write anymore, couldn't face life with diminishing talent—why go on when you've lost the ability to do the one thing that gives life meaning and purpose?

To my mind, the thing that gave life meaning and purpose was getting laid, and at one point in the Fiesta of San Fermin, Suzanne sounded like she was going to let me have my way with her. But we were both too drunk and threw up all over our room instead. The next day I decided to wait until we got back to France, back to civilization where I could find some hookers.

When Ronnie finally got over to France that summer, she drove down to the Riviera with Mom to meet us. Ron's description of that drive illuminated a side of our mother I hadn't seen before.

"Steve, you wouldn't have recognized Mom. She drove nonstop, all night from Orléans to Nice, right through the foothills of the Alps, clutching the wheel in one hand, a container of coffee in the other, and a cigarette hanging out of her mouth. She ate chicken salad sandwiches as she drove and only stopped to pee. At first I thought she was worried about you and in a hurry to see if you were alright, but I think she was just really happy and excited to be away from Daddy for a while."

By the time Veronica graduated from Penn, she'd gained another year on me—I had to repeat my senior year at Orléans American High School, due mostly to absence and general lack of interest. I figured I might as well pursue what I knew best—a life of crime and self-indulgence.

The hipster, the hophead, and the hustler were fast becoming my role models. I idolized musicians like Chet Baker and Jackie McLean and didn't have time to consider that maybe they created that music *in spite of* the drugs, rather than because of them.

In 1962 Dad's three-year commitment in France wound to a close, and he and Mom began to pursue their plans for retirement. Once again we packed up to move, and this time, the thought of leaving the romantic sites and sounds of Orléans and Paris was infinitely more disappointing than when we'd left Philly or Heidelberg. I was glad I'd failed my senior year and stretched it into two, no matter the consequences of a poor scholastic record. I had no idea what I'd do with myself when I got back to The World (as the GIs called it). I had vague notions of going on the road, à la Jack Kerouac, and exploring the historic birthplaces of the music I'd come to love—joints like Birdland, the Five Spot, the Village Vanguard, and Minton's Playhouse in Harlem.

I'd found a way to make fast money in France on the black market. Surely there'd be similar opportunities stateside for a quick-witted guy like yours truly. The world, as they say, was my oyster. After all, how many young white guys could scat-sing Coltrane solos?

part three

back in the world

chapter 4

Once we got back to the States, it didn't take me long before my nose for adventure got me into serious trouble. It's not like I'd planned or had any desire to be a bona fide criminal. It just played out that way, evolving gradually like a bridge hand where you run out of trump and get stuck. I mean, what the hell? I was a nice fella, charming and bright, experimenting with the seamy side like other young guys as I teetered on the edge of manhood. But I was determined to linger on that edge as long as I could. It was the early sixties, the Kennedy years. Youthful rebellion hung in the air like a siren song. Anything seemed possible.

I went through the motions of doing the right thing, drove down to Florida with Mom and Dad where they bought a new home in Clearwater, a two-bedroom bungalow that bordered an orange grove. The asphalt streets and lush lawns of their suburban community were surrounded by the fading remnants of a much older Florida—small cattle farms, horse ranches, and endless cypress and weeping willow trees dripping with Spanish moss. Pogo and Albert's Okefenokee Swamp seemed like it was just around the corner. The place had some soul, but sitting around the Florida room with Mom and Dad, eating off TV tables while we watched *The Beverly Hillbillies* and *The Dick Van Dyke Show*, wasn't my idea of a life. A local junior college was willing to overlook my poor grades. Prompted by my parents, I enrolled for the following September.

Eager to "expand my horizons and supplement my education" through travel, I arranged to meet up with Wilfred, my old black-market buddy, who was getting his discharge in New York. We'd drive across country, see life On the Road, have a grand old time and a last fling before school. First I had to persuade Mom and Dad to finance this worthy expedition since I hadn't figured out yet how to make money. I told them I wanted to stop by Philly to visit Ron at Penn and seek her advice about scholastic matters. Then, I told them, I planned to take a short trip to the West Coast with an old high school friend and "finally see this wonderful American countryside of ours."

"Nuts!" Dad said. "Where the hell is this kid gonna get the money to go gallivanting all over the country?"

But Mom said, "C'mon, Charlie. Give him a few bucks and let him go sow his wild oats before he settles down. After all, weren't you traveling all over the globe at his age?"

She probably hoped I'd get the wild streak out of my system once and for all. Against his better judgment, Dad gave me a few hundred bucks and I got on a Greyhound.

A shiver of anticipation ran up my spine as I rang the doorbell to Ronnie's apartment, which was right in the heart of the neighborhood surrounding the University of Pennsylvania. No matter the time and distances we'd traversed, the predicament was always familiar—standing outside the door to my sister's room, wondering what the hell she was doing in there.

The door opened and there stood Suzanne, my big heartthrob from Pamplona, grinning at me and looking vastly more mature. Her hair no longer hung over her shoulders but was clipped and coiffed, and a skirt, blouse, and heels had replaced the old peasant dress and sandals.

"Ronnie, it's your brother, Steve," she said as I slouched into the apartment. Suzanne gave me a kiss on the cheek as I went past and added, "You're starting to look like Vincent van Gogh."

I wanted to grab her, crush her in my arms, and stick my tongue down her throat, she looked so good. I regretted not balling her when I'd had the chance because the way she kissed me on the cheek made it clear that that opportunity was past.

Then I spotted Ron, getting up off a window bench that overlooked the tree-lined street, walking over to me with a soda glass in her hand and a delighted grin on her face—what an attractive young woman she'd become at the age of twenty-one, so svelte and poised. The image of that smart-alecky kid that persisted in my memory no longer fit her.

She stopped at arm's length, cocked her hip, and studied me for a moment, then laughed. "I never thought of it before, Suzanne, but with that little goatee, he does look sort of like van Gogh. Now sit down, Steve, and let me get you a Coke. Then I want to hear what you've been up to and what your plans are, okay?"

"Ronnie," Suzanne called from the doorway, "I have to go pack, but big kisses to you both, and keep in touch."

I detected a brisk sense of transition in the air, young women embarking on careers, brimming with confidence, all jacked up after four years of college and eager to create their new lives.

When Ron came back I said, "What do you want to leave this place for, Ron? This is the coolest apartment I've ever seen. Tell Suzanne to come back and we could all just stay here. You write your stories and I'll get a job with Jocko as a deejay or somethin'."

Ron laughed. "I wish it were that simple, and we'd both love nothing more. But Suzanne has plans in Boston, and I'm moving to New York. What I want to know is—what do you plan on doing now?"

It was the sixty-four-thousand-dollar question—I'd spent a lot of time and energy avoiding it and didn't appreciate it coming from her just then. I gulped my Coke and stared at my shoes and tried to suppress the irrational resentment that she'd gotten the Ivy League education while I had to mooch off Mom and Dad.

"I dunno. I'm gonna meet an old friend from France tomorrow, ride out to the West Coast in his car, then go back to Florida and start school. You know, some junior college down there."

"Look, Steve," Ron said, picking up on the change in me, "I'm sorry. I didn't mean to give you the third degree, and I know you just came by to visit me. Let me make you a sandwich and we'll go to the movies tonight, okay?"

"Okay." Ron always knew how to cheer me up, when she wanted to.

"Here, I got this for you when I heard you were coming." She picked up a flat package off the coffee table and handed it to me. Inside I found a brand-new copy, still in the shrink-wrapping, of John Coltrane's album *Blue Train*, featuring Curtis Fuller on trombone and Lee Morgan on trumpet. I would later come to love that album so much that I could scat-sing their solos on the title track almost note for note.

It was a British movie we went to that night, *Whistle Down the Wind*, with a young Hayley Mills. Afterward we ran into a couple of guys Ron knew from Penn at a local diner, and we all ended up riding around in their car, supposedly to go to a club for a few drinks. A prolonged silence in the car prompted me to speak up at one point.

"Hey, Ron, listen. I'm really beat," I said, stretching and yawning in the backseat, trying to beg off gracefully, but still hip. "I need to, like, go catch a few Zs, know what I mean?"

Ron started laughing and her friends followed suit. My sister always found my attempts at striking a hipster pose ironic and funny, and the guys didn't know what to think of me with my wispy goatee, long hair, and the stooped posture I'd come to associate with the druggies and beatniks I was trying to emulate. I wasn't really sleepy. I was feeling so uncomfortable that I wanted to go somewhere and weep. I felt like the Alan Bates character in the Hayley Mills movie, impossibly alienated and doomed.

Ron took pity on me and had them drop us back at her apartment. She never took my "tortured soul" act very seriously and probably suspected that I was playing it tongue-in-cheek. On the other hand, it was much funnier to her *because* I was so serious, a quality Ron always recognized as an essential element of humor—misplaced seriousness. Feeling awkward and self-conscious as we stepped out of the car, I judged her friends harshly and zeroed in on the absence of sexual tension going on between her and these guys. I might've been naive about my sister, or about the rigors of an Ivy League education, but I could've told these jag-offs a thing or two about sex. I sneered at Ron's college friends—they were all a bunch of squares who'd copped out and didn't have the spit to go face life on the street.

The next day I caught the train to New York, travelin' light. Spent the day in a great triple-bill horror movie on the Deuce—*Dracula, Franken-stein*, and *The Wolf Man*. Then I went downtown to meet Wilfred at the old Five Spot on Cooper Square with thirty-cent beers, sawdust on the floor, and Roland Kirk hooting up a terrific storm. Talk about getting your well-rounded education.

Kirk, blind since two years old, rocked back and forth as he played in a way that only a blind man might move who'd never watched and mimicked the physicality of other musicians. He had three saxophones hanging from his shoulders, the body of each horn stretched out longer than the next, and on tunes like "Three for the Festival" he jammed all three in his mouth and blew them together in harmony. He had a flute stuck in the bell of the tenor, and a circus whistle around his neck that he tooted on to punctuate transitions from one horn to the next.

But this was no freak circus act. Roland Kirk was one of the most exciting virtuosos of his time, particularly on flute. He had a kick-ass rhythm section of old pros like Charlie Persip and Horace Parlan behind him, pushing him into increasingly impassioned efforts, and when he yanked that flute out of his tenor and started growling and moaning into it, man, it was tasty. When he finished a tune, he'd grope around for the three horns that were now slung all around his body, sweat pouring down his face, and Wilfred and I clapped and stamped our feet and hollered for more. That session at the old Five Spot, crammed into that little bar with Roland Kirk blowing right into my face, stands out in my memory as the best live set I ever caught.

Wilfred, who was getting his discharge at Fort Hamilton in Brooklyn, had had his supercharged Austin Healy Sprite shipped back from France. He'd removed the grille and painted the cavity black, giving the nose that scooped-out Lotus look. The rest was painted silver with a wide black racing stripe and a roll bar on the driver's side—a real labor of love. Tossing his old army uniforms in the first trash can we saw, he folded the top back on his car and we headed out across country to enjoy our newfound freedom from parents and Uncle Sam.

I remember little of what we talked about on that cross-country drive. Wilfred had installed an Abarth exhaust system on his car, giving it the growl of a much larger grand-prix model and making conversation or even playing the radio difficult. But whenever we stopped to eat or fill up the tank, Wilfred reminisced about his family, a big Italian one, and as he talked the hipster image faded away and an irrepressible grin would animate his craggy face. His voice rose with fondness as he told me stories of him and his brothers sneaking in and out of the kitchen all day to dunk bread in Mom's tomato sauce and Dad sitting at the dinner table with a big bottle of dago red at his feet.

Down-shifting into curves with the engine howling and then powering out the other side, we headed southwest to New Orleans. To our whacked-out, youthful perceptions, the French Quarter in New Orleans held the promise of weird drugs and loose women, a stateside version of what we'd enjoyed in Pigalle. All we found were a lot of clip joints full of slick Bourbon Street broads with glossy-mouthed come-ons. Bottles of champagne would materialize on the bar, and if you looked like you didn't want to pay for it the bartenders and bouncers got mean.

We stopped in Austin, Texas, to visit Riley, an old black-market buddy from France who was working as a security guard at the University of Texas. Riley, a big lanky Texan and wannabe hippie, fed us peyote buttons ground up with green Jell-O that made us nauseous. Wilfred and I took turns sleeping with his sexy cousin, who had a great body, and we'd lie on each side of her while she checked out who got stiff first. We drove to Nuevo Laredo, bought some amphetamines at a Mexican pharmacy, and got busted trying to cross back over the border with them. The only reason we didn't get locked up was that LBJ was coming across the border at the exact same moment with a huge entourage and the border guards couldn't be bothered.

When we hit San Francisco we discovered that Augie, the main mover behind our black-market capers in Paris, had forsaken his love of larceny to study television production at San Francisco City College. Wilfred also copped out to the establishment shortly after and went to live with his parents in Salinas and study hair styling and cosmetology. This was somewhat understandable, though, since Wilfred would go to any lengths to get his hands on a broad.

The last time Wilfred, Augie, and I were all together, we went to a jazz joint in the Fillmore District called Jimbo's Bop City. Ben Webster was playing that night with a young guitarist named Carlos Santana, who at the time was known only in local jazz circles. Nobody threw down on a ballad like Ben Webster—made us cry in our beer when he did "Danny Boy"—and I loved the contrast of old boozy-sounding tenor against electric guitar chords and licks.

Another contrast unfolded in the wee hours of the morning when Jimbo's closed and everybody staggered several yards up the block with drinks in hand to an after-hours joint called The Plantation Club, musicians too, bass player dragging his huge bass fiddle. As the sun began to light the horizon, men in suits and girls and women in Sunday dresses came strolling by on their way to a Baptist Church. And as they passed by the guys who were shooting craps and drinking beer on the steps outside the Plantation, there was a lovely collision, night people and day people, hipsters and working stiffs; all-night loners ghosting a husky tenor man were afforded a glimpse of their doppelganger opposite in a doffing of porkpie hats and a sudden surcease in cursing. Each time someone came in or went out of the club, jazz music and cigarette smoke billowed onto the street and enfolded both the Good and the Bad in a seductive embrace.

Now that Wilfred and Augie had gone legit, I hooked up with Augie's brother, Pasquale, who was looking for a crime partner to hang out with. Like me, he was younger than Augie, but he had an older, rougher aspect. If Augie reminded me of a Fellini movie, Pasquale was John Garfield out of film noir. We spent a few weeks prowling North Beach while Pasquale gave me a tour of the jazz joints and coffee shops. My favorite was the twenty-four-hour Hot Dog Palace at the triangle of Columbus, Grant, and Broadway, where speed freaks with monikers like Fast Walkin' Jack and Gray Eyes zipped in and out all night, their pockets clinking with Methedrine ampoules and Art Blakey on the jukebox.

Methedrine was a tease—made us restless—and one night we hotwired a car for a trip to Long Beach. Pasquale said he knew guys there who were into serious drugs, heroin and cocaine. My curiosity eclipsed my skepticism as I watched Pasquale, half drunk, fumble with a chewing-gum wrapper that he used to jump the car's electrical system. We didn't get out of Russian Hill before the car, a nice little TR3, shorted out with the lights flashing and the horn honking. When we tried to push it over to the curb, the car rolled out of control down one of those steep hills that San Francisco is famous for, carrying Pasquale with it. He was hanging half out the door trying to reach in and hit the brake when he bounded off a parking meter and smashed into an exquisite old apartment building. As I helped Pasquale out of the wreck, we noticed that a patrol car had pulled up into the same street. It was four a.m. There wasn't a soul around. Everything geared down into slow motion.

"Hey, Steve," Pasquale said. "I can't take a pinch. I'm out on bail on a narcotics beef."

Now he tells me. And here I thought he was such a sweet guy.

"Fuck it," I said. "Let's run."

We took off just as the cops pulled up across the street from us and were climbing out of their patrol car. We ran back up the block, turned the corner, and started to sprint. Bullets banged off cars next to me as the cops opened fire. Pasquale got shot in the back, bent over as he was running, and the bullet, I found out later, exited up by his shoulder, striking no vital organs. I got away momentarily but was recognized as I tried to walk out of the neighborhood, now swarming with harness bulls. When the cops told me that Pasquale had been shot, my reaction incriminated both of us.

It was my first arrest, so Pasquale forgave me for stupidly giving us away. We strutted around the big dormitory bullpens in San Francisco City Jail for a few days, trading war stories with the other cons, Pasquale with his cop-shot shoulder all taped up, smoking cigarillos and cracking wise. Then we got shipped out to San Bruno County Jail for a few months.

Pasquale got sent to a different tier because he had other charges, so my first experience with a county jail was solo. The tier was a block-long cement hallway with single cells on either side. The first week the cells got filled to capacity, so an old stew bum was put into my cell.

"Put him in with the kid," I heard the trustee say to the hack when the cell doors were cranked opened.

He was in rough shape, smelled bad, and spoke little. Since there was only one bunk, he slept on his mattress on the floor. Like many an old-timer he was stoic about his miserable condition and seemed grateful to lie down in peace. He curled up on the floor and slept soundly through most of the days and nights, and while he slept, I could not resist studying the creases and scars on his ravaged face, a tragic story detailed like a map in the harsh glow of prison lighting. A chow wagon came around and trustees slid metal trays of starchy food under the bars. This was the only thing that aroused my cell mate to consciousness.

"Say youngster. You gonna eat that potato?"

I could not deny him. I always gave him my baked potato, which he wolfed down, holding it in his tobacco-stained fingers like a ripe pear. Something about him struck a chord in me, as though I was seeing a potential version of myself in thirty years.

After we finished our meals, the entire tier was locked out of the cells for several hours. Most of the guys gathered at the far end of the tier and lounged around on spare mattresses listening to KJAZ on the radio. The disc jockey played three cuts from different jazz albums, and everybody tried to guess who the musicians were before the credits were announced at the end of the three tunes. The older black guys were amazed at my ability to pick out not just the leading horn players but who the rhythm sections were. I could scat-sing solos note for note, like Cannonball's and Coltrane's solos on "So What."

Aside from the pathetic old guy in my cell, it was not a bad time. It was the first of many incarcerations, and I relished my ability to find a kind of beauty in such things, real-life drama and experience that I knew was beyond the grasp of my brilliant sister. You take the high road, baby, and I'll take the low.

Finally Pasquale and I came back to court, the charges of Grand Theft Auto were reduced to Joyriding, and we got sentenced to probation. So ended my version of *On the Road*. I was only too happy to head back to my parents' house in Clearwater, Florida, lick my wounds, and go to work sawing up chickens in a Kentucky Fried Chicken until I saved up enough cash to go back to the Big Apple.

Mom and Dad had heard the tale of my arrest when I'd called them frantically from the police precinct in San Francisco, begging them to wire me several thousand dollars for bail money. Surprisingly, they'd sent the cash immediately, but it got lost for a while in the penal system, and finally went toward a fine for the damaged car and a plane ticket back to Florida. When I got home they claimed to be happy to see me again and thankful that I'd made it back in one piece. But they were more subdued around me. Sometimes I'd catch Mom peering at me through her cigarette smoke. Then she'd smile faintly and look off as though lost in thought on some other matter. I remembered how she'd taken my back when I wanted to go on that trip—then I'd gone off and betrayed her trust. I was suddenly aware of Mom's quiet dignity and inner strength and felt the sting in her forgiveness.

I'd have felt better if she'd lashed out at me or told me to get lost, because I no longer felt like the nice guy of six months ago who was just "experimenting with the seamy side." Something clingy and dark had followed me from that county jail and I sensed its proximity, pursuing me even here in sunny Florida, in the innocent home of my parents. I made a vow to myself that, from then on, I'd never tell Mom and Dad if I got busted or ever ask them again for bail money. I'd just take my lumps as they came and try to keep my shady troubles from their doorstep.

To appease my parents I attended classes at St. Petersburg Junior College for a semester, but it wasn't long before my resolve was forgotten. Restless, and lacking direction, I fell in with a few jovial lushes and we lurched around campus leering at the girls and sneering at the squares.

Ron, meanwhile, had arrived in New York and was hanging out at The Hip Bagel, a typical early-sixties, Greenwich Village eatery that was on either Thompson or MacDougal between Bleecker and Houston. Bleecker and MacDougal streets in those days were lined with sleepy coffee shops like the Fat Black Pussycat, Rienzi's, the Figaro, and the Feenjon, but The Hip Bagel had good food and featured a jukebox with one of the best jazz collections in town. Ron loved the place and once told me she'd have been happy to work there as a waitress for the rest of her days.

But my sister was paying her dues too. She got a job at Lord & Taylor's and found a roommate, Susan Goldberg, who worked at Macy's or Bloomingdales and had a spare room in her apartment up in Yorkville. Susan had introduced my sister to a crowd of bright young men, like Danny Fields, David Kaufelt, and David Neuman. Some of them had been to Penn, and their faded khakis and polo shirts offset their dark, big-city intensity. Ron had a crush on Danny Fields, for all the good it would do her. These guys were about as straight as a pair of waltzing mice.

Danny once told me that Susan Goldberg "invented" Veronica. There was an amusing proprietary ring to the expression and I laughed when he said it, never having heard it before. I pictured all these gay blades and fag hags running around inventing one another, endowing my sister with a hip new persona as they ushered her into their precious inner circle. They were a resourceful crowd, though, and Danny Fields would later make an impact on the music scene when he championed people like Iggy Pop and the Stooges, the Ramones, and Nico. Who knows? Maybe he invented them.

My sister's first romance in New York was with a guy named Michael Maslansky, who became a film publicist. Their crew hung around San Remo's and the Bleecker St. Tavern, called themselves the YJS, or Young

Jewish Set, and Danny recalled that Veronica's affair with Maslansky was less than satisfying.

"He would call her," Danny told me, "and ask her what she'd been doing all day, and she'd say, I've been waiting for you to call. We all thought your sister was beautiful, but her intensity apparently turned Maslansky off."

Here was a prelude to a string of heartbreaks for my sister. She was, perhaps, a little too bright, and cared a bit too much about love affairs, which required a lighter touch. I remembered how her eyes shone when she talked about guys she liked, and naive though I was, I sensed in her a deep longing for intimacy and for a guy to cherish her enough to propose marriage. If that seemed incongruous with her circle of gay friends—well, being a fag hag was, as Danny put it, the smart move for a hip, career-minded young lady in the big city.

chapter 5

Yo, Flocko! What's the word?
      Thunderbird!
What's the price?
Thirty twice!
Hey, man. Lemme do the lead on "Life Is but a Dream."
No way, Jack. You white boys ain't got the chops for lead. Just do the blows.

It was 1964. I was twenty years old and hanging out in Washington Square Park, singing doo-wops with a couple of Puerto Ricans and a bottle of Thunderbird, only a block away from Ron's beloved Hip Bagel. I'd caught the first bus out of Florida as soon as I'd saved enough money working every day at a Kentucky Fried Chicken. After being cooped up with my parents, this was just the balm I needed, lounging around the park all day, passing a bottle and a joint and doing "the blows" in three-part harmony—*whooooooooooooooo, whoo-be-doooooooooo*—throwing down a cappella with Flocko and The Thunderbirds. Knew damn well Ron couldn't blow no doo-wops.

Greenwich Village had the atmosphere of a carnival that never stopped, and as I strolled around on a summer day I always had the taste of cotton candy in my throat. People didn't wear clothes, they wore costumes—porkpie hats and bowlers, Chinese silk jackets, embroidered smoking jackets with velvet lapels, hooded cloaks like Dracula, beatnik-baggy boatneck sweaters, or wheat jeans with madras shirts and sandals (gay Ivy League), sheepskin vests and cowboy boots, jellabas and kufis, some with elaborately carved walking sticks and huge sheepherding staffs—and it was perfectly acceptable to spend the evening catnapping on a bench in Washington Square if you failed to pick up a mate. Why go home, ever?

Getting my sex education from Pigalle hookers had left me shy with girls and inept at seduction, but there were plenty of guys offering me a bed for the night. Problem was, I didn't like sex with men, which I knew was the unspoken deal when one offered to take me home. I tried it a few times but realized quickly that I could get more sleep on a park bench or a seat at the bus station. Yet if I picked a mark who was stoned enough, I could get by with a minimal amount of pawing and begging off before he passed out, giving me the added bonus of raiding his refrigerator and medicine cabinet. All the nellies were into drugs like dexies (uppers) and goofballs (downers). One of the guys I met had a pint of paregoric in a mouthwash bottle. In the morning when he had to go to work, I paid close attention so reentry into his vacant and well-furnished apartment was not a problem, then made nice-nice with the doorman so I could go back and pick up that Rolex on the nightstand. Why the hell anybody would want to go to work was simply beyond me.

The only communication I had with my sister was when I was in a jam and needed a few bucks to eat or a place to sleep. Ron soon parted ways with her roommate in Yorkville and got a thirty-five-dollar-a-month walk-up on Bedford Street, where once in a while she let me fall out on the floor. Being Ron's little brother I was occasionally tolerated by her friends, and throughout my life I would reap side benefits from her encyclopedic knowledge of the arts. The least little throwaway remark from her—*Scorsese is the next great American filmmaker*—would gain me the center of attention in hip circles of conversation even before most people had seen *Mean Streets*.

Once I ran into one of Ron's friends Danny Fields in Washington Square Park and tried to spark his interest in purchasing an ounce of grass, figuring I'd pull the old catnip gag. I mean, he was just some *guy* she knew and something of a Village character even back then. In hindsight I felt lousy doing it, but mainly because her friend, who'd seen a few scams himself, took one sniff at the nip and reneged on the deal, making me look like an amateur. I knew very quickly that the profession of beat-artist, although popular and lucrative at the time, was not for me.

Getting busted in San Francisco had interrupted my quest to try serious drugs, but once I hit the Village it didn't take me long to get connected. I'd read in one of those books by Burroughs or somebody the description of a rooming house on Ninth Street and Fourth Avenue that was a haven for heroin addicts and small-time criminals. (This building was torn down several years after I discovered it.) I checked into a room there one day and scored for smack my first night when I introduced myself to Sonny St. Claire, one of the old-time resident junkies.

Knock knock. "Sonny?"

From inside came the patter of someone tapping lightly on a bongo drum, floating out into the ratty old hallway where I stood. Silence, then the creak of floorboards as someone approached the door.

"Who?"

"Steve."

The door opened a few inches, revealing a sliver of Sonny's brown face with long goatee. Then the door opened wider and he stuck his head out to glance up and down the hallway.

I held up a few joints that I'd brought along by way of introduction. "You guys smoke reefer?"

"C'mon in, man. Sheeit, I thought you was Doc looking for the rent. Yeah, baby. You just in time to get down on a nickel beezag with me and Abdul Wadu."

Abdul Wadu sat on Sonny's bed tapping on a bongo drum in the light of a bare, red bulb in the ceiling. A radio was softly tuned in to a local jazz station and I recognized Red Garland on piano from one of those early Miles Davis cuts, like "Workin'," or "Cookin'."

"Say hey, little brother," said Abdul. "Did I hear somethin' 'bout some smoke? Come on in, cop a squat. Party's 'bout to begin."

He played a little riff on the bongo. Abdul looked like a shrunken version of Sonny, with an Afro, scraggly goatee, baggy boxer shorts, and a colorful bathrobe with a matching little cap. Sonny, his muscular torso bare over flannel pajama pants, offered me a stool next to his armchair. If these guys ever went out and hustled money for their drugs, you couldn't tell by their attire. Sonny St. Claire was rumored to be a good second-story man, but I rarely saw Sonny or Abdul Wadu wearing anything besides pajamas, bathrobes, and shower shoes, although occasionally they'd don jeans and peacoats to go score smack.

The room was spare of furnishings but still felt crowded. Sonny sat back down and proceeded to cook up a shot, holding several matches under a bent spoon.

"Abdul, get the kid a bowl a oatmeal over there on the stove."

I don't think I ever went to Sonny's crib when he didn't have a big pot of oatmeal simmering on his hot plate. Sonny grinned at me and winked. He took a tiny piece of cotton stuffing from a torn hole in his stained mattress, popped it into the spoon, and drew up his shot into an eyedropper-and-needle rig, then put a few drops back in the spoon for me—a gee-shot.

This was a time before the availability of plastic disposable syringes that can now be obtained free at needle-exchange clinics in the wake of the AIDS epidemic. Back then, hypodermic needles were precious and by prescription only, but they were stainless steel, endured through many fixes, and were passed around from one hungry junky to the next. Everybody shared *works*, or *gimmicks*. At shooting galleries, works could be rented for a dollar, and people rarely carried them on the street. "Possession of paraphernalia" would get you a skid-bid in the Tombs or Rikers Island, so you stashed them behind toilet tanks, in the busted mailbox of an abandoned building where you liked to "get off," inside the light fixture of a phone booth near the cop spot.

"Hey, man. You got gimmicks?"

"Yeah, for a gee-shot."

"Bet."

I watched Sonny carefully strip the edge off a dollar bill and wrap it around the end of the dropper so it fit securely into the female end of the needle. The strip of paper, usually the edge of a dollar but sometimes half of a match or a strip off a brown paper bag, was called a collar or a gee—hence, gee-shot—the amount of liquid contained in the tapered nose of the dropper that was wrapped with a gee.

"That oatmeal made with milk and honey, baby. You want to start with a warm, full belly cause after you take off on some a this here good Harlem doojie?" His eyes went soft and dreamy. "Man, you won't be thinking 'bout no food."

"Amen, brother," said Abdul Wadu. "S'like it says in the Koran. Man's always got to pay attention to his health."

Since I didn't know what I was doing, Sonny tied me off and hit me. He grinned when he saw my eyes dim as the warm glow spread through my gut and the taste of cotton candy bloomed in my throat. To turn somebody on to their first taste of heroin was known as "giving someone their wings." Chet Baker, a notorious heroin addict, came on the radio singing a Rodgers and Hart tune. Suddenly I knew exactly where Chet's mellow sound came from.

"If God made anything better than this," said Sonny, "He kept it for Himself."

"Listen," said Abdul Wadu as he tied up for a shot. "If I OD and go out? *Please* don't wake me up."

I felt like I finally found what I was looking for, not just the cozy high, but all the minutiae of the ritual. Hell, this was better than sex. A half hour later I looked down at my hand and noticed that my cigarette had burned right through my fingers.

One night I was leaving Sonny's crib with a chick named Sometime Annie, a waifish, gypsy type with short black hair and darting eyes, and she says to me, "Hey, Steve, you don't have to be mooching cotton shots off these creeps. Christ, you look like an NYU student, like butter wouldn't melt. C'mon, I'm gonna show you how to be a booster, stand on your own two feet 'stead of groveling for dope like a hippie." This from a ratty little wisp of a girl, but one who could spot great potential in another human being.

Sometime Annie was as good as her word. I practiced for hours in front of a full-length mirror making things disappear under my coat— the hand is quicker than the eye. I was so proud of myself. Annie showed me how to distinguish which textbooks in the NYU bookstore would be used for the next semester, then how to unload them at a dollar over half-price at a bookstore around the corner. *Wow,* I thought to myself. *I always wanted to go to NYU!* A couple of textbooks would net me an easy twenty bucks, enough for a few bags of scag, a cheap hotel room (television with a coat-hanger antenna), a bottle of Yoo-Hoo, and a couple of Ring Dings. Hey, it didn't get much better than that.

But it did get better—much better. I got good enough to make a rare art book the size of a *World Atlas* disappear under my sport coat. One day I grabbed several handfuls of jazz albums from the record browsers in a bookstore and crammed them into a shopping bag, just for the hell of it. They sold so well that I began to practice making stacks of records disappear under my coat, and it wasn't long before I could handle twenty to thirty at a clip. After walking up and down Eighth Street for a year or two, hawking records out of shopping bags, I got the moniker Record Steve. I loved it. Selling records retail on the street was occasionally time consuming but it was also fun, in your face, and people loved that I offered a good product at cut-rate prices. Clerks in the stores that lined Eighth Street would wave me over, "Hey, Record Man, you got any Rolling Stones?" Hell, it was like being legit, and if the cops ever hassled me (first thing after a hit was peel the store tags off so the records couldn't be traced), I told them that the records were remaindered and I bought them for a buck apiece. What did cops know about the record biz anyway?

Like attracts like, and once I started boosting I fell into the company of other boosters, like Shoppin' Bag Billy, Jimmy Porter, and BJ the Queen of Crime. They all had their particular styles. Billy, with his light brown hair and gray eyes, had the washed-out, bland aspect of a weary shopper, and his casual indifference as he shoved items into shopping bags somehow made him invisible to store dicks and earned him his moniker. Jimmy Porter preferred burglary, but he affected such a gay, effete manner that he made good scores boosting in antique shops and jewelry stores, wooing the shopkeepers with his banter, ascots, thin mustache, and phony business cards.

BJ was short for Barbara Joanne—femme fatale, speed freak, coke-head, junky, and sometime dyke. She came on like a big, tall, sexy Jersey housewife but was one of the most treacherous, volatile characters I ever met. She'd once escaped from a women's penitentiary and was proud of her moniker, the Queen of Crime, which she probably gave to herself. I remember having an argument with her that ended with a boiling hot cup of coffee in my face. A couple of hours later we were in the sack. BJ wore Ace bandages wrapped around her midriff, jammed merchandise underneath them, and strolled out of stores with priceless rare books and anything else that wasn't locked in glass cabinets or nailed to the floor.

Accepting me as one of their own, they steered me to their fences and offered priceless business tips. At the time I thought it was all a fascinating adventure. The junk enfolded me in a warm cloak of coziness, and the characters were deadbeat and Runyonesque. There were archetype speed freaks like Panama, a spectral black guy with a skull-like head and snow white hair who fell off the roof of a building and walked away unharmed, "Panama be indestructible, baby!" There was the notorious Bill Heinie, who lived over on Jane Street with a wispy girl who fluttered around his basement apartment like a wounded butterfly, wearing only silk scarves that she tied to her wrists and arms. Trannies like Jackie Curtis and Ondine or beat poets like Herb Huncke would pop into Bill's for a blast. Jimmy Porter would blow in with a shopping bag of lapis lazuli antiques he'd boosted, have himself a shot, and then perch painstakingly for an hour in front of a tiny tanning device to rid himself of his prison pallor.

These characters stayed up for days at Bill's shooting methamphetamine-hydrochloride, purchased in quantity from pharmaceutical spooks in Philly, groping, twitching, and chattering with such chemically induced radiance you'd think they were solving the problems of the universe—so much talent going nowhere fast. Meanwhile some freckle-faced woman from Iowa weaved among the denizens like a deranged Florence Nightingale, "Would you like an alcohol swab with that?"

Bill was a tremendously talented artist and musician and could play long, involved Coltrane riffs on a two-dollar recorder or a hand-carved flute, but his drawings were so complicated and dense that by the time he finished fiddling obsessively with them, the entire surface was blacked in. Even his paintings, done on tiny wooden squares, were incomprehensible to me. Bill scratched himself in one spot behind his ear so obsessively that he finally managed to burrow out a deep hole in his head. The devoted wannabes who gathered in his busy apartment sat around determinedly scratching behind their ears, trying for a hole of their own.

"Hey, Bill," I confided in him one night, amid the usual wired-up or nodded-out cast of freaks. "I think I'm developing a heroin problem."

Bill gave me his beatific smile. "Oh, baby, how could you say that? Look at you, you're the very picture of health."

Bill's girlfriend skittered by and, with a dancer's flourish of her scarves, flashed her bare, emaciated body. I never heard her speak in a known language—she sort of tittered incessantly and reminded me of a vampire.

"Bill is absolutely right, Steve," said Huncke, who came over just then to add his two cents' worth. "Any fool can see that heroin is keeping you young. You're glowing. Whatever you been doing, baby, keep doing it."

"Cloizeenay, baby," said Jimmy Porter, a cigarette hanging from his lips. "That's where the money is. I had your good looks I'd charm these antique dealers out of their fucking socks." His immobile face gleamed yellow as he held it inches from the red coils of the tanning device, which looked like a primitive space heater. "Now come over here, babe, and lemme tell you about cloizeenay."

Meanwhile, Ondine sprawled naked on Bill's couch like a beached whale, and some part of my mind registered a loud, ratcheting sound coming from across the room. Turns out it was Panama grinding his teeth.

Veronica, for whatever reason, disdained even the most casual offer to smoke grass, at least as far as I know. The entire subject of drugs totally turned her off, and whenever I visited her or met her anywhere, I always made a fastidious inspection of my person, checking shirtsleeves and trousers for tiny telltale bloodstains and burn holes, left in the wake of shooting up and nodding out with a lit cigarette. I'd check my eyes in a mirror to make sure I wasn't too zonked out, afraid that if I didn't keep that part of my life hidden from her, I'd lose her. But I wondered if she'd be impressed that I'd met a beat poet and two infamous drag queens at an enclave of underground artists. Hey, I had my own entrée into the world of the literati.

Ron preferred the more socially acceptable route of actually working her way into that world, and I had no doubt that she'd do it. Every fiber of her being was aimed at a life of working with the literature she loved. Finally outgrowing dead-end survival jobs and sleeping on a couch at her friend Betty Ann's place in Brooklyn (she'd somehow lost her apartment on Bedford Street), Veronica adjusted her sights, found herself an apartment on Seventy-fifth and Riverside Drive, and made her first baby steps into the publishing business. She started working as a research editor for *Collier's Encyclopedia*. They issued coupons with each set of books, and then clients used the coupons to submit essay, survey, and other research questions for editors like Ron to work on. After Collier's, Veronica took a job as an editor at Platt & Monk, which published children's books, like *Winnie the Pooh*.

What a coincidence that her first jobs in publishing reflected the books I'd seen as a kid prowling in her room in Philly. On the bottom shelf of her bookcase had been a long row of burgundy spines with elegant gold lettering—ENCYCLOPEDIA BRITANNICA. On the top shelf were all the Pooh books. It was a comfort, though, to know that we both started out in the same industry—the first thing I'd done for a living when I got to New York was *stealing* books.

Ron had cats in her apartment on Riverside Drive, and I'd catch her chiding them inanely, going on and on like Alice after a trip down the Rabbit Hole. She'd always hated the way Dad gushed in baby talk to dogs, and here she was, acting just like him and worse. It made my skin crawl.

The only children's story that resonated in my life was "Wynken, Blynken, and Nod"—for hours I'd be standing outside Gem Spa candy store on St. Marks and Second Avenue, zooted out, a Yoo-Hoo in one hand and a Ring Ding in the other, my head dipping toward the pavement like a dowser's wand, and just when the Yoo-Hoo was about to spill on my shoes, I'd snap back erect.

One day I was walking through Tompkins Square Park with Little Ralph, a hard-boiled runt of a guy who sounded like a drill sergeant on a bad day but who always knew where to cop a good bag of scag. Ralph waved at someone way across the park, and I recognized Sonny St. Claire, looking unusually muscular in a cut-off T-shirt. I hadn't seen Sonny around for over a year.

"Yo, Sonny!" yelled Ralph. "Where you been?"

Sonny was on a mission, same as us, so he didn't stop to chat. He waved back from across the park in a long, slow, sweeping motion that seemed full of history and yelled back at Ralph: "Been up and down the moors!"

We just waved and went on about our business. When I asked Ralph what Sonny was talking about, he laughed and made an offhand reference to Sonny being locked up, but the phrase stuck in my head for weeks. It seemed like one of the most romantic things I ever heard—*up and down the moors*—like something out of Dickens, or Sherlock Holmes. I had an image of Sonny trudging stoically up and down some dark, dismal landscape, the fog and poisonous vegetation hiding pools of quicksand, and I figured "up and down the moors" was hipster patter for being in prison. Later I found out that Sonny had actually said, "Up in Dannemora," which was the name of a New York State correctional facility.

* * *

None of us, back then, anticipated any dire consequences from our drug use and sharing works. I laughed at stories that depicted *Man with the Golden Arm*–type horrors of heroin withdrawal. I kicked junk habits many times during the sixties, always cold turkey and often in a jail cell. It was akin to having a really bad cold for a few days, and then feeling vaguely restless until the first good night's sleep, which might take days, a week, or even a month. But the dramatic and excruciating agony of withdrawal turned out to be a myth, no doubt perpetuated by addicts to elicit sympathy, sell books, or justify continued use. It was easy to kick. The hard thing was *staying* kicked, and the real pain of addiction, I realized later, happens to the people who care about you.

Greenwich Village during the sixties was a time of lighthearted fun, and to me, the different political agendas (Norman Mailer's bid for mayor comes to mind—"No More Bullshit!") were just another excuse to socialize and flap your jibs, show how hip you were, all in aid of getting some free dope and strange pussy. Same deal with the spiritual movements— Hare Krishna and Nam myo ho renge kyo—free macrobiotic meals and the girl washing dishes giving up hand jobs in the meditation room.

You could watch firsthand as the Beat Generation slowly morphed into the stylized, drug-addled characters of the later sixties and seventies (*Tune in, turn on, drop out!*), panhandling flower children running up against MacDougal Street beat-artists selling catnip to squares from Jersey, hustling up money for a fix, hissing at passersby from a bench in Washington Square or a MacDougal Street stoop.

"Pssst! Grass 'n' hash. Grass 'n' hash."

There was a kind of incense that could be bought in a local herbal store called "Opium" that looked and smelled remarkably like a huge block of hashish. Wrap it in tinfoil and you could palm it off on some square for anywhere up to a thousand bucks—the more you charged, the more authentic the deal seemed.

You could double-door chumps at places like the Hotel Albert. "The connection don't meet strangers, so give me the money and wait by the gate. Else forget about it, s'up to you." Take the money, go in the front door to the Albert on Tenth Street and University Place, past the desk, down the hallway toward the restaurant in back, and right out through the back door onto Eleventh Street. I got double-doored at the Albert myself when I was still new at the game.

Deadbeat hipsters hunkered outside the Village Gate, catching the Modern Jazz Quartet for free as the music drifted up through the sidewalk grating or the basement window.

"Hey, babe. Got a dollar?"

"Say what?"

"Room and board for a dollar, babe. Can you believe?"

I sat down next to a guy in a porkpie hat and leaned my back against the Village Gate. The tasty vibes of Milt Jackson came drifting up through the sidewalk grating.

"MJQ, right?"

"Yeah, babe. Bags cookin' some serious voodoo in there."

"So what's this room and board for a buck?"

"See this place next to the Gate? Greenwich Hotel, babe. Ninety cents for a room, and ten cents for a hard-boiled egg at the deli cross the street. Haw! Room and board, you dig?"

There were still sailors in white uniforms crowding the bar in places like Googies or the Kettle of Fish. Occasionally I caught sight of Veronica through the plate-glass windows of the Bleecker St. Tavern, between Mac-Dougal and Thompson streets—a typical Village watering hole with exposed brick walls, peanuts in a huge barrel, a great jukebox, and cheap mugs of draft beer. I rarely went in there, though. The crowd was too intellectual and gay and their effete patter and burning glances made me feel awkward and uncomfortable.

The West Village was not so overrun back then. It could be a small world with the same gaudy characters reeling past on MacDougal Street, popping up over and over like bad checks until they gained a certain notoriety or celebrity status in your head. Once I saw Ron in the Bleecker St. Tavern standing at the bar next to some guy whose medicine cabinet I'd robbed, and I cringed at the thought of her hearing about those capers. It was one thing to steal from stores that insured their merchandise against theft, but ripping off individuals implied such a total lack of integrity that I couldn't justify it to myself, let alone in the face of my sister's innocence. Professional and personal ethics, from that point on, would not allow me to stray from my chosen niche—shoplifting.

chapter 6

Mom and Dad would go for years not hearing a word from me during the midsixties, and I avoided my sister as much as I could. When I did occasionally go over to Ron's place on Riverside Drive, usually for a free meal, and she'd ask me what I was doing, I'd lie.

"The record biz, Ron. You know, buy remainders cheap from a cut-rate distributor and sell 'em in retail joints or in bars. The other day I made a couple hundred over at Loeb Student Center in about half an hour."

"That's great, Steve," she'd say with that faraway look that meant the conversation was about over. I wasn't sure if it was lack of interest, or if she suspected I was lying, but when our parents called her and asked what I was doing, she'd pass along my story—Steve's working in the record business.

Don't get me wrong. I wasn't schlepping around those days in a cloud of guilt or longing to get a job. I was thrilled with this alternate lifestyle, proud as punch of my shoplifting prowess and my ability to score junk all over town, from Harlem to the Lower East Side. I sneered at junkies who hung around the cop spots begging for a taste: "Hey, Stevie, can you help me out, ba-ba? I'm sick as a dog." Forget about it. *Hope-fiends* I called them.

I'd finally found a way to make fast money, and as long as my luck held out I lived in cheap hotels just below Midtown. I felt like Nick Charles in *The Thin Man*, ordering up from local diners and nodding out to the tones of "The Syncopated Clock" that blinked the lights out one by one in the flat cityscape logo of *The Late Late Show*, introducing the next B-movie, and then blinking them out again for *The Late Late Late Show*. And on and on through the night, cherishing the grace period between the last score and the next, staving off the morning and the moment when I'd have to go out and throw another brick. For a while I shared an apartment down on East Sixth Street with Floyd, a guy I knew from France and who knew where to score good grass. But in the world I moved, it didn't pay to have an apartment with furniture and belongings. You had to be ready to move fast, and there was always a place to crash when you had some drugs in your pocket. Life couldn't have been sweeter.

Of course, if you steal every day for a living, odds are you'll take a pinch now and then and eventually spend some time in the joe. And if you were a blond-haired, blue-eyed kid like me, guys would try to take advantage of you if you didn't know how to handle yourself.

One day I got pinched boosting in a discount department store off Union Square—Klein's or Mays—and the store dicks told me, almost apologetically, that they couldn't cut me loose. The insurance companies were insisting that stores get tougher with shoplifters if they wanted to collect. So off I went handcuffed in a squad car to the local precinct, then on to Central Booking, and finally sat around in the bull pens at the Tombs, waiting for my name to be called for court.

The first few days after an arrest are a horrible ordeal. You get shuttled around in jam-packed paddy wagons, enduring the stench of people in much worse shape, scrounging for cigarettes until the short butts lying next to the toilet bowl start looking good. You get nothing to eat but stale baloney sandwiches that back up on you all day and are finally reduced to lying down on the filthy, sticky floor you've been disdaining but are so drop-dead exhausted from anxiety and lack of sleep that you no longer give a rat's ass.

When I finally reached court, I was offered a ninety-day sentence for Attempted Petty Larceny, a class-B misdemeanor. Three months was a lot—thirty days was par for such a beef but the judge was in a foul mood. My rap sheet listing my previous arrests was sitting on his desk, so pleading not guilty in hopes of getting released on my own recognizance was definitely out. There's always a shot at probation on a misdemeanor, but in order to qualify I'd have to let the courts contact a local family member, and I remembered my vow never to let them know about my arrests. So I took the deal, copped out, and was happy to get on with it. Figured I could do three months standing on my head, take a break to kick my jones, put on a few pounds, and get a fresh start.

It was the first time I ever did a bid on Rikers Island, and I unwittingly got assigned to a dormitory in C-76 that was about 90 percent black. This dorm housed inmates who worked on a labor crew that went out to Hart's Island every day to dig graves at Potter's Field—F-Troop, to which I was assigned. They were usually picked for this work detail because of their brutal capacity for hard labor and indifference about the dead, but occasionally men were assigned simply because of a shortage in manpower. The two or three white guys in the dorm were mostly old men doing skid-bids for bad checks or drunk driving. They went out to the police shooting range to pick up spent ammo. I had nobody to take my back.

The first time I took a shower in that dorm, two black guys who were showering at the same time started singing that Motown song, "Heaven must have sent you from above. . . ." I had a suspicion that I was going to have trouble.

There was one huge gorilla of a guy named Slim who took to winking at me at night as we lay in our bunks, and I knew right off I'd have a problem if I didn't put a stop to it quick. Unfortunately, I didn't have any experience of how to go about this. I walked up to Slim one day when I caught him winking at me while we were waiting for meds in the dispensary and spoke to him in my best Humphrey Bogart imitation.

"Look here, Slim. You got something wrong with your eye, I'll be happy to remove it for you."

This is what's commonly known on the street as a wolf-ticket, and often done more as a bluff than an actual challenge, but implies that you got the ass to back up your mouth—in this case, that I was cold blooded enough to jab his eye out. I don't know where I got the balls to do this, but the effect it produced was not what I hoped for.

"Ahma see you back inna dom," Slim mumbled, which was Neanderthal-speak for "I'll see you back in the dorm."

Later that day I was lying down on the top half of my double bunk when Slim and another guy rolled up into my aisle. It was way in the back of the dorm and far from the hacks that worked in the booth near the front.

"Alright, white-baw," says Slim from the foot of my bunk. "Somefin you wanna git off yo chest?"

I knew there was no way around this—it was fight or be humiliated and submit to being somebody's jailhouse punk. I was kicking a drug habit and not in the best of shape, but I swung off the top of the bunk determined to do as much damage as I could. Before my feet even hit the floor, Slim, who stood about seven feet tall (I couldn't have picked a worse guy to fuck with), stepped into the enclosure between bunks and nailed me with a straight right hand. He had a ring on one finger and it gashed my cheek open just under my eye, nearly accomplishing the very thing I'd threatened *him* with.

As I flew back against the tin lockers I knew that I couldn't stand back and trade punches with this guy—his arms were twice as long as mine—so I ran right up in his chest, threw my hands around his neck, and tried to sink my teeth into his face. This strategy nearly proved fatal and all I managed to accomplish was to bleed on Slim's overalls. We toppled to the floor gouging and punching and I quickly fell victim to his superior strength and weight. At one point he managed to wrestle me onto my stomach and it looked like he would've raped me there and then were it not for the prison overalls we all wore. His partner took this opportunity to lean in and stab me in the calf with a pencil, which I didn't even notice until much later, being in the heat of battle. Just then the rest of the black guys in the dorm stepped in and pulled Slim off my back.

"The hell you messing with this kid for? He don't bother nobody."

"Yeah, but what make him any diffent from Gene over dere," said Slim, pointing at some pathetic white guy who was reclining in his bunk, munching a candy bar, thumbing through a porno magazine, and pretending like this whole thing wasn't happening. Gene must've been reduced to punk status before I ever showed up and his porno book and candy were perks for submission. I caught his eye as I stood up and he winced in helpless shame.

Slim said, "I oney gonna brang out whas in 'em anyways."

What—this idiot figured I had it in me to be a homo or a jailhouse punk? That infuriated me. A red haze blurred my vision and I threw a couple shots that bounced harmlessly off Slim's skull and shoulders before the other guys pulled us apart again. The rest of the guys in the dorm decided, over Slim's protestations, that I should get a pass on this treatment simply because I fought back. Later at the dispensary where I went to get butterfly stitches on my cheek, the doctor asked me what happened.

"I fell out of my bunk." Snitches in jail suffered a worse fate than punks.

"Oh," said the doctor, who pointed at the pencil sticking out of my calf. "So did you get that falling out of your bunk too?" I was so filled with rage and terror I never even noticed the pencil till then.

In the mess hall some of the older white cons remarked on my shiner and butterfly tape and asked me what happened. After I related the story, they went, unbeknownst to me, and asked one of their crew who worked as a runner for the assignment captain to see if he could get me transferred to a different dorm.

I knew I'd have more trouble with Slim, so I carefully plotted my revenge. That night I would take a sharpened pencil, now that I knew what an effective weapon it could be, creep up to Slim's bunk while he slept, carefully place the point of the pencil into Slim's ear, and drive it into whatever tiny brain he had with a quick stroke of the flat of my hand. Along about two in the morning when everyone was asleep, I actually did tiptoe over to Slim's bunk, pencil in hand, but discovered him sleeping with a blanket over his head and I couldn't determine exactly where his ears or eyes were. It was one of the most fearful and rage-ridden nights I ever spent, and my determination wavered as I put it off until the next night. There was an off chance that I might actually kill him, but I'd read somewhere that such an attack, if done quickly and efficiently, would produce no outcry from the victim, leaving me to creep back to my bunk undetected.

Fortunately, my new friends from the mess hall persuaded the assignment captain to move me to another dorm before I got a chance to test that theory. I finished my bid in the tailor shop, surrounded by an affable crew of white cons.

Back out on the street after my three-month bid, whenever I got hit on for spare change for food from some barefoot flower child in raggedy jeans and a fringed suede jacket, my reply was, "Why don't you go steal something? That's what I do." When I was hungry and broke I simply went into a supermarket or a deli and stuck a package of lunchmeat and a roll in my pocket. I could not understand why anyone need go hungry in New York. Another hustle I practiced from time to time was boosting steaks, usually porterhouse since they were the most expensive, and selling them for half price in bars. This hustle was popularly known as "cattle rustling." After a few days of cattle rustling, my pants and Jockey shorts would be stained with beef blood and I'd have to go boosting for clothes. If I had any steaks left over that didn't sell, I'd take them to Sonny's or Bill Heinie's for a feast, feed the protein-starved junkies and speed freaks, and maybe get a taste.

It never occurred to me that the ordeal I barely survived in Rikers Island would never have happened in the first place if I hadn't been arrested for stealing. While Veronica had been gifted with prudence as a survival tool, I'd been gifted with the ability, like Wile E. Coyote, to not let anything get me down for very long. But I'd be wracked by terrible feelings of loneliness and jealousy each time I glimpsed my sister and her friends through the plate-glass windows of a Village saloon. I felt like a hobo watching from a street curb through someone's window as the family sat down to a cozy dinner, always on the outside looking in. Those people went home to real apartments, got up the next morning, and went to real jobs. How the hell did they do it?

But I would not allow sentiment to get me down. Being an outlaw took a certain kind of nobility, courage, and fortitude. If the weather was bad and I was down on my luck, I could always get "room and board" at the Greenwich for a dollar (the rooms were tiny partitions with a cot and chicken wire across the ceiling to keep the guy next door from crawling in), go crash at Sometime Annie's pad in Alphabet City, or nod out in an armchair at Sonny St. Claire's. If the weather was nice, there was nothing finer than kicking back on a bench in Washington Square, nodding off under the stars to the sights and sounds of night creatures as they mixed and mingled on benches or sprawled out groping in the bushes. Those squirrels were definitely cracking nuts.

chapter 7

From editing children's books at Platt & Monk, Ron moved on to Holt, Rinehart & Winston, where she edited textbooks for a year or so. She never talked about work, but I sensed that she was striving for greater things. Her life had begun to spiral upward and outward, and though I was proud of my sister, I was increasingly uncomfortable around her as my skewed take on hardworking, legit people drove a wedge between us. And then there was my stonerlike unpredictability: failing to show up to meet her somewhere, calling her up in the middle of the night to ask if I could fall out at her place, or even nodding out in the middle of a conversation over dinner.

"Hey, Steve. Are you alright?"

I looked up and saw Ron standing over me, pulling on a pair of flesh-colored rubber gloves, like a doctor preparing for an intrusive examination.

"Wazzit?" As my mind struggled to grasp the last thread of conversation we'd been having, I realized she was getting ready to wash the dishes and had been clearing the table around me as I dozed. It was a familiar scene for Ron, having endured all those years of Dad drinking too much and falling out snoring in the middle of a house full of company.

"Huh? Yeah, I'm just beat to hell, Ron. Mind if I fall out here tonight?"

She must've thought I had Rip Van Winkle syndrome.

She was full of good spirits, tremendously self-disciplined, and in love with New York and being a New Yorker. When we talked, she always kept it light. She might ask casually what I'd been up to, but I sensed that she didn't really want to know. Her mind was whirring away on career matters, or maybe longing for a better romantic life, areas that were none of my business. I knew little about careers or intimate relationships, nor did she know the first thing about street life. It was like a silent pact we'd made not to burden each other with personal troubles. There we sat, having dinner, the love between us stretching out like a tightrope over this gap and neither of us eager to walk out on it. As I spiraled down further into my own sleazy world, my behavior became increasingly erratic and incomprehensible to her.

Things came to a head one night when Ron was going out of town for a few days and offered to let me stay at her apartment while she was gone. She had no real idea of my criminal life, and I brought along a guy and his girlfriend, dead ringers for Pacino and his moll in *The Panic in Needle Park* and both heroin addicts. They'd let me flop at their hotel rooms on occasion, so now I could return the favor.

When I woke up the next morning with the sound of my sister's key in the door, I discovered that my "friends" had left in the night along with my sister's jewelry. The missing pieces included a few family heirlooms that she'd inherited, along with her own day-to-day earrings, rings, and bracelets. She was furious and told me to get out and stay out. I could hardly blame her. It was pouring rain on that freezing winter night, but I was so filled with remorse, and so furious with myself, that I tramped through the Village streets all night, uselessly searching for my treacherous companions, weeping and gnashing my teeth for being such a chump. My relationship with my sister was damaged almost beyond repair. She mentioned that night briefly in a later story, "A Lot in Common."

I don't want to name the deep trouble my brother got into around that time; it scared me, and one night I refused to let him stay in my apartment even though it was raining. I still think about this, although he forgave me and later a psychiatrist told me science couldn't say what I should have done.

My attraction to lowlife was as mysterious to my sister as her progress in socially acceptable circles was to me. After all, we both grew up in the same household, with the same parents and with similar opportunities. The growing disparity in our lives seemed inexplicable. I'd be sitting in a jail cell and my mind would track back through memories of childhood, trying to pin down some essential difference in us, like the contrast in how we'd reacted to Dad's "Tuesday" routine.

"Hey Dad," Ronnie used to say. "Could we go to the zoo?"

"Christ, do you kids have any idea where the zoo is?"

"Isn't it in South Philly where you work?"

"In South *Philly*? Who the hell told you that? There's nothing in South Philly but jungle bunnies."

"Well don't they keep the bunnies at the zoo?" I'm not sure Ronnie understood the racial slur at that age, but she kept it deadpan.

"Oh c'mon, Charlie," Mom would say. "Don't teach them that nonsense. Take them to the zoo."

"Alright already. We'll go to the goddamn zoo."

"Well, when are we going?"

"Tuesday."

And we knew it was not going to happen. Whenever we asked our father to do anything that he didn't want to be bothered with, he'd say, "Alright, we'll do it on Tuesday." It was code for the day that never came—a taunt, vague yet arbitrary. Ronnie and I got so caught up with life from day to day that when Tuesday finally rolled around, we'd often forget any promises made on the previous days. But if we *did* remember, it didn't do any good. Not even my sister's diamond-hard logic could pierce our father's obstinacy about Tuesday. After a few years of this treatment, we came to accept Tuesday as synonymous with the completely arbitrary "Forget about it!"

Someone once told me that our father's "Tuesday" routine came from an old *Popeye* character, Wimpy, who was always stuffing himself with hamburgers and promising, "I'll pay for these on Tuesday." The discovery of this piece of trivia made me look back at our father with a bit more humor. My sister, however, never forgot this measly treatment, and heaven help the editor in chief who got arbitrary, or tried to get her to go for the okeydoke. "Yeah, sure, Veronica. We'll buy that story . . . on Tuesday."

I, on the other hand, didn't learn a thing. I became glib. For me, the okeydoke and the flimflam became perfectly acceptable, although at times regrettable, approaches to life, business, and survival.

As my shoplifting career branched out from Manhattan, so I could hit stores where my face wasn't known, I got busted in New Jersey and arraigned before a small-town judge. It was 1965 and I was twenty-two.

"Young man," the judge said to me over his half-moon glasses. "Have you ever been arrested before?"

"No, Your Honor." I didn't travel with a lot of bail money in those early days, so convincing everyone that I was a first offender was crucial to getting an ROR—Released on my Own Recognizance.

"Are you sure, son? Are you *positive* you've never been arrested anywhere at all before?"

"Your Honor, I haven't even had a parking—"

The judge cut me off. "Maybe you'd like to take a moment before you answer that question again, young man."

Okay. I looked around the small courtroom. There were a dozen strangers out there and they were all looking at me. The detective who'd arrested me was smirking in the front row. I looked back at the judge and licked my lips.

"You see, son," he went on, picking up a telephone and laying it on top of his desk. "All I have to do is pick up that phone right there, dial a certain number, and in a few moments I can have your entire criminal record. So think real good before you answer that question again."

It was the "dial a certain number." Nobody talks like that. What the hell was he going to do, call J. Edgar Hoover? He obviously had my entire rap sheet right there on his desk and the phone thing was just a taunt.

"Well, Your Honor, in all honesty, now that I think about it, I do recall that I have been arrested several times before. But I'm just scared and I didn't want to admit it. I'm scared and really fed up." I was getting warmed up now and a few tears rolled down my cheeks. "Seems like my whole life I've been shuttled around from foster homes to county jails." I stole a look at the arresting officer, who was rolling his eyes.

"Son," said the judge, "I am just tickled pink that you decided to be honest with me here today." I could hear a few chuckles. The judge pushed his glasses back up his nose and picked up my rap sheet, which was considerable, and which *had* been sitting on his desk all along. He flicked through several pages of arrests and finally plopped it back down on the desk. "Yes indeedy. You sure have been arrested before. But before I make a decision on your bail, would you be so good as to tell me one thing?"

"Of course, Your Honor." I resigned myself, then, to the fact that I was going to jail. Resignation always makes the final blow easier to swallow. Yeah, sure you'll get released. On Tuesday.

He ran his finger down my rap sheet and said, "What the devil is *Murphy game*?" Then he threw his palms up, shrugged his shoulders, and mugged for the courtroom.

It was a reference to the time I got knocked outside the Metropole Cafe on Broadway with some guys who were playing short con—Dis-Con 6, or Disorderly Conduct 6 in the Criminal Code, otherwise known as Murphy game, a short confidence hustle played on unwary tricks from Jersey. Murphy players were a common sight around Midtown in the sixties, guys standing out on Broadway or Eighth Avenue hissing at the passersby, "Sssaaaay, fellahs. How 'bout some a them girls tonight?"

One variation that I was familiar with involved a sleight-of-hand envelope switch at the end, which requires the player to carry envelopes and a folded newspaper at all times, as well as an assortment of wallets, fake watches, and phony money. You never know what a trick will stuff in an envelope. The game is best played outside the entrance of a hotel where there's a public phone booth handy. You point out the hotel and tell the trick he's got to check his valuables at the hotel desk so he won't get ripped off by the girls, or claim later that he got ripped off. It's all for security so nobody gets hurt, protects him and the hotel, and you reassure him that you never touch his money. He doesn't pay you a dime. You get paid a commission from the hotel, all on the up and up. If he goes for it, you hand him an envelope to put his valuables in, watching carefully to see what he crams into it. Then you step over to the phone booth, supposedly to call the girls and make sure they're available, and stuff another envelope to approximate the one he's got. You place the dummy under your newspaper and return to the trick.

"Okay, you glued it shut? Good. Now I just have to put my initials on your envelope so the hotel will know who to give the commission to."

You place his envelope on top of the newspaper, the dummy held underneath, and turning for a second to get some light to write by you flip the paper over, which brings the dummy to the top and turns the real one underneath. You write your initials on the dummy right in front of him and hand it back. When the trick runs on into the hotel to check his "valu-ables" at the desk and get laid, you take the real envelope and hightail it over to the Ames Pool Room or the Guys and Dolls until things cool off.

On the occasion when I got knocked I was not in the neighborhood to play Murphy game. It wasn't my hustle. Hell, I was a booster. I was in Midtown only to score some smack, but when Walter walked by with two white, middle-aged tricks in tow, he whispered to me out of the side of his mouth.

"Hey, Steve. C'mon and play this thing out with me." Walter was a dapper old black guy and figured a white boy like me would put the tricks at ease.

I shook my head, but Brother Fats was standing there and said, "Go make that money, man. Cop-man won't show for another hour."

So I fell in step with the two tricks behind Walter and made noises about how hot the girls were. The tricks were sad-looking guys in sport shirts and windbreakers over beer bellies. One of them had a can of beer in a paper bag. Walter steered us all into a tenement building off Seventh Avenue. Up the stairs we went, and when we got to the third-floor land-ing, Walter stopped, tossed his jacket over the stairway railing, leaned ca-sually against the wall, loosened his tie, and whipped out a small pad and pencil. I felt like I was standing in his office or the comfortable foyer of a whorehouse. Walter was good.

"Okay," he said to the tricks. "How much can you guys afford?"

They both mumbled something about ten bucks.

Ten bucks? This was pathetic. I felt sorry for these guys. What did they expect for a sawbuck? Right then I knew I'd made a mistake.

Walter nodded and said, "Alright. Ten it is." Then he turned to me. "You can go on up, man. I owe you one from last time."

I knew two flights up brought me to the roof, and so this was my cue to go on out and over the roof to the next building and meet Walter back at the Ames. Besides, a con man like Walter never lets another thief see how he caps it off.

As I took a step toward the stairs, one of the "tricks" sly-rapped me right on the nose with a roundhouse punch. I sat down on my fanny and watched dazedly as they whipped out thirty-eights from shoulder holsters.

"Here's how Midtown vice cops take care a you douche bags."

They gave us a pistol whipping and threw us a few kicks. I was only the shill so I didn't get the worst of it, but I felt bad for Walter, who was a frail old guy. He took his beating stoically, knowing that beatings were usually dished out when the cops didn't feel like doing paperwork, the implication being that we'd get cut loose. Instead, these pricks took us downtown and booked us too. I did thirty days on Hart's Island at the old workhouse, with the stew-bums and the deadbeat dads, and now the expression Murphy game was forever stamped into my dossier.

It all came back to me in that moment in the Jersey courtroom. Caught off guard, I blurted out, "Your Honor, Murphy game is where you procure for women who don't really exist!"

There was a brief moment of silence. Then the judge threw back his head and burst into laughter, followed by the rest of the courtroom. The judge did better than release me on my own recognizance. He gave me a suspended sentence of ninety days and then called me up to his desk. He asked me if I had any money, and when I shook my head he handed me a ten-spot for bus fare back to New York.

"You're either a damned good con man," he whispered as he handed me the tenner, "or a very sincere young man. In either case, good luck to you. Now get the hell out of my courtroom. If I ever see you back here again I'll make you do that ninety days and then some."

The arresting officer was fit to be tied. Before I got out of that courtroom he got in my face, unleashing a cruel insight that cops are sometimes capable of, they being in the same business and therefore knowing the nature of a criminal.

"I know guys like you," he said, little bumps of frustration and bitterness popping out on his jaw and forehead. "Probably a bright kid, but now just another piece of shit that breaks the hearts of his family and everybody that cares about him. Don't ever let me catch you in Jersey again."

It was a good try on his part. On the bus back to Manhattan I even thought about what it might be like to be a cop, but I was too intoxicated with my near lockup and breathtaking reprieve. Sure, I'll clean up my act—on Tuesday. Decades went by before I got beat up enough to try something legit.

Although I knew at a very young age the difference between right and wrong, instilled in me by my parents in spite of their age and their own failings, I did the wrong thing anyway. It looked like a hell of a lot more fun. But there was no getting around the cosmic principle of reaping what you sow. The best I could do was to avoid the baffled eyes of loved ones as they watched me slide downhill.

Mom and Dad were always willing to send me the fare for a plane ticket home, even though they wouldn't hear from me for a year or more while I was in New York. I was lucky that I hadn't burned that bridge. Street life can take a rough toll on you, even on a hardy young guy like me in his twenties, and the occasional vacation in Florida allowed me to remain in relatively good health. Not that I gave much thought to physical fitness. The fact that I recovered rapidly from physical neglect and drug abuse made me cocky, and I took my youthful fitness for granted. Little did I know that the growing conflict in Southeast Asia, which had ignited a huge draft by the armed forces, would one day in the not-to-distant future put my physical prowess, and all my conniving expertise, sorely to the test.

chapter 8

I n 1966 I went down to Florida for a little R & R. Mom and Dad had
fallen into their own groove and no longer troubled me about careers
or jobs. They were content to have me around again and, like Ron, seemed
to have entered into an unspoken pact to avoid prying into personal troubles. Mom probably feared that if they pried too much they'd drive me off.

"You'll always have your room here," Mom said. "Just don't expect
me to clean it up for you. You're a grown man now, and you can pitch in
a little around the house, right, Charlie?"

"Listen to your mother," Dad said, "but I don't give a damn if you live
like a pig in there, as long as you don't ask me for money."

I was always pleasant when I showed up down there, happy for the
momentary reprieve from the stress of big-city life. Ron, on her occasional
visits to Florida, had left behind a collection of Raymond Chandler, Ross
Macdonald, and Dorothy Sayers. I ate well, did my push-ups, and tanned
in the backyard while I followed the dogged exploits of Marlowe, Archer,
and Lord Peter Wimsey.

As a retiree, Dad wasn't quite sure what to do with all the free time he'd
worked so hard to secure. He played a little golf at a nearby par-3 course
with some other retirees, drank beer, and played billiards at the Elks Club,

puttered around the front lawn and backyard, and watched a lot of television. I noticed that he'd have a shot or two of whiskey early in the morning,
and he spent a lot of time just sitting around brooding. One or two of his old
army buddies lived nearby, but they turned out to be not as much fun as my
father had once hoped. Dad began to pick up some of the household chores,
like cooking, although his idea of a meal was a couple steaks seared in a frying pan. Fine with me. We ate them off those folding aluminum TV tables
while we watched *F-Troop* or *The Andy Griffith Show* in the Florida room.

Mom, encouraged by my sister at some point, had begun to paint. She
did watercolors, still lifes, oil portraits, and even those prefab canvases
where the idea for the painting is already sketched out and the student fills
in the colors, practicing the blending of hues on a palette. She took to
wearing a beret and a smock, which effectively hid her spreading figure.
There was a portrait my mother did of Dad that was quite good.

Then Ron came down to visit, either to pay her obligatory respects or
just to get a little suntan. Things perked up with her arrival and old con-
flicts reemerged. Nothing galvanized Dad more than my sister's presence.

"Christ, you people better get it in gear. Where the hell are your
bathing trunks? You can't go to the beach in dungarees."

Dad had had the family car—a sturdy little Ford Taurus that they'd
bought years ago back in Heidelberg—shipped back to the United
States, and we'd all pile in and drive to the beach. Dad organized these
outings like we were going out on military maneuvers, synchronizing
watches and fidgeting with beach blankets and other gear hours before
we were ready to go.

"And make sure all these windows are locked. I don't want to come back
here and find the house flooded by a hurricane. Rose, leave those dishes. We
don't have time for that. When's the last time you put gas in the car?"

"Charlie, relax."

"Re*lax*? Christ, you wait around here all day, we'll never find a place
to park."

"But the sun's just coming up."

"Leave him alone, Mother," Ron said. "He hasn't had this much fun
since the Battle of Bull Run."

"Miss Smarty-pants. You live in New York now, so what the hell do
you know about Florida?"

"Hey, Dad. Do we have a transistor radio I can bring?"

"Wait a minute. Who the hell stole my goddamned Bain de Soleil?"

"I have it, Ron. I was just, you know, borrowing it."

Driving in a car with the entire family was always a royal pain in the ass. Since our father didn't drive, Mom was usually at the wheel, but even driving all over Europe hadn't improved her technique. She gripped the wheel in a two-handed death lock and had a heavy touch on the gas and brake. Dad sat next to her on the front seat and made running commentary.

"Alright now, watch this guy over here on your left. Christ, where the hell's the fire? The speed limit's only thirty. Didn't you see that stop sign? Watch it now, that guy's got his signal on."

My sister would attempt to hold on to her sanity by keeping her nose in a book or a magazine, and I'd sit in the back with her and grind my teeth. It was about a fifteen-minute drive to the beach, across semirural Bellaire Road that ran past an orange grove, then down Missouri Avenue with all its strip malls and medical arts buildings, to the main drag, and finally out across the causeway that spanned Clearwater Bay and connected the mainland to the island of Clearwater Beach.

There was a huge bronze statue at the beginning of the causeway—a soldier on a fierce charger, the horse's front legs rearing up and pawing the air as the soldier brandished a musket or a saber, a yell frozen forever on his lips.

"See that guy over there?" Dad said, pointing at the statue when we stopped at the intersection. "Know what he's doing?"

"No, Dad. What's he doing?"

"He's chasing the jigaboos off Clearwater Beach."

"Oh, Charlie. Stop with that," Mom said.

"You mean jigaboos as in colored people?" my sister asked.

"What do you think, smarty-pants?"

"Mom," Ronnie said. "Let me off over there by Maas Brothers, please. I suddenly lost my interest for the beach."

"Yeah," I said, anxious to go check out the security in Maas Brothers. "I'll get out here too."

"How the hell are you two gonna get home?"

"Don't worry," Ronnie said. "I'm sure Steve and I can find a ride with some jigaboo taxicab driver."

I never noticed the racist tendencies in our father while we were in Europe, but now that he was living in the South it didn't take him long to pick up whatever negative mind-set was near at hand. By the time we got to the beach we all needed a dip in the Gulf to cool off.

Ronnie wasn't much of a swimmer, but she loved to lounge around on the shaded wooden deck at the Palm Pavilion by Pier 60 that faced the Gulf of Mexico. The Palm Pavilion attracted a lot of Europeans, and the familiar German and French Canadian accents gave the place a comfortable, nostalgic ambience for Ronnie and me. They had a block-long row of big, comfortable deck chairs with armrests for balancing drinks, cigarettes, ashtrays, and matches. Ron would sit there for hours, coming up out of her book from time to time to squint at the pelicans and other storklike birds, egrets I believe they were, that roosted on the old wooden pilings exposed above the surf at low tide. Neither of us minded the dearth of conversation. I loved just being around her. We all did. She was our hope for a family success story.

Mom's enthusiasm for painting fell somewhat short of satisfying her need to be useful, and she applied for a job doing secretarial work at city hall in downtown Clearwater. Dad didn't go for it.

"Aw, what do you want to go to work for? I worked my whole life so we could retire, and we don't need the money. You should stay home and relax."

"Relax and do what?" Ron said, jumping in. "You want Mother to sit around the house all day and watch television and wait on you hand and foot? Or is it maybe because you can't drive? What you need is a chauffeur. Why the hell can't Mother have a life too?"

Dad was furious. He hadn't forgotten Ronnie's and my attempts to drive a wedge between the two of them when we were kids, trying to enlist Mom for our own agenda. There was so much history between all of us that the least little argument could set any of us off on a rampage.

Ronnie had come down to Florida planning to stay for a month and really work on her tan. But after hardly a week she jumped on a flight back to New York, unable to bear any more of our father's obstinacy. For my own part, I found myself sympathizing with Dad on the subject of Mom going to work. The idea of *any*body going to work when they didn't have to seemed awfully drastic to me.

When Ron went back to New York, I was sorry to see her go and started planning my own escape. Then two things arrived in the mail that changed everything. The first one came in the form of a check, a totally unexpected inheritance from our godfather, Daddy Pitman. He'd died long ago and left Ron and me five thousand bucks each, to be given us at a specified date in the future. That date had apparently just arrived. With my sudden windfall I bought a little Vespa motor scooter so I could tool around to the beaches, and soon I was frolicking in the surf up and down the west Florida coast, picking up girls at the beach and taking them back to their apartments on my scooter for sex. I found juke joints on the tiny highway that ran between the Gulf of Mexico and the Inland Waterway, hidden among cypress trees and bait shacks, as I weaved on my scooter through little beach towns between Clearwater and St. Petersburg. There was a piano bar in Passagrille where a sexy woman did a fair imitation of Billie Holiday, and she invited me out after her gig to a midnight party on the beach. A bunch of Spanish guys and their girlfriends were sitting around a campfire with a conga drum, drinking wine and doing Smokey's "Hello Stranger." The girl laughed, and I dragged her over so we could blend our voices to the background—"Seems like a mighty lo-ong ti-ime . . . shoo-bop sh'bop, my babee-ooooooo . . ." I was so happy to be singing again that tears rolled down my cheeks.

"What's the matter?" the girl asked.

"This song—it really has been a mighty long time," and then we started laughing at how corny I sounded. But I'd unearthed a soulful little pocket of lighthearted romance, and Florida became fun for the first time.

Then my draft notice came in the mail. My carefree little romp in Florida was coming to a screeching halt. I don't remember coverage of Vietnam dominating the news media yet, being indifferent to politics and current events anyway, but the very idea of going into the army filled me with foreboding. What worried me most was the loss of freedom that the military implied. I'd lie awake all night trying to figure out how to find drugs in hick towns where there weren't any on the street. I wanted to have one last blast before I had to straighten up and be a STRAC trooper, and getting stoned was the best cure I knew for being freaked out.

I started cruising through hospital parking lots on my scooter, snatching doctors' bags full of drugs out of cars. One day I was nodding out on a public bench by a beach pier and got rousted by some suspicious patrolmen. They noticed the tracks on my arms and hauled me in for bullshit like Public Intoxication and Loitering. They impounded my scooter, and when they broke open the trunk, lo and behold, they found all the *coznotics*. Their beady little cop eyes lit up with glee.

Luckily I had my draft papers with me, and when I showed them to the detective in charge he decided to let me go into the army rather than lock me up. It was an offer I couldn't refuse. And though I was grateful they didn't notify my parents, I always suspected that the cops violated search-and-seizure procedure—I'd surreptitiously dropped the keys to the scooter on the beach when the bulls rolled up.

I'd been drafted as part of a massive effort to revamp the entire Ninth Infantry Division that hadn't been mobilized since Korea, to replace either the Fourth or the First divisions that were getting their asses kicked in Vietnam. Mom and Dad saw me off with hopeful words that belied their concerns about my survival.

"Do what they tell you, Steve," Mom said. "Change your socks a lot so your feet don't rot and fall off and you'll be fine." Good ol' Mom, a real army wife.

"Don't worry, Rose," Dad said. "The army'll either cure him or kill him."

I went through basic training at Fort Riley, Kansas. I was pretty good at drills and playing soldier, being the son of a career officer. It took me a couple of weeks to get in shape, but once I hit my stride it turned out to be great sport, running around with a rifle, bayoneting dummies, and screaming "Kill, kill!" The officers and drill instructors strutted around in starched, tailored fatigues, while the grunts made do with the ill-fitting, baggy stuff we were issued. Eager beavers went to the Post Exchange and bought fatigues that looked more tailored. The terrible reality of our situation had not yet sunk in, and we preferred to nurture rumors going around that we were shipping out to Hawaii. Even the M-14 rifles that we went through basic with and qualified with on the range (I made Marksman) were anachronistic. It wasn't until we came back for advanced infantry training that we got the famous jungle weapon the M-16, space-age-looking black plastic and six hundred rounds per minute on full-auto, empty a thirty-round clip with one good, firm squeeze of the trigger.

On the last day of basic training we all gathered around our company commander while he read off the list of who was going to what schools. My buddy Fred and I were assigned to Radio-Teletype school at Fort Dix,

New Jersey. Fred looked and talked like a young Lenny Bruce, and when we heard our names read out, we looked at each other and grinned. Hey, man! Dix was right across the river from New York City. Alright! After two months of harassment and running around with rifles we all felt indestructible and ready to kill *some*body, but Fred and I had been given a momentary reprieve. Dix meant party time.

Capone, one of the guys in my platoon, overheard me telling Fred a deprecating story about my old man being a career army officer. Capone was a New Yorker, considered himself a ladies' man, and his fatigues were always meticulously cleaned and tailored. He asked me what branch my father had been in.

"Quartermaster," I said.

"Quartermaster? Jesus Christ, Steve, your old man's my hero—running around with a box of shirts under his arm instead of these goddamned M-14s."

We laughed, and for a moment I saw Dad in a new light, but I already had my eye on goofing off at Dix.

After basic we got a week's leave before school and advanced training. I shouldered my duffel bag full of gear, hopped a space-available flight in my uniform, and went back home to Clearwater. Dad immediately made me spread out the entire contents of my duffel bag on the living room floor and then spent hours inspecting all my uniforms and paraphernalia, shaking his head and commenting on the cheap fabrics.

"Jesus Christ," he said. "They're gonna send you to Southeast Asia with this crap? Listen, I still know a few buddies high up the chain of command who can get you out of this chickenshit outfit. Why don't you let me make a few phone calls?"

"That's alright, Dad. I can handle it."

Famous last words, but I was resistant to the idea of my father influencing my life in any way, shape, or form. That would be the last time for many years that I would see him enthused over anything I tried to do.

Radio operator's school, which was a prerequisite for Teletype and cryptology, was also at Fort Dix. Instead of attending boring Morse code classes, Fred and I would pay off the corporal who was in charge of keeping head count so we could spend the day in New York smoking weed and chasing girls. After a few weeks, the company commander called me into his office.

"Listen, Geng. You haven't been in class two days since you've been here, but I'm going to graduate you from radio school anyway and send you back to your division with a critical MOS [military occupational specialty]—radio operator. That's an MOS with one of the shortest life-expectancy rates next to door gunner in a chopper. No Teletype-crypto for you. The army's wasted enough money on slackers. You think you're such a smart ass, let's see you get out of going to 'Nam now."

Oh yeah? I'll show you, I thought.

That company commander at Dix knew what he was doing. When we got back to the division at Fort Riley, Fred and I were made the Brigade Intelligence Radio Operators—since we arrived back ahead of everybody else, they thought we'd graduated head of the class. I had no idea what I was doing, but I realized real quick, sitting in the brigade intelligence communications tent with the officers in charge of us, that these guys were not playing around. Game time was over, and you could see it in the way the brigade officers talked and carried themselves. The more psychotic and homicidal an officer seemed to be, the more respect he got. This was not the ball-busting bravura of basic—this was business. These guys were career soldiers hungering for a chance to go kill people, and their eyes were full of wistful death. Terrific, except it probably wouldn't be their asses charging up that hill.

Unlike during basic, there were always passes to be had now. We'd go into Junction City, Kansas, a typical army camp town that was flourishing with all the new troops, stop at a drugstore for some codeine cough syrup (the streets of Junction City were littered with broken Robitussin bottles—"Time to Robe-up!"), and then go shoot pool and flirt with the hookers. Even guys from small towns in the Bible belt were getting stoned, many for the first time in their lives. There was a funky ho-stroll through the middle of Junction City, packed with juke joints and gambling dens, weird poker games where the dealer had one eye riveted on the table while the other eye swiveled all around the room, reaching out randomly to flip over a wooden counter that changed the game from high-hand to low-hand winner. You had to be a real fatalist to get in one of those games. Our futures were uncertain and nobody wanted to think about the reality of our situation. There was a song that kept playing on everybody's transistor radio, "For What It's Worth" by Buffalo Springfield—as soon as you heard the opening guitar lick your radar picked up on the fear.

There's somethin' happenin' here. What it is ain't exactly clear.

Marijuana grew wild in the weed-choked fields surrounding Fort Riley. We'd go out and harvest it in big laundry bags, come back to the barracks, and run it through the dryers in the laundry room to "cure" it. Everybody walked around the base with a corncob pipe full of grass and even stuck stems in the canvas covers of our helmets for camouflage. Maybe we'd go to Manhattan, Kansas, to smoke reefer and shoot pool with the students from Kansas State.

A ragged-looking corporal with a thousand-yard stare, who was finishing his tour of duty after 'Nam as an instructor, came into our barracks one night after lights-off and told us a bedtime story in hillbilly monotone.

"You fellas want to know what the Delta's like, listen up. I'm walkin' behind a deuce-and-a-half layin' commo-wire, see. It's monsoon and every swingin' dick's in the truck trying to stay dry. All of a sudden a fifty-millimeter opens up on us, the jungle and the rain so damned thick you can't see where it's comin' from, the noise so loud and right on your ass like it's comin' from everywhere at once. I get under the truck and guys pile out, trying to return fire, but they get cut down to a man. Me and the driver the only ones to survive."

At this point in our training we were all intimately familiar with the paralyzing roar of a large-caliber machine gun at close proximity, and images of myself in that situation filled me with trepidation. I don't think anybody slept too good that night.

Fred and I relieved each other on the radio net, twelve-hour shifts. I caught him staggering out of the brigade intelligence tent one day, his fatigues all baggy and unkempt, his eyes bugging out of his head, tiny insects crawling down out of his hairline. He'd been jacked in for hours, not just to the radio net, but tuned in to the craziness and fear.

"Freddy, what's up?" We'd been fuck-up buddies since basic and cut out of Morse code classes at Dix together to prowl around New York. On one of those jaunts Fred had confessed to me that two of his heroes were Che Guevara and Ho Chi Minh.

"Steve, we need to get out of this outfit. These guys are off the wall."

"What happened?"

"You see that operations map of Vietnam they got tacked up in there? That shit's classified, and they got it marked out where our outfit's headed—some spooky little ville in the Mekong Delta called My To, or

Mak Tho, down there in the rice paddies where the VC get their gro-
ceries. So Major Dickhead points at the map with a swagger stick, see, and
he goes, I don't give a rat's ass if Westmoreland wants to restrict ops to
daylight. I say we can whack Victor Charlie just as good at night, goddamnit. Steve, these guys are all bucking for the Big Putsch, battlefield
promotions, and we're doomed to be at the mercy of their decisions."

Fred was right. It was one thing to run around Fort Riley stabbing
dummies, crawling under machine-gun fire on a practice range, going on
maneuvers, pitching tents, and shooting off clips full of tracers across a
Kansas field at night. I loved it. It was another thing entirely to hump the
jungles of Southeast Asia in a country where the natives were all shooting
at you with real bullets, and some gung-ho lieutenant goes, "Hey, Geng.
Go run up there on that ridgeline and take a look, see if you draw any
fire." Meanwhile the enemy is zeroing their artillery in on my radio signals. Sharpshooters always try to zap the enemy's radio so they can't call
for support.

I was in peak physical shape and, other than some grass and cough
syrup on weekends, I'd been drug-free since my induction. But after years
of getting stoned and busted I'd developed some deep sense that I wasn't
too good at taking care of myself, so the idea of shipping out to a country
where a hostile and highly motivated population would be trying to kill
me didn't hold a lot of merit. I developed a plan and started going to the
dispensary complaining of anxiety and lack of sleep, then saved up all the
pills they dished out. One day Fred hovered by my shoulder at the water
cooler in our barracks and watched me wash down a huge bottle full of
tranquilizers.

"Sure you know what you're doing?" he asked with great concern.

"Yeah," I replied. "Drugs are my thing. Just make sure you find the
pill bottle when I pass out so they'll know what to do."

"I don't know, Steve." Fred shook his head dubiously. "I got your
back, but I think I'll pass on this route." Fred had no faith at all that these
army doctors would save his life.

I passed out in the motor pool an hour later, but all it got me was a
stomach pumping and the scorn of the other guys in my outfit, aside from
Fred. While I was in the hospital a captain told me that if I tried a stunt
like that again they'd make me do my time in the stockade, give me an un-
desirable discharge that would haunt me the rest of my life.

"Fine with me," I said. "Run it." But I knew it wouldn't happen. They needed cannon fodder too desperately. I'd grown obstinate by this time, and equally determined that no one control my life or tell me what the fuck to do, especially these army whackos. My old man had been one and I sure as hell didn't let *him* tell me what to do.

One day I was watching my unit's equipment getting piled into huge Conex containers to be shipped overseas, and I came up with the great idea of taking a few sugar cubes of LSD (here again drugs were my ace-in-the-hole and I knew art students at Kansas State who could score acid) and paying a visit to the head psychiatrist at mental hygiene at Fort Riley. My buddy Redd, a black hipster from DC who was part of our Junction City tip, worked in the psych clinic and hooked me up with an appointment. Redd told me that dope fiends were tenacious, clever survivors, and he had no doubt that I could survive 'Nam, but he was also intensely curious to see if our plan would work.

The acid started kicking in as I stepped into the waiting room of the base shrink. I felt a goofy sense of anticipation, and a wave of paranoia swept over me when I noticed several other people waiting to see the psych. There was a middle-aged woman with a teenage boy, and another guy in uniform with a thousand-yard stare. We all kept trying to sneak looks at one another. Suddenly I realized that they too were probably out of their fucking heads. Why else would they be here? And that's when I started peaking. The floor started undulating and the faces of the other patients began to distort. The door opened just then and I was summoned into the inner sanctum. I walked through the office door in slo-mo, my feet sinking deeper into the carpet with every step.

The psychiatrist was a bald, overweight captain with wire-rimmed glasses who was bursting out of his khakis, and his voice sounded like insect chirps coming out of a mound of pink flesh stacked up behind his desk. The walls whirred around in a fascinating kaleidoscope and the floor disintegrated into molecular squiggles.

"What seems to be the trouble, soldier?" the captain chirped as I sat down.

Seems to be the trouble? Christ, was he blind? Couldn't he see that I was stark raving loony toons? I was so overcome with the absurdity of the question that I burst into hysterical laughter. The entire half-hour interview (it might have been five minutes—I had no sense of time) went pretty much the same way. He asked me where I was *from*, and my mind reeled dizzily at the possibilities: *Where was I born? What outfit was I attached to? Where did I come from an hour ago?* It was too hilariously funny and I could not stop laughing. The air in the room shimmered like boiling fur.

There was one brief moment of lucidity when the captain asked me if I'd ever taken LSD. Suddenly the walls stopped spinning and I was stone cold sober. I looked him straight in the eye as I replied with great conviction: "Certainly not!"

Finally his first sergeant came in and led me by the hand, still laughing, over to the psychiatric ward of the base hospital where I was shot full of Thorazine and recommended for a general discharge.

"We don't really believe that you're crazy," said the army psychiatrist, standing in front of my hospital bunk with my discharge recommendation on a clipboard. "But we do think the army made a mistake when they drafted you." I ended up getting recommended for a General Discharge, Honorable Conditions.

One day, about a week after I'd arrived, Fred appeared on the psych ward. I was sitting on my bunk, watching people stroll by in the hallway, waiting stoically for my discharge papers to come through, and suddenly that familiar, hawk-nosed profile drifted by as though in a trance. Overjoyed, I sprang out of bed and pursued him down the hallway.

"Hey, Fred. Wait up!"

He ignored me, and I finally caught up to him when he crawled onto his own bunk.

"Hey, Fred, jeez, it's great to see you. How the hell did you manage to avoid shipping out? C'mon, man, I can't wait to hear the story."

But Fred stared straight ahead as though struck deaf and dumb. In his bloodshot eyes I glimpsed a hint of whatever terrible ordeal had brought him to the psych ward.

"Aw, Freddy, relax. You made it here, so everything's gonna be alright." Tears welled up in my eyes. He looked so terrified and alone. Finally he flicked his eyes at me, and I leaned in close to hear whatever sounds he might make in such a state.

"Steve," he whispered with great urgency. "My bag is catatonia, so I can't react to anything or they'll know I'm bullshitting. Go back to your room and I'll try to come by later."

"Yeah, but Fred, the game's over. You're here and your discharge is no doubt being processed as we speak."

"I can't break character!" he hissed furiously at me. "Don't you get it, you dumb fuck? Get the fuck away from me! Go see if you can find me some bread or a fucking potato. I can't show any interest in food either and I'm starving to death. Now get away from me before you blow my whole thing."

Poor Fred. About an hour later he staggered into my room like Frankenstein, eyes riveted on some distant landscape that no one else could see. Once inside my room he scampered into the toilet and sat on the bowl where he was hidden from view by the bathroom door. I tossed him a sandwich that consisted of two slices of bread with a baked potato in between. Fred devoured it in three huge bites.

"Water!" he croaked.

I got him a cupful, then sat on my bunk and kept chippie while he related his hair-raising tale. One day he just flipped out in the company area, went berserk, jumped in front of a speeding jeep, snapped into a salute and froze up, nearly missing getting run over. He would not move. MPs grabbed him and hurled him into the stockade where he was starved, beaten, dragged out in the middle of the harsh Kansas winter at night, stripped naked, and doused with freezing water. Colonels and generals waltzed in and out of his cell to see if they could make him salute, and when he didn't, they beat him some more and stepped up the constant harassment. Finally, after stoically enduring all of that for several weeks without ever reacting to any of it, he was brought to the psych ward and recommended for a psychiatric discharge, a mental case, which would not only keep him out of 'Nam but earn him a disability pension for the rest of his life.

Fred was a free spirit, who dreamed of nothing more than stocking a Land Rover with survival gear and driving across country, across the Rocky Mountains and down to Mexico. Of all the guys I met in the army, Fred seemed like more of a soldier than most, a crack shot who could excel at any physical test of skill. But about twenty-five years later I ran into him in Washington Heights and he was a crackhead.

Playing crazy as a means to get what you want is not something I recommend. It's like making a pact with the Devil, forever looking over your shoulder, wondering when he'll show up to collect his due. It also smacked of cowardice, and I always suspected that the army knew what it was doing when it discharged me, that maybe I really was nuts.

By the time I finally got out I was only six months short of doing my two years anyway. The army had shifted me around from one holding company to another while I waited for my discharge to come through. Once I was in an engineer company, working as the first sergeant's jeep driver, and the next thing I knew they were packing up to ship out for 'Nam. Maybe the army was giving me another chance, hoping I'd straighten out, but after I went AWOL for a few days, they transferred me to a fuck-up company where I had very minimal duties, and that's where I stayed until I had my papers in hand. The army doesn't pass out discharges easily, and it'll get its time out of your ass one way or another.

A terrible mixture of guilt and relief hit me later when I heard that my old outfit—guys from Yonkers and small towns in the South, guys who I'd cracked jokes with and crawled through mud and reminisced about home with (I'll never forget a young pimple-faced kid from a hick town in Georgia who used to lie in his bunk at night and sing in a sweet Southern accent, "Well it's cryin' time agin, you're gonna leave me")—shipped out to a meat grinder in the Mekong Delta and got greased.

After my dubious military career, I went back to New York and my old life of boosting and using drugs, trying to get the taste of cowardice and insanity out of my mouth by indulging in street life. It took me a year of mainlining heroin every day before I felt relatively sane again.

I never discussed my early discharge with Veronica. When I finally saw her again, I made some vague allusion to bullshitting my way out of going overseas and getting a general discharge. She never pressed me for details. I was at her apartment for dinner and noticed that she'd saved some snapshots I'd sent her of me and my buddies, lounging around in fatigues and goofing off during basic training. She'd put them in little plastic frames and had them sitting on her mantelpiece. When I looked closely at the guy in those photos, the one with "Geng" on his name tag, he seemed to be some other brother who no longer existed, who'd gone off to war and perished with his friends, or maybe survived in an alternate reality. It was the strangest feeling. I could still see the youthful cockiness in his eyes in those pictures, and wondered whatever became of him.

I never even called my parents after my discharge and avoided going back to Florida for as long as I could. I knew that Dad, at least, had nurtured hopes that I'd make a career of the army, and I knew he'd be heartbroken when he found out what had happened.

These were the heydays of LSD, Lucy in the Sky with Diamonds, baby. Pop a tab of acid and go catch The Doors live at some club under the Fifty-ninth Street Bridge, get all weird on the dance floor, gyrating in slo-mo like a stalking beast and spooking the other dancers, or hang out at endless loft parties that went on for days. But after my experience in the army, acid served only to push my mind farther out to that place we all dreaded—the "bad trip" that knocked you off your pins and left you gibbering on a street corner, stranded, and maybe never find your way back.

Another pleasurable (and, as it turned out, equally risky) pastime was sex. I seemed gifted with a positive genius for attracting troubled women and bringing out the worst in them. At one point after my discharge I moved in with a girl named Lorraine, the ex-girlfriend of a guy I'd run with during the early sixties. She was part American Indian and part black, an exotic-looking, oversexed girl with coffee-and-cream-colored skin and a great ass and legs that she loved to flaunt. She wore glasses with oversized aviator frames, had a pillow-lipped mouth, and fine, wavy, jet black hair, which she usually covered with a slouch hat. She dressed in the sexiest, micromini dresses she could find, and didn't come off much more African American than I did. A talented girl with a sure hand for classic arts like oil painting, calligraphy, and etching, Lorraine also had a keen eye for bad-boy types and I definitely fit the bill. She was the first girl I ever had a prolonged sexual relationship with, and she did much to restore my self-confidence that had flagged from too many hookers and too many drugs.

She had an adorable daughter about five years old, who often stayed at friends' apartments or with her estranged father, while her mother went to work and boogied around the Village with her shady boyfriends. Playing big brother or substitute dad for that kid was a gas, strutting through Washington Square with her sitting on my shoulders while she laughed and waved at every passerby. It filled me with a new sense of well-being to finally be useful to someone, if only a small child. At night I'd tell her children's stories in goofy accents.

"So Little Red Wisenheimer walks in Granma's house, see, and

Granma's wearing a wig and a zoot suit with a Stetson hat all broke down ace-deuce-trey, and Red goes, Vas ist los heayah?"

"No, Stevie!" the kid protested, punching me in the arm and laughing. "That's not how it goes."

"Okay, okay. Listen up. So Granma whips off the lid and the wig, see—it's the Big Bad Wolf, and he goes, Zo, if it ain't Little Red Riding Schnitzel . . ."

"Come *on*, it's Little Red Riding *Hood*. Tell it right," she'd insist, feigning anger. "Mom, make him tell it right."

Lorraine, applying a cucumber facial in front of a mirror, choked on her reefer and said, "Stevie's folks were German, bunky, so that's probably the way he heard it."

These were the days of rock and roll hot spots like the Electric Circus, which was down on St. Marks Place and swarming with stoned-out hippies, and Steve Paul's The Scene, off Eighth Avenue and Forty-third Street, one of the forerunners to Max's Kansas City. Lorraine liked to say how she'd gone to high school at Manhattan's much lauded Music and Art, but she was originally from Baltimore and had a lot of that soul sister about her. She loved to smoke grass, drop acid, and hit the discos in her miniskirt, get down with the Jerk and the Shing-a-Ling, shake her booty to Mick Jagger doing "Satisfaction." Or we'd just lay around her apartment having sex and smoking reefer with Otis Redding or Aretha blaring on the box. Like me, she was a dedicated hedonist and we had an enormous amount of sex and fun. We'd be watching a movie and all I'd have to do is touch her and she'd go, "Stevie, let's go home." We'd get up, leave the movie, and race over to her place and start tearing our clothes off.

But the whole setup was troubling. I mean, what kind of girl would leave her kid in my hands, a guy who was stealing and using heroin? I never shot up around Lorraine, but she knew. Even the kid seemed to have more sense—in spite of her delight at my clowning around, she'd occasionally shoot me a baleful look as though anticipating my departure, and finally her eyes would drop with resignation. Obviously, she'd been through this before with her mother's lovers.

There was also something about Lorraine that was wound up like a steel spring. Occasionally she'd talk about giving herself an abortion, if need be, with a coat hanger, in such a way that sent chills up my spine. In fact, she had a particular coat hanger set aside for this purpose, and had given it a name, Willy. If things got too complicated, Willy was the backup plan. I chose to ignore this (maybe I was too stoned when she told me the coat hanger bit and I'd misunderstood) in favor of the ego gratification of having such a good looker on my arm. At the time, though, I thought it was love.

One night I took Lorraine and her daughter to Ronnie's place. I'm not sure why I did that. Maybe it was an attempt to show my sister that I was alright—Hey, Ron, look at this swell girlfriend I've got, and things are just peachy keen. Or maybe I wanted to see if Ron thought this girl was as nuts as I suspected.

Ron was much taken with the kid, but she regarded Lorraine skeptically and with a forced politeness that bordered on indifference. When we left, Lorraine was pissed and inflicted my sister's coolness on me, no doubt blaming Ron's reaction on the color of her skin. But I doubted that. I figured my sister's reaction had more to do with Lorraine's cable-knit micromini dress that you could see her nipples through and barely covered her pubic hair.

When I ran into Ron on the street one day, she said, "Steve, that little girl was so adorable it's almost scary." But when I asked her what she thought of Lorraine, she got a look on her face like she needed to hail a cab—which she did.

Lorraine seemed to genuinely care for me, though, on some level. For one thing, she grew increasingly intolerant of my using heroin. I felt that was a little hypocritical, what with her smoking reefer every night, and the only effect her disapproval had on me was that I got evasive and stayed away for days while I hung out with my cronies. And then she was always after me to find a job, she being a skilled graphic artist and never having any trouble getting gigs in art departments.

"C'mon, Stevie," she'd say. "Do you think I'd live with a guy who wasn't capable of more than petty theft? There's plenty of jobs out there. I know people with half your brains who are doing damned well. Just pick something that strikes your fancy and see where it takes you."

Her tenacity was both inspiring and intimidating. I've always found the spirit of working girls in New York, especially single moms, totally disarming, so I gave it a shot. I stopped using drugs. And one day I was passing by The Cheese Village, a gourmet deli on Sixth Avenue and Eighth Street, and saw a sign in the window saying "Help Wanted." I went in there and they hired me. Lorraine was delighted.

Trouble was, whenever I stopped using drugs, my nutrient-depleted body cried out for food. I'd go for weeks with a bad case of the chucks, my stomach growling and saliva flooding my mouth every time I walked into that delicious-smelling deli. The owner encouraged me to sample the vast selection of cheeses so I could talk easily about them to customers. But I still found myself sneaking into the stockroom and wolfing down entire jars of brandied peaches and furtively hiding the empty bottles. Finally, the day arrived when I was too embarrassed to return to The Cheese Village—there were so many empty jars and cans of food stashed around the stockroom that I knew the boss would tumble me sooner or later.

Discouraged, I proposed to Lorraine the idea of my going to Florida for a while to clean up. I was feeling claustrophobic, by this time, in her one-and-a-half-room apartment, sex or no sex. She was making noises that smacked of commitment, something that was anathema to me. But she wasn't about to let go easily. An artist by nature, she'd found in me an unformed piece of human clay and was trying to sculpt and mold it gradually into the guy she needed.

I skillfully pressed home the great point that my chances of staying drug free in New York were slim, which she couldn't deny, and so she reluctantly got behind the Florida caper. She promised that she and her daughter would come down and stay with me.

"Don't worry, Stevie," she said. "We'll be with you all the way."

I'm sure that was meant to be supportive, but secretly it terrified me. This chick had her hooks in and it looked like nothing would get them out. Plus, the idea of melding my life with a single mom, not to mention running around Florida with a black girl (suddenly her color seemed much more apparent), was completely unrealistic. I could barely take care of myself. How could I take care of a woman and child, and what would Mom and Dad think of the arrangement?

Sure, I said. Y'all come down to Florida, that would be great. But I knew it was a lie, and figured she could hardly be serious either. So off I went to Florida to clean up, relieved to escape this intoxicating but worrisome relationship. Facing Mom and Dad seemed like light stuff in comparison.

part four
soul on ice

chapter 9

The jalousie windows in the Florida room were cranked open, and a breeze from the orange grove brought in cool, moist night air and the chirping of crickets. My mind had drifted for a moment from *The Tonight Show*, where George Gobel, a nerdy little comedian with a deadpan midwestern delivery, had just sat down in the guest chair next to Johnny Carson. Next to Gobel on the guest couch were Dean Martin, looking charmingly pie-eyed as usual, and Bob Hope, who was holding a golf club between his knees. They were still broadcasting out of New York in 1968. Dad was dozing in his chair and Mom was knitting. The television droned on.

"I wanna say somethin' here," says Gobel, "say I was very glad to be here, an' I'm gonna tell ya—without *me* here, your show tonight woulda been *nothin'*!" He let the laughter die down, and into the lull he delivered the unforgettable line, "Do you ever get the feeling that the world is a tuxedo and you're a pair of brown shoes?"

The audience cracked up. Carson, Hope, and Martin guffawed. They were all clutching big plastic cups full of something, and every time Gobel looked over at Johnny, Dino flicked his cigarette ashes into Gobel's drink.

Hope appeared distressed and started fussing and flicking at ashes on his dark suit.

Everybody tuned in Carson in those days. It was like putting balm on a festering wound, what with the media swamped daily with horror stories about the Vietnam conflict. Sitting in that little Florida room with Mom and Dad, my past disasters receded into the distance with each line of talk show banter.

Dino dumped more ashes into Gobel's drink and Hope started pawing the carpet with his golf club.

"I asked you this before," Johnny said when the audience quieted down. "You were a pilot, right?"

"Oh, yes," says Gobel. "I was a pilot, uh, during the *war*. Uh, you remember the war, was in all the papers 'n' everything?"

Dad was suddenly awake and watching. He shot me a look. Maybe I was being too sensitive, but I heard a message in his expression, like, *Speaking of war, what happened to my son, the slacker?*

Gobel launched into his routine about being an instructor at an air force base in Oklahoma. "And if you think back, and I'm not mad at anybody or anything, but remember—there was not *one* Japanese aircraft that got past Tulsa."

More laughs and more cigarette puffing and ashes flying around.

Dad sneered. "What's this bozo talkin' about? Christ, we didn't fight the Nips in any goddamn Oklahoma."

I shot a look at Mom, trying to see if she was putting out any *my son the slacker* vibes. But as far as I could tell she was just relieved to see me again. My sister had apparently told our parents that I'd gotten discharged honorably. Again, I didn't volunteer details and they didn't press me for any.

Dad, rather than being heartbroken that I hadn't pursued a career in the military, seemed to feel even more self-righteous and justified in his original appraisal of me—that I was a bum. The only difference was that now he'd begun to accept it.

I was in my midtwenties then and still hadn't a clue what I wanted to do with my life. *The Tonight Show* offered a momentary reprieve, but in bed at night I'd rehash debacles of the past that seemed to be following me around, and not like a shadow anymore, but more like a lumbering elephant, increasingly hard to hide and causing my family members to lie to one another—*Steve's working in the record business. He's fine.* And down there in Florida I didn't have the drugs to calm the beast. A sinking feeling of uselessness nagged at me, and so, remembering Augie's example in California, and perhaps inspired by *The Tonight Show* crew, I started going to St. Petersburg Junior College again, to study TV production.

I was grabbing at straws. It seemed like fun when I thought about it, but sitting in a control booth learning how to sync up camera shots, zooms, lap dissolves, jump cuts, and so forth, while communicating with everybody else in the studio through a headset mike, was way too technical, not to say intimidating. I got frustrated and rapidly lost interest.

One day after class, I was driving around St. Petersburg on my motor scooter and found myself in a funky black neighborhood. There was a strip of bars, gambling joints, and soul food diners along Twenty-second Street South, not unlike the stroll in Junction City, Kansas, but minus the obvious hooker trade. I had an unerring instinct for spotting the druggies and hipsters, and made fast friends with a group of shady characters in the neighborhood—Tommy, an ex-boxer and ladies' man who was light on his feet and one of the best dancers I'd ever seen; Arthur, or Heavy, as he was called, a small-time con man; and Tight, a retro-looking little guy with conked hair who wore porkpie hats, bow ties, two-tone wingtips, and played bass fiddle. All these guys had women who fed and housed them.

We hung out on the strip, drank "shake-em-up" (Silver Satin wine and grapefruit juice), smoked reefer, and drifted around to wherever the music was good, the women loose, and the drinks cheap. If we ran short of cash, these guys would do anything from stealing other people's money off the bar to impromptu card hustles and dice games. Tommy, Heavy, and Tight had a hipster patter that was a musical mixture of Southern dialect, old bebop, and jailhouse cynicism.

A girl walks by on Twenty-second Street. Tommy goes, "Damn, girl. Get on with yo fine self. Mmmm-hm! That thang you shakin' gonna *hurt* somebody."

The girl smiles and goes, "Tommy chile, you need to get yo'self a damned job."

Heavy takes a pull on the wine bottle and goes, "Saaay, girl. Is you crazy? Whachoo thank we standin' out here fuh? We on the job right now." He fans a deck of cards at her.

"What job is that?" the girl says. "Holdin' down the sidewalk?"

"Girl don't know a hardworkin' man when she see one," says Tommy. "Too busy shakin' that monkey ass."

Tight spreads a blanket over the hood of his car to set up for a three-card Monte game, goes, "Un-ass that weezine, Heavy, you want to run off at the jibs."

"Hey, Tommy," says Heavy. "You peep how she flashed on Steve? We gonna git some a that pile."

Tight goes, "I seen better-looking trim in the penitentiary." Tight was spoiled. He had a girlfriend who looked like Tina Turner.

It wasn't like we were doing anything earth-shattering, but it sure as hell eclipsed whatever was going on at St. Petersburg Junior College. When the sun went down the whole neighborhood pulsed with a lazy hum of sex, intrigue, and soul music.

There was a big ballroom-type saloon on the strip called something like Toppers, or The High Hat, where guys like Wilson Pickett once played on tour before St. Pete was considered small potatoes. We'd hang out in there, crack wise, finger pop, and dance around to Jimmy Smith and Shirley Scott on the jukebox, fatback and beans music, or catch local musicians like Tight jam. We spent the rest of our time seducing the local women.

Heavy turns to a voluptuous black woman they'd lured into the car. "Say, baby, you know what they say about white boys?"

"You tell me, Arthur," she says as she looks me over. "I'm just a small-town girl."

"They ain't afraid to give up some sky."

Everybody burst out laughing. The woman leans her head on my shoulder and goes, "Ooo baby, you and me gonna have some fun tonight."

I think these guys used me as bait for women who were fed up with their hit-and-run antics. Fine with me. I couldn't get enough of it. To these guys, sex was like making music, to be savored occasionally in the company of friends. They'd peek in the bedroom and comment on my moves, fascinated with a white guy's performance.

"Looky here, Tight. Steve got a soulful little ass-roll when he joog dat pile."

There was a barbecue joint on Twenty-second Street named Geech's, and on any given day you'd see this big guy stripped to the waist in the back lot, looking like a statue of John Henry come to life with his muscles rippling as he chopped up hickory wood that Geech used to smoke the barbecue. Geech was famous for his mustard-based sauce, which was so delicious.

One night we were in Geech's eating chicken sandwiches. When I finished mine, Heavy looked at my empty plate and goes, "Say, man. The hell you do with the bones?"

"What bones?" I shot a look at their plates, all piled with little bones. I realized that I ate the entire breast, chewing happily through bones and everything it was so good. They were all laughing at me.

"That's a cryin' shame," says Tight. "White boy throw down on some trim, but you bring him in Geech's he liable to chizoke to death on a chicken bone."

My memory can still catch the fragrance of Geech's barbecue, the aroma of fresh-baked sweet-potato pie, and the heady scent of a Southern black woman's bush.

Neighborhoods like Twenty-second Street South were no doubt the inspiration for the "dusty road" lyrics in songs like "Soul Man." Many of the streets were unpaved, but the soulful and lighthearted energy of the locals was evidence of a vanishing era.

I kept getting calls from Lorraine in New York, and at one point she said she'd given up her apartment and was catching a plane down to Florida the following week. I was no good at saying no, and her seductive voice hinted at more great sex, eclipsing my memories of how disturbed she could be—a thousand miles away and this girl still had her hooks in. Besides, who the hell was I to judge someone else's sanity? Now I could have an old lady like Tight and Heavy had, to keep house and cook up some greens while I was hard at work. Lorraine must've had high hopes for my cleaning up because she even brought her daughter and her furniture with her.

Mom and Dad had no clue any of this was going on, and I wanted to keep it that way. I told them I needed to be closer to school and was going to rent a room near the campus.

Anticipating Lorraine's arrival, I traded in my motor scooter for an old V8 Chevy and rented the entire first floor in a quaint house on the south side of St. Petersburg. The house was on the borderline between the soul section and a once-elegant white district of three-story, wooden homes with porches and balconies. The neighborhood was a little run-down now and the houses were beginning to sag, but it was racially mixed, and far enough away (thirty miles) from Mom and Dad that I felt confident I could keep the elephant hidden. I actually went out and got a *real job* at the *St. Petersburg Times*, working as a darkroom technician. Once again I felt the cozy confidence of being the man around the house, bringing home a paycheck, and being rewarded at night with hours of great sex.

The first morning Lorraine woke up in that house she shook me awake.

"Stevie," she said, pointing at the open window, her face full of curious excitement. "What's all that noise?"

It was dawn and the sun was slowly beginning to light the horizon.

I listened to the ruckus for a moment and said, "Birds, and the wind blowing in the trees. There—that right there is a bobwhite. Couple of blue jays too, I think. Most of the racket is coming from some sparrows that live in the eaves of the house. Maybe a coon or a squirrel or two. You know—life."

"A *coon*?"

"Little furry creatures that raid the trash cans."

"Yeah, but a *coon*?" She rolled out of bed and started pulling on clothes. "Stevie, if there's a goddamn coon out there I sure as hell want to see him."

We broke up laughing. She'd grown up in big cities like Baltimore and New York, and I was touched by her amazement over something I'd quickly taken for granted.

Lorraine's daughter was spooked at first, shooting us baleful looks as she doggedly laid out her things and constantly rearranged the bits of furniture in her bedroom to suit her mood. Soon she began going to public school with a child who lived upstairs from us and loosened up. We'd stroll around town shopping. The occasional double take from passersby had little to do with our color. It was either some guy checking out Lorraine's ass or some gal admiring her clothes, no different from New York.

One morning I woke up and Lorraine was sitting by the bed, sketching me in different positions of sleep. She'd done half a dozen of them in ink on heavy vellum, in unerring freehand with a rapidograph pen, every hair on my head. Amazing. It almost seemed as though we could be happy there.

But with my inevitable nose for trouble, I'd stumbled into some guys who were into forging prescriptions for narcotics. One day I came home with my pupils pinned and started nodding out. Lorraine got icy, but spoke not a word about it.

The next day, I strolled through the front door of the house after work and found the entire apartment completely empty, stripped "down to the bare walls" as they used to say at closing sellouts on Canal Street, a few bits of packing strips on the floor, not a trace that she'd ever been there. Lorraine had gathered up her daughter and her furniture, arranged for a moving van, reservations, and plane tickets, and packed up every stitch of her things and moved back to New York—all in the eight hours I was at work. Didn't even leave a note. I was stunned. The iron will and decisiveness of that woman was terrifying. As usual, I was torn between relief, resentment, and heartbreak—another perfectly fine reason to go get shit-faced.

Shortly after Lorraine left I started forging my own prescriptions for Dilaudid, a popular opiate derivative with a good kick. I was back living with Mom and Dad, and one day I found Dad snooping in my room, as he'd always been fond of doing. I went off on him, punched my bedroom door and almost broke my hand, yelling about how I'd never had any god-damned privacy my entire life. Of course, I had plenty to hide at that point—my failed relationship with the screwy girlfriend, not to mention the pads of prescriptions, syringes, and plastic vials of pills that were hidden in my mattress. As I stormed through the house toward the front door, I passed by Mom, who was standing by the dining room table, wringing her hands with tears rolling down her face.

"Oh God, Charlie," she said in an anguished voice. "Why is he so unhappy? What did we ever do to make him so unhappy?"

"Let him go," Dad said. "I always told you he was a bum."

Their words stung deeply. They were much too old to deal with such turmoil and had no idea what was wrong. Whatever remained of my conscience made me heartsick and full of self-recrimination, but that only increased the longing to get away from my parents, and the need to get stoned. It wasn't long before I got arrested for Obtaining Narcotics by Fraud—came back to a pharmacy to pick up my prescription one day and the cops were waiting. It was a felony that carried a five-year penalty, and Mom and Dad bailed me out. I was grateful and wanted to show a little discretion, but the beast was out in the open now and out of control, no longer content to follow, but dragging me around willy-nilly. All I could do was hold on and hope for minimal collateral damage. I tried an old stunt, breaking into a doctor's car in a hospital parking lot for the intern's bagful of drugs, but I got caught, and this time the cops, lawyers, and family friends all urged my parents not to bail me out again. I had a drug problem, they said, and would only return to drugs if they did. Now I had two felonies hanging over my head.

Dad came to visit me in Pinellas County Jail during the year I awaited trial and sentencing. All my life I had thought he hated me, yet here he was, showing up on visitor's day with cigarettes, books that I'd asked him to bring me, and bags full of clean underwear. It didn't seem fair, though. I was dependent on his mercy, had no choice in the arrangement, and I sensed that his attitude was still sneering—Look at you! I *told* you you'd get your tit in a wringer. I saw right through his glib concern.

"How you holding up in there, bud?"

I kept my mouth shut and tried to look pathetic. I was still pissed off that he refused to bail me out.

"I brought you some more underwear," he said into the phone, hoisting a huge shopping bag onto the metal counter outside in the hallway where the visitors had to sit.

"Jesus Christ," I howled. "How long do you expect me to be in this goddamn place? I don't need any more underwear. I need you to get a bail bondsman and get me out of here."

I was furious. How the hell had this happened to me? The guys I was locked up with were nitwits and brutes. I was a nice guy, bright, with lots of potential. Couldn't my father see that?

"Dad," I pleaded, looking back over my shoulder in feigned terror. "These guys in here are animals. I don't know how much longer I can hold out against them."

"I brought boxer shorts this time instead of Jockeys," he said. "And Pall Malls instead of the Marlboros."

I started banging the phone against the glass window in front of his face. "Get out of here and don't come back without a bail bond, you sonofabitch. I know damned well you have the money, you cheapskate."

Dad gave me a look like he didn't know who I was. He stood up and went off down the hallway, his fishing hat bobbing rapidly out of sight. He came back several weeks later, though, with more cigarettes, more books, and, infuriatingly, more underwear.

I stayed in Pinellas County Jail for almost an entire year. As usual, once I accepted the situation, my good spirits rapidly returned. There were no drugs available so the yen passed quickly, and once you learn how to jailhouse (which I prided myself on), being incarcerated is not as bad as it's cracked up to be. I read the great Russian novels, books that I'd never had time or patience to read on the street, James Joyce, and Shakespeare's plays. The food was starchy stuff, lots of beans and cornbread. I grew a mustache and got into a competitive routine with a couple of other guys doing push-ups and chin-ups after every meal. After six months I could jump down and do 150 push-ups nonstop, usually on a bet. There were no mirrors in the county jail so I couldn't see the effect these physical routines had on my physique, but I could see a change in how the other prisoners treated me. The crazy black guys who blamed *whitey* for their troubles, the rednecks who usually hated slick northerners, they all gave me a grudging respect. If a young white guy rolled into our sixteen-man cell, I could tell when his effort to chat me up was an attempt to secure protection.

There were moments that were magical, lying on my bunk at night in the dark while three or four local guys sang doo-wops or old gospel tunes they'd had to learn when they'd been locked up in a Southern juvenile reformatory called Marianna. There was one I used to request over and over. The refrain went something like, "And the wheels kept a rollin'—kept a rollin' kept a rollin'—my brother to the graveyard," and when they did it, you'd hear the voices of lost boys who'd left their youths behind in that grim reformatory. Late at night some guy would stand by the bars, gazing moodily out through the window slats, and do a ballad by Joe Tex or Sam Cooke with such longing he'd have us all in tears. There was a young guy named Pee Wee who could do such a sexy, convincing version of Aretha's "(You Make Me Feel Like a) Natural Woman" that we all started looking at him with moon-eyes. But Pee Wee was a treacherous kid, forever filing his toothbrushes into shanks, and nobody made a move on him.

Occasionally I'd get a request: "Hey, Steve. Do the one about the German spies," which was a reference to the line in "My Ship" by Gershwin and Weill that goes, And of *jam and spice* there's a paradise in the hold. It was one of my all-time favorite ballads and I could do a fair imitation of the version by Johnny Hartman, Count Basie's old crooner.

Telling stories or "running reels" is a traditional pastime in jail, and there was no shortage of dramas in this place: stories of escapes from road gangs (chain gangs were anachronistic in Florida by this time, but they still had the shotgun bosses and bloodhounds), stories of armed robberies that went awry.

"We pull up front of the liquor sto'. I get out the car, pull the stocking down over my face." Bama slowly drew his open hand down across his face, miming the gesture, his scarred and muscled frame giving the tale a spooky weight. "Time to step up and throw down. If I'd known that cracker kept an M-16 under the counter I'd a stayed in the goddamned car. Sheeit. I come *flyin'* out that liquor sto', bullets whizzin' 'round my head like bumblebees."

Three of us sat on a bunk in the eight-man sleeping chamber of our sixteen-man cell, listening to the hair-raising tale.

"I got shot here, here, and here," said Bama, indicating the puckered holes in his anatomy. "Drove three blocks fo' I passed out at the wheel."

"What happened to your partner?" I wanted to know.

"Sheeit," said Bama. "Nigger didn't even make it out the sto', may God rest his soul. Man cut him in half point blank with the first burst."

A wiry, long-haired redneck named Roy rolled into our cell one day with a handcuff key in the sole of his shoe and a big spiderweb tattooed around his belly button. First night he was there he told us a story—he's a kid living on a farm, goes in the barn one day, gets up on a stool behind the mule, and pulls down his drawers to get himself some round-eye. But it got good to the mule, see, who backed up and pinned Roy against the wall with his legs dangling in the air, pants hanging off his shoes, just as his mother walked in—You in there, boy?

At the far end of the cell a prisoner hunkered down over the steel toilet facility, cooking up a batch of hot chocolate (water and a Three Musketeers bar) in a metal coffee cup over a Bunsen burner made of toilet paper, the tiny burner balanced precariously on the toilet's rim. "Burning" in the cells was strictly against the rules, so the toilet was the handiest place to cook—a quick flush sucked away fire and fumes. Light from the flames bounced off the con's angular face and gave our cell the wistful aura of a hobo camp. Whatever criminal life I'd enjoyed on the streets, I found it in a more compressed, boiled-down version in jail.

The day redneck Roy went to court, he was so cocksure he'd go free he swore to us that if he came back he'd give everybody some round-eye.

Sure enough, the turnkey came around later that day and told us Roy had escaped from court, somebody had smuggled him a gun, big shoot-out, hostages, car chase, the whole nine.

I finally got sentenced to five years on each felony, to run concurrently. My lawyer, luckily, arranged a deal with the DA to suspend adjudication of guilt and allow me to do my time on probation. But first I had to go through a three-month treatment program for drug addicts at Raiford, Florida State Prison. Thank God my parents had put their money on a good lawyer instead of foolishly bailing me out. At this point in my life, being locked up was the only way I could stay sober.

Bama got fifteen years. It was his first offense. Never did hear what happened to ole Roy, far as I knew he was still out there. I never saw any of those guys again.

One time during my stay in Raiford, Mom and Dad drove all the way across the state, from Clearwater to Starke, Florida, to visit me. They looked so out of place in such grim surroundings, Mom in a loose navy blue pantsuit and Dad in golf slacks and a McGregor windbreaker. They looked like they were on the way to a backyard barbecue. Having visitors in jail is not always a treat. After a while you adjust to your surroundings, forget about the outside world, and time zips by, but visitors snap you out of your routine. In retrospect, I realize how different I must have looked from the nice young guy they'd tried their best to raise. I was a hunkering brute, with a bristling, red mustache and enormous back and shoulder muscles from all the chin-ups, push-ups, and mountains of beans and cornbread. (When I finally did get out and was able to look in a mirror, I was shocked at what looked like a tiny head sitting on top of massive shoulders.)

I'd always been something of a chameleon, so my speech probably reflected the black humor and broad syllables of the Southern penal system.

"Hey, bud," said Dad as we all sat down in the visitors' room. "You staying out of trouble in here?"

"I'd have to be pretty stupid to cause trouble in this place. On the other hand, what're they gonna do . . . lock me up?"

Mom looked much more grim and unforgiving than Dad. "What do you plan on doing when you get out?" she said.

Dad covered for my lack of response. "Are they feeding you alright?"

"Look at me. I look like I'm not eating?"

"We don't want you coming back to Clearwater again," said Mom.

Dad softened the blow by adding, "Not if you're only going to get into trouble again."

"How's Ronnie doing?" I asked.

"She's a big-shot New Yorker now," Dad said with a sneer. "We're lucky we even get a goddamned phone call."

I could not understand his bitterness. I was thrilled that my sister had made a life for herself, and I cherished the thought of her far away in some glamorous existence, far removed from my own dark struggles.

"She's doing great," Mom said. "She's getting work now as a writer and editor and couldn't be happier." Then, noticing my troubled reaction, she added, "And don't worry. We didn't tell her you were in here."

I appreciated her saying that, but once again I felt horrible knowing that my life of crime had caused my poor family to worry and lie to one another. I'd grown comfortable living in a world of deceit, and I renewed my vow to keep it from my parents' doorstep.

Finally they got up to leave. "You need anything?" Dad asked. "Books or cigarettes?" He knew better than to mention the underwear thing.

"No. I'm good. I'll see you."

"Yeah," Dad said, and then made an attempt at his old cornball humor. "See you in the funny papers."

After they left, I spent the next half hour in the bathroom on the stool, one of the few places in prison where you are afforded a minimum of privacy. I didn't want anybody to see me weeping.

chapter 10

"**H**ey, man. I seen Steve the other day."

"Steve who?"

"You know, *Record* Steve." Word was out in the old hood.

When I finally got out of jail near the end of 1969, I managed to finagle a probation transfer to New York, claiming I could get better rehabilitation for my drug problem there. The only rehab in Florida at the time had been the one I'd endured in the penitentiary—lock you in a padded room for three days and shoot you full of Thorazine, then a few months of "group therapy" with a Cuban doctor who didn't speak much English.

I returned to my familiar haunts in Manhattan, my old crime partners, and my dependable routine of shoplifting and drugging. One day I was strolling across East Tenth Street toward Tompkins Square and a treacherous lowlife named Midtown Charlie leaned out of a doorway and hailed me.

"Yo, Rec! Where the hell you been?"

I swelled with pride. Record Steve, a neighborhood legend now, right up there with Shoppin' Bag Billy and BJ the Queen of Crime.

* * *

My sister was getting articles published regularly in magazines like *Ms.* and *Cosmopolitan.* Ron wasn't crazy about this kind of writing and told me that she felt like she was selling out, writing about the proper kind of lipstick to wear with Levi's. She even did some of that stuff under a pseudonym, Phyllis Penn. But the grande dame of *Cosmo,* Helen Gurley Brown, apparently liked Ron and gave her a lot of encouragement and plenty to do. When Ron wasn't writing her own pieces, she contributed anonymously to the "Speakeasy" column that advised young women on how to catch a man. I hadn't a clue how much courage and tenacity it took for her to accomplish even such feats as those. I figured she was always a smartass and now it was paying off. She moved into a studio apartment on the Upper East Side where she lived and wrote from that point on.

It was around 1970 when Veronica moved to East Sixty-fourth Street. Call it love at first sight—a rent-controlled, fifth-floor walkup in a little brownstone between Park and Madison, right across the street from the Hôtel Plaza Athénée. She'd look out her window and spot photographers lurking around, waiting for a shot of Elizabeth Taylor or Clint Eastwood coming out of the hotel. In the drugstore around the corner on Madison Avenue, she'd bump into guys like Henny Youngman and Sid Caesar. Going west a block and a half brought her to the children's zoo at Central Park, and a brisk walk past the Wollman Rink and the softball fields would take her to Lincoln Center, where she was becoming a big opera fan. This was prime real estate, and about as far removed from her family as she could get. She was still struggling in the publishing business and had not yet arrived at the *New Yorker.* But she'd found her physical niche, a spartan little nest where she quickly covered the walls with shelves packed with books and records.

When I first got locked up in Florida I'd written a letter to Lorraine at her old address, desperate to hold on to some thread of my past life. It got forwarded, and with amazing good humor she'd written me letters during the entire time I was locked up. She confessed that she still cared about me, so when I finally got back to New York I assumed that she'd take me back and we could pick up where we'd left off. But she seemed changed somehow, older, no longer the hip little soul sister. She'd had her wavy hair clipped close and bleached blond, and the soft peach fuzz under her arms was shaved to stubble and powdered with deodorant. She'd moved into a little storefront apartment, and the top of her old dining room table had been converted into a loft bed. Of course, the first thing I did when I moved in there was to drag her up the loft stairs for a good romp and a long-awaited meal on the old tabletop. Her daughter wasn't around so much anymore, having grown up enough to stay with her little school buddies.

The real trouble was that Lorraine had become involved with other men, had other boyfriends, and jealousy and rage began to tie me in knots. I'd grasped little of how to behave in intimate relationships from Mom and Dad, so I sought counsel wherever I could, from macho street hustlers I knew like Boston Bob, who was something of a ladies' man.

"Listen, Steve," Bob says to me one day when I was crying the blues. "Why you think she keeps fucking with your head, balling other guys and flaunting it? A bitch don't know you care about her till you show her your teeth."

Sadly, women did not appreciate it when I showed them mine.

One day Lorraine flatly told me to pack my things, get out, and don't come back. Little wonder—I was back to stealing and using heroin again. On my way out the door, I stopped and turned to her, my head filled with rage, jealousy, and hurt pride. My grasp of reality was already tenuous, after all the drugs and a long incarceration, and this seeming betrayal pushed me over the edge.

"There's a thing I always wanted to do ever since I've known you."

"What's that?" she asked with a smirk.

I hauled off and slugged her. It was the first time I ever struck a woman and I instantly regretted it. She leaned back against the wall by the front door and put her hands to her face, that exquisite face that I'd come to feel like I could not live without. I immediately apologized and tried to comfort her but my continued presence only made it worse. All I could do was comply with her wishes and leave her the hell alone. I'd never felt worse about anything I've ever done.

Several weeks later I was renting an apartment nearby on St. Marks Place and got a call from Lorraine, asking me if I'd return an Indian blanket she'd given me. I went over there in high hopes of begging her forgiveness. When she opened her door at my knock, I held out her blanket. She grabbed my wrist and yanked me into the darkened apartment. Her brother, who was lurking behind the door, stepped up behind me and caved my skull in with one terrific blow on the head with a claw hammer. Then another guy came out of hiding wielding a club and the two of them beat me into unconsciousness.

I woke up terrified and unable to move. No wonder—I was gagged, my hands and feet were tied, and I was wrapped in something rough and restrictive. I couldn't see much in my mummy-like shroud, but being faced with death can really perk you up. Senses I didn't even know I possessed snapped into red alert. Some might get addled from a blow like that to the head, but for me it was a wake-up call:

Bang! Pay attention, dummy!

From its texture and smell I recognized the rug I was wrapped in, the one that Lorraine had spread over her loft . . . where we'd made love so many times.

Voices of people arguing broke in on my reverie, and my auditory sense swept out like radar, searching for a clue to my chances. Lorraine was still there. Her voice was soft, and the words indistinct, but the texture was unmistakable. Amazingly, I could've sworn she was pleading my case, because her brother suddenly started barking something about it being too late. She'd started all this, goddamnit, so just clear the hell out and let him finish it, he said, and that I deserved it after molesting a child. Apparently, in an effort to get her brother to carry out her vengeance, Lorraine had told him that I tried to sexually abuse her daughter. Which was completely untrue! But that explained why he suddenly wanted to kill me. Maybe Lorraine had had a change of heart, but the wheels were in motion now, out of her control, and rolling implacably toward my demise.

Somebody said something about moving the car closer. Immediately I envisioned being carted off in the trunk for disposal. What a sad little epitaph—*Man found in Dumpster beaten to death.* Those thoughts sent another surge of adrenaline to my senses, but to no avail. I was completely helpless. At that point I heard the door open and everybody go out, leaving me alone.

The need to breathe must be the most powerful urge there is. The gag and rug were suffocating me, and with the strength born of terror I freed my hands, got the gag off, and wriggled out of the rug. The first thing I noticed was a pool of my own blood, like a small red lake spreading out over the tiny black-and-white tiles of Lorraine's storefront (the place had once been a candy store). Struggling to untie my ankles, I looked around frantically for a weapon. My hands trembled. How much time before they came back? Please, God, give me a few more moments. Suddenly the front door opened. Both guys came back in and found me sitting on the floor untying my feet.

"Damn," said the other guy to the brother, shaking his head. "Ain't it amazing what a dope fiend can survive?"

Lorraine's brother was a big, dapper black guy, and I remembered her telling me how nuts he was, an S&M type with a taste for street boys. The minute he saw me he picked up his claw hammer and stepped forward, but the other guy put his hand on his shoulder and stopped him. This guy looked streetwise, rough-and-ready in a cheap leather jacket and jeans. When his eyes locked on mine I detected a flash of someting human (the brother's eyes were unreadable red slits) and I seized on that like the drowning man that I was. I launched into a heartfelt plea for my life, addressed to the brother but appealing to the street kid next to him. It was a speech that I would remember the rest of my life, filled with every ounce of cunning I could dredge up out of my manipulative junky soul as I hovered on the brink.

"Okay, look. I know I'd done wrong to punch Lorraine, and I probably deserved a beating. But, c'mon, man. I never did anything to her daughter. I loved that kid like she was my own." With an inspired touch of stoicism toward my tough lot in life, I added, "And, hey, no hard feelings. I've had worse beatings than this from the hacks in prison. But enough is enough. I learned my lesson. Just let me get to the hospital and I'll forget it ever happened and never bother your sister again."

The street guy nodded and they conferred briefly out of earshot. Thankfully, they relented. When I reached up to tentatively feel my head, the street guy came over and stopped my hand. "Don't touch it," he said. And though his words made me fear for the damage, I figured he wouldn't have bothered if they were going to kill me.

They walked me, drenched in blood, through deserted late-night streets on First Avenue, one guy with a shank pressed against my ribs in case I yelled for help. Several blocks along I noticed a uniformed cop on a corner on the other side of the avenue. Sly hope rose in me. But he was talking to someone and seemed miles away, while close at hand the knife pushed insistently into my side—they must have spotted the cop too. Moreover, I was so acutely aware of my caved-in skull, stepping gingerly to keep my brains from spilling out, that I feared a sudden struggle would do me in. Finally, a block or so past the officer, they let me stumble unassisted up to Beth Israel Hospital—but not before the brother gave me one last blow to the head with his hammer. Luckily I was lurching forward at the moment so it was only a glancing one.

I was greeted in the emergency ward with gasps of horror. Luckily, a skilled neurosurgeon happened to be standing there lecturing several interns. He took one look at me and told them to immediately prep me for surgery, then spent hours piecing my cranium back together. Miraculously, I suffered no noticeable ill effects from the beating, other than an eggshell-sized dent in my skull that would remain for the rest of my days. As usual, I quickly took good fortune for granted.

I spent several weeks in the hospital recuperating, stoned to the gills on drugs that my associates smuggled in to me. But they sounded skeptical when I told them what happened. "Yeah, but Steve, they obviously tried to kill you, so why did they let you go?" It annoyed the hell out of me. I needed the sympathetic fury of my friends at those people, but my hysterics must have sounded far-fetched. I briefly tried feigning motor-impairment, staggering up the hallway and then suddenly collapsing, thinking I might get disability. But I'd never had the patience for long, involved con games anyway. Some detectives from the local precinct came by and questioned me about what happened, since it was a violent crime, but I was so stoned and terrified that my descriptions must've confused them. When they went to Lorraine's apartment, nobody answered the door, and they claimed they didn't have enough evidence for a warrant to break in.

What I didn't know was that during the time I was laid up in the hospital, my mother was dying of cancer in Florida.

When Ron came to visit me I'd been out of surgery a few days and must've looked pretty bad with my dome all wrapped in bandages. I was so relieved to see her I just blurted out all the horror, betrayal, and fear, occasionally bursting into tears of disbelief at the viciousness of it all, trying to purge it out of my system where it was burning a hole in my gut. Ron, who'd always loathed violence, stood silently at the foot of my bed, stunned, trying to impart some small feeling of sympathy or comfort and all the while doing her best to conceal her bafflement. I felt like a complete and utter fool.

"Jeez, Steve," she said, wiping away a few tears of her own. "That sounds horrible. Can I get you anything?" At least Ron believed me, and I loved her for it.

"Talk to me a little. What are you up to?"

"Christ, nothing this dramatic. Writing articles for women's magazines about how to catch a man."

"Don't make me laugh. It hurts my head."

"You think that's funny? What about the women who actually took my advice?"

"C'mon, Ron. Stop."

"You sure you don't want me to get you some magazines or cigarettes or anything?"

"Nah. I'm good."

She certainly didn't glean a lot of useful information from me about how to conduct romantic affairs. I was grateful she didn't hit me with the old *So now what're you going to do with your life?* I was lucky I'd survived. Whatever I did after this it was all gravy. I was glad she'd come. As soon as she left, I revisited the terror I'd felt when I was wrapped up in that carpet, not knowing if I'd ever see another day.

Just before I left the hospital, I called Ron, and that's when she told me that Mom had died. She'd just come back from the funeral. I burst into tears, and then I was furious.

"I don't believe this," I ranted into the phone. "Why the hell didn't you tell me Mom was dying? She's my mother too." I was nearly hysterical. "Jesus Christ, cave my goddamned skull in, I don't give a flying fuck, but please don't tell me that you stood right here, knew Mom was dying, and never said a goddamned word? Oh, Ron, how could you do that?"

I don't think I've ever been so sad about anything in my entire life. Yeah, I got whacked pretty bad and probably had it coming after the life I'd led. But poor Mom, who'd put up with my crap all those years, not to mention putting up with my snotty sister and our crazy father, who'd taken care of me since day one, cooked and cleaned and wiped my nose and never complained or raised her voice to a soul, who'd anguished over how unhappy I was and probably blamed herself . . .

"Steve, get hold of yourself," Ron said. "I'm sorry too, but you'd just had brain surgery, for God's sake, and I was afraid if I told you about Mom that you'd have lurched up out of bed and gone down there."

My sister had spent her life constructing a wall of reason to shield her from the irrational, the tragic, and the emotionally disturbing. Ron once told me, for example, that she didn't feel any loyalty to our family just because she was *born* into it. But that didn't mean she could avoid the pain of our mother's death. She'd always rallied to Mom's side against our father, and she'd been closer to Mom than I was to either of our parents. But blinded by my own misery, I was unable to appreciate Ron's difficulty in dealing with Mom's death alongside her brother's near demise. All I could see was that nobody was giving me any consideration, and I was not sure if I could forgive any of it—Ron for not telling me, myself for getting in such a bind that I was unable to show up for Mom's last days, and especially the sonsofbitches who cracked my cranium. And thus rage offered me a way to sidestep the tragedy of my mother's death—to face it head-on, I feared, would have destroyed me.

When I got out of the hospital, I bought a K-55 shank and a baseball cap to hide my ravaged scalp and went over to the little playground across the street from Lorraine's storefront apartment. Finding an unobtrusive spot to sit with my back against a wall, I settled in for the long haul, fury giving me extraordinary patience as I waited for somebody, anybody, to enter or leave that dread place where I'd almost met my maker. And then, I swore to myself, I'd take it out of their hide.

No lights came on in the apartment when the sun went down. People walked by, going about their lives. When the sun rose the next morning my rage was undiminished. A house sparrow lit on the playground fence and cocked its head at me. Then it fluttered to the ground, hopped a couple of times, and pecked at something on the asphalt. It had been a long night. The sparrow suddenly flew off, chirping raucously at some unseen affront. Tears came to my eyes as memories of Mom crept back unbidden and I almost lost my resolve. But when I looked back at the covered window of that storefront apartment, I couldn't help wondering if they'd mopped up the huge pool of blood I'd lain in. The fury was still there, right where I wanted it. After a while some kids came by, shot a few hoops, and left, hardly glancing at me as I sat and stared through a red haze at the door across the street. Nobody, goddamnit, had the right to instill that much terror or cause that much damage to another human being.

I'd been there for almost an entire day when one of my hustling acquaintances, a lanky, older guy named DJ, came by and squatted next to me in the playground and listened to my tale.

When I finished he said, "Give it up, Steve."

"I can't, DJ. Can't allow somebody to get away with that."

He looked sideways at me. "How long you prepared to sit here?"

"Long as it takes."

"Spare me," DJ said. "You're punishing yourself. I know 'cause I've been in that same spot a few times my damned self. Think about it. If somebody does show, which it ain't looking, y'understand, any too goddamned likely that they will, and you do manage to get some satisfaction, then what? You prepared to go upstate with a homicide?"

He let that sink in for a minute before he went on. "Ahhh, never mind me runnin' off at the jibs. Hell, it ain't me that got my melon mashed. Those people were definitely way outta line, so do what you got to do, babe. I always did. Who knows? You'll probably pull a light bid, justifiable and shit, maybe max out in five, read some good books, play a little handball."

This guy was starting to get to me.

"Meantime," he said, getting up and stretching, "my old lady's burning a mean pot of greens and I got a half-load of good Harlem dope stashed in my shaving kit."

Later at DJ's, there was a fleeting moment when it occurred to me that none of that trouble would've ever happened if I hadn't clocked the poor girl with a left hook or been so eager to overlook the signs of deep disturbance in a woman in order to get laid. When I told DJ and his old lady that, they laughed. Finally we were laughing so hard I had to beg them to stop, it was hurting my head so bad.

That whole business had taken some wind out of my sails and colored my carefree life on the streets, so several weeks later I went down to visit Dad. Figured I'd let my head heal and maybe assuage the guilt I felt about missing Mom's funeral and her last days. Dad seemed relieved to see me. I knew damned well Ronnie hadn't told him anything about me getting my skull caved in. But Dad suspected I'd been in dire straits not to show up for my own mother's funeral. When he got over being pissed off at me about that, he told me about Mom having a mastectomy. I winced at the very thought, but Dad said no, it hadn't seemed to bother her that much, that everything was alright for a while. Then he told me the sad story of when he'd found her.

"I was out cutting the grass and Lilly [their neurotic, high-strung pooch] started barking and nipping at my trousers. Dat poor wittle dog knew dat sumpin was da matter. She was frantic and barked and barked, and when I went into the bedroom, there was Rose with her head on the pillow, just as peaceful as could be. Jesus, your mother was such a good little soldier, never complaining. . . ."

He looked so sad and lonely and he wept unashamedly. I wanted to take him in my arms and comfort him, weep with him, but I felt so cut off from them all. There was a hint of accusation in my father's tale, and I thought of the Christmases they must have sat around wondering what had become of me, which only accentuated my feelings of remorse. I wanted to head right back to New York to escape this new regret—that Mom had soldiered on into the next life without ever knowing if I'd turn out alright. The implications of my mother's death were too overwhelming, and I pushed it down into that inner sanctum where all my other regrets dwelt, resurfacing from time to time but thankfully eluding the harsh light of day.

Before I left, Dad gave me their car, since he didn't drive himself. I think it was a last-ditch attempt to get me to stay in Florida, trying to bribe me to remain there with him. The car was a Volkswagen camper, and I had to listen to tales about camping trips that he and Mom had made in it. I told him to sell it, that I didn't want the damned thing if it meant staying in Florida where I'd done nothing but cause him and Mom trouble.

We exchanged angry words, and that's how we parted, me driving off in their car, and Dad slamming the front door as he went back in the house. I felt horrible leaving him like that, but I feared I'd only cause him more pain, not to mention lose my mind if I stayed there. Besides, I was still on probation and there were some small-town cops in Florida that really had a hard-on for me.

Back in New York, I used the car for a while to go boosting, but it reminded me of Mom and I didn't like doing anything illegal in a car that was registered in my real name. A few months later I sold it and blew the money on drugs. Too young and cocky to be concerned for my immortal soul, I nevertheless had a hustler's notion of karma, the run of the cards, and poetic justice. That car had been inextricably connected to my parents, and after I dumped it and squandered the money, an eerie feeling came over me that that was the move that brought on the next bit of bad karma in the year 1971.

"The court will now recess for an hour and reconvene at one o'clock," said the bailiff, whereupon the judge gathered up his robes and departed with the bailiff via a side door to his chambers.

I looked around at the other prisoners who were seated in our little peanut gallery on one side of the Nassau County courtroom. They were a sad, unkempt crew of petty criminals who looked like they belonged there, unlike yours truly who was at that point facing extradition proceedings and hence a serious felon. But the sheriff, whose job was to bring prisoners from the bull pens into the courtroom handcuffed to each other, paid no more attention to me than the others when he took the cuffs off, permitting us to go singly before the judge to be arraigned.

It had started out as a standard pinch for shoplifting, this time in a mall in Long Island, and as usual I gave the cops an alias, hoping to skate by as a first offender—Harold Wilson, 110 Downing Street, Greenwich Village. I wasn't being flip. It's just what came out of my mouth in a desperate moment, knowing I was still on probation from Florida. But as chance would have it, my prints brought back my rap sheet, and the cop who'd taken down my information had come back to the holding cell red in the face.

"Well, look who we got here—the fibber. Between us and Florida we're gonna stick it up your ass and break it off."

The idea of facing hard time in the Florida state pen was not appealing.

I glanced around the courtroom. The sheriff in charge of us was standing by the door that led to the hallway, watching the free people file out for a smoke during the hour-long recess. He seemed bored stiff and never glanced over at us. People walked out of the courtroom right past him and he paid no attention to them. Suddenly it occurred to me that I might do the same. A charge of adrenaline ran up my spine.

The last people remaining in the free section were sitting directly across from me, and when they got up to leave I simply stood up and followed close behind them. They took no notice of me as we walked away from the prisoners, through the seats over to the windows against the far wall, and up to the front of the courtroom. The sheriff never wavered from his gazing. I removed my sport coat and draped it over my shoulder to vaguely alter my appearance and hoped that Saint Nicholas, patron saint of thieves, would bless me once again with a shoplifter's cloak of invisibility. Time ratcheted down into microseconds. We crossed in front of the vacated judge's bench, then stepped toward the exit where the sheriff stood, leaning against the door frame and still staring into the hall. I stole one last glance at the other prisoners and they were all looking wide-eyed as I shouldered my way past the sheriff, but once out in the hallway I detected no ripple of disturbance from behind or calls of alarm.

I walked out of the building, my heart pounding, up to the bus stop, and finally got the subway back to Manhattan. There aren't many highs better than that. I was grinning and laughing at the straphangers on the train. Sure, I thought to myself, I'll do my time—on Tuesday.

Unwittingly I'd committed a class-C felony—Escape Pending Extradition. The very next day, two warrant detectives from Nassau County came by the hotel I'd once given as an address in Midtown where I used to go cop. When I knocked on the door to my connection's room he told me to get scarce, that he'd seen two huge cops knocking on my hotel room door.

I had a really helpful probation officer at the time, so I went to her office and told her my tale of woe. She said she might be able to keep me out of Florida if I went voluntarily into Daytop, a long-term therapeutic community for drug addicts.

At the time, Daytop had a small outreach-intake office down on Chrystie Street, so I started going there in the morning, trying to get admitted into one of their live-in facilities and hopefully dodge the long arm of the law. It was a musty old storefront with lots of folding chairs, and other junkies like myself would sit around in meetings bragging to the Daytop guys how much pure heroin they'd been using. I gritted my teeth and came back day after day. Anything was better than the Florida pen.

But the warrant detectives were persistent, and one day they went to Veronica's apartment and inquired about me. Ronnie knew I was trying to get into Daytop. She told them to buzz off, that her brother was going into a facility for drug addicts to try to get himself together. One day I was playing basketball with the Daytop people across the street from the storefront and two big detectives rolled up on me.

"Are you Stephen Geng?"

Suddenly I was the only person left on the court. I had several bags of dope and a set of works in my coat pocket. I looked around to see if maybe I could get away—not a chance.

"Now look, Steve. We can do this the easy way or the hard way."

As we crossed the bridge on the way to Long Island, one cop goes, "You got any drugs on you? Because if you do, deep-six them into the river now. Our job is only to bring you back and clear the books."

I was in a black mood contemplating extradition to Florida, but it was nice to know that not all cops are ballbusters. When they finally got me back to Nassau County Jail, the cop who'd been in charge of the court cases on the day I escaped was still working down in the holding cells.

"Hey, Frank," said one of the warrant detectives. "Look who's back. Speedy Gonzales!"

I stayed locked up in Nassau County Jail for nine months and enjoyed notoriety on the tier since a few of the cons had been in court the day I escaped.

"You was looking *in*tense, Jack, like walking in slow motion. When you took your coat off? Damn, we thought you gonna throw it over the screw's head, go for his pistol. Couple hours later we back in the bull pens. Cops come around, want to know what happened to Wilson, you dig? Don't nobody say nothin' 'cept this one chump. Say *he* know what happened to Wilson—if they let him make a phone call."

Florida finally agreed to continue my probation in New York and I got time served on the shoplifting and the escape, but part of the plea bargain was that when I got out I went right into Daytop. I was relieved that my sister unwittingly gave me up. Escape is intoxicating, but it's no fun being on the lam.

When I was finally accepted into Daytop, I was sent to its live-in facility out on Staten Island. It was a beautiful farm that someone had donated, with a huge A-frame house, a nicely landscaped driveway, dormitory rooms to accommodate fifty residents, and a barn and stable with two horses, all on several acres of grassy property. Daytop Village was the East Coast answer to Synanon, a self-contained therapeutic community for drug addicts that featured confrontational encounter groups and ego deflation as the vehicles for change. I loved the place. The food was great, there was constant camaraderie, and the harassment dished out to new-comers for the purpose of ego deflation was, to me, like a Sid Caesar ver-sion of army boot camp.

The first job they gave me was animal care. There was a horde of cats, several dogs, and two horses in the barn, making for a lot of cleaning up and feeding. I arrived with another newcomer, a young black guy who confessed to a terror of horses, so we decided that he'd care for all the house animals and I'd take care of the two horses. I fed them, mucked out their stalls, replenished the straw, and, once I got comfortable with them, even groomed them and exercised them with bridled walks and short rides. One was a swaybacked old nag and the other a spirited bay named Rusty. I became quite devoted to these animals and smuggled them many an apple out of the dining room. On several occasions I jumped up on Rusty bareback with nothing but his bridle on, gave him the reins, and thrilled as he galloped around the huge field behind the barn.

Back in the house, anyone caught indulging in negative or "dope fiend" behavior was given what was called a "learning experience." The residents who dished out learning experiences were called "coordina-tors." Learning experiences usually came in the form of humiliating signs, like sandwich boards, slung around the offender's neck, with specifics of the offense listed like advertising on the front and back. If you got caught stealing cookies from the kitchen, you got a sign saying, I'M A SLIMY THIEF . . . PLEASE CONFRONT ME. That's a simplified example, and the ex-otic variations of learning experiences that I saw during my stay at Daytop were a real tribute to the creative minds of the coordinators.

If, for example, you were caught falling asleep in morning meeting, they made you wear a Rip Van Winkle beard made out of cardboard with Zs inked down the face and hung from your ears. If you came on like a tough guy, they'd make you wear a dress. If you were caught lying, you'd get a Pinocchio nose tied around your head, which was replaced with still longer ones for further offenses. The many beards and noses decorating all the fuck-ups gave a wonderful ambience to the house, like characters in a Brecht or Ionesco play. I'll never forget a guy who wore a tinfoil halo and cardboard wings that he got for constantly "spacing out."

There were a few cardinal rules (no drugs, violence, or illicit sex) that when broken would get you a shaved head or thrown out. These grand violations resulted in a "house meeting," where the entire population voted on the punishment. You had to sit up there in front of fifty people while they stood up one at a time, frothing at the mouth, and screamed at you all the details of what a degenerate asshole you were.

I, myself, was awarded a small Pinocchio nose, a "pop sheet," and a "can of lies." This consisted of a number-ten can slung over my shoulder with a piece of twine and labeled A CAN OF LIES. Inside the can of lies I carried the rolled-up pop sheet—a typewritten list of every person in the present population of the residence. I had to encounter each person on the list and explain to them why I needed to tell lies, then check their name off. When I'd gone through the entire fifty or so people in population I would have fulfilled the learning experience. When they asked me why I lied, I lied. I gave teary-eyed therapeutic answers I thought they wanted to hear, like, "I'm afraid you won't love me if I tell the truth."

I tried to keep up a good front, but the people were getting to me. They'd have talent shows and I'd end up in a doo-wop group and develop close friendships with some of the guys. Then when those guys graduated to "reentry level" and moved on to another house, I'd fall into fits of sadness. Guys would find me in the laundry room weeping and ask me what was going on. I developed a terrible crush on one of the girls, which was a real no-no in that place. When they brought the girl and me into an encounter group and told me what a sick, perverted dope fiend I was with no business lusting after one of my "sisters," I started looking for a way out.

But my fondness for the other residents, and they for me, continued to grow, making me ever more uncomfortable. I was getting giddy and defenseless and my emotions felt out of control. Even the damned horses were getting to me. I kept wandering out to the barn to check on them. Maybe I'd read too many Dick Francis stories about steeplechasers, but sometimes those horses would look me in the eye and tears would run down my cheeks. Once I went out there late on a winter night and discovered that they'd been chewing on the wooden beams around their stalls and I went around the house frantically asking people what was wrong with them. Nobody knew. I felt like I had to get out of that place or I'd go nuts.

Daytop was a long-term, in-patient rehab—a year and a half minimum—but after six months I'd had enough. I was in good health, and my mental synapses were firing on all six cylinders; my emotional breakdown I attributed to the constant presence of all these people. So I left, sneaking out the back door in the middle of the night like the thief that I was. I lasted about half a day before I was stoned again. Resignedly, I went over to my sister's apartment on East Sixty-fourth Street and started dumping all my troubles on her—my inability to stay drug free or move my life forward, the can of lies that I still seemed to be lugging around and using mainly on myself.

Ron had been sitting and chewing a fingernail during my litany, but at one point she stood up and glared at me.

"You think you're the only one in the goddamned universe who has troubles?" Tears were rolling down her cheeks. "You think I don't have troubles? You ever think what it might be like to be me? You think I don't get lonely as all hell sitting around in this tidy little apartment year after year, totally incapable of keeping up any kind of an intimate relationship without—hell, I don't know—sticking them under a magnifying glass or whatever it is I keep doing? Every time I see you, you're dragging some little tart over here, parading her around under my nose, and now you sit there complaining like you're the only person in the world with troubles?"

"Jeez, Ron," I said, much taken aback. "I didn't know any of this. Maybe I could show you a few tricks about—"

"Oh, just shut up for two minutes. Do you have any idea what it's like to be wracked with insecurity, I mean about just *func*tioning out there in the cold, cruel world [she laughed wryly for half a second here], but still have to get up every goddamned day, all by yourself, march down five flights of stairs, and go to work because if you don't, then who else is going to pay the bills? You really don't have any idea what that's like, do you? You think you're having trouble? You don't even know what trouble is."

Here she was living on the Upper East Side, writing stories for *Ms.* and *Cosmo*; it just never occurred to me that she would be anything other than delighted with her accomplishments.

"Well, of course I know what it's like, Ron. I mean, every time I make a hit and have to walk out past security guards, the paranoia is unbelievable, and it's everything I can do to maintain that carefree aura of the—"

"Oh, that's just great. I wish I had a tape recorder so you could listen to yourself."

The humor was lost on her and I felt hollow and stupid saying it. Tears continued to flow as she snatched up a pack of Virginia Slims or whatever the hell she was chain smoking in those days. I just sat there, stunned, totally disarmed, my heart breaking for her now rather than for myself. She was exposed to me in this way for the first time, and it jarred me out of my own self-centeredness. As she stood there drying her tears, she turned to look out the window onto Sixty-fourth Street, giving me a view of her delicate back, her shoulders hunched up around her ears. It was clear that she was just as human and complex as the rest of us.

Unfortunately, passing epiphanies can no more overcome a life of self-indulgence any more than my six months at Daytop Village were able to change me. It wasn't long after that scene that I was back out on the street doing my thing.

Although my sister's outburst had little lasting effect, I was occasionally motivated to seek employment by the women I shacked up with. One girl helpfully went through the employment section of the *New York Times* with me.

"Look, Steve. Here's something you could do."

The French-American Banking Corporation was looking for a young man who spoke French to help in their letters of credit department.

"I mean, you speak some French and you really look great in a suit and tie."

So I reluctantly went on down to Wall Street and they hired me. My girlfriend was delighted to see me put on a suit and tie every morning and go off to work. French was the common language of international finance, so I had to translate these letters of credit, for huge sums of money, from banks all over the world, from French into English. No big deal. It was mostly all numbers and words like *corporation*, which were spelled the same in English. But I wasn't much of a typist, and the paper used for these negotiable bonds was extremely expensive and about six copies thick. I also knew that I'd never make it through the day without a drink or some drugs, so I always brought a few four-ounce bottles of codeine cough syrup to sip on at my desk.

"I got a dry cough," I'd say, coughing discreetly into a handkerchief and taking a sip.

Every once in a while I'd go to the men's room to check myself out in the mirror, see how my front was holding up, and my eyes looked like two BBs in a glass of tomato juice. By the end of the day I'd be stoned and I'd have a wastebasket jammed full of that beautiful bond paper from all the typos that were impossible to correct through all the copies.

Astonishingly, I lasted almost three months before I was let go, supposedly because I couldn't be bonded to work with negotiable letters of credit. I didn't even bother to go back to my girlfriend's apartment but collected my last paycheck and checked into a fly-by-night Midtown hotel to get loaded and celebrate my freedom.

I simply hadn't learned anything else quite as thoroughly as stealing and getting stoned. The scenario with my sister, losing my job and my girl-friend, became several more in a collection of remorseful scenes that I played back over and over on that little VCR in my head, whenever I needed a tasty dose of self-pity to justify the hours of being stoned or sit-ting in a jail cell in the Tombs or Rikers Island.

One day I paid Veronica a visit and spotted a middle-aged guy in a full beard making himself comfortable on her studio couch. She introduced me to him when I stepped inside the door, but Ron was acting so strange, leaning languidly against the door frame with a goofy smile on her face, that I declined an invitation to join them. It was Donald Barthelme, my sister's favorite writer at the *New Yorker*. Apparently my sister had just looked up his phone number in the telephone book and called him to say how much she loved his stories and he'd asked her out to lunch. He was married, which made him even more attractive to my sister, who gravi-tated toward unavailable guys. From what little I could gather, Donald Barthelme was the one who brought Veronica to the attention of William Shawn and the magazine that she would come to work for and love.

chapter 11

Veronica's writing career began to take off as she continued to get published in magazines and catch the eye of the literary crowd. The piece that caught the attention of people at the *New Yorker* was a parody of their famous movie critic, Pauline Kael, in the *New York Review of Books.*

THE CURRENT CINEMA
BY VERONICA GENG

Ho, Ho, Ho

Robert Altman's not just working at his talent's peak now; he isn't just putting to-gether movies better than any director's ever done. It's as if he's trashed the en-tire form. By junking the LA hacks' formulas, and the Europeans', he's reinvented movies at some new level, so that the word "movie" 's relevant now only when it's preceded by the word "Altman." In *St. Pete,* we're at a convention of department-stores' Santas in St. Petersburg, Florida—seniorsville at its sappiest and most brutal. The picture's knockout. There's nothing the matter with it. It's Altman's farewell to movies, with their Esperanto sensibilities, their bogus art and darling "actors." It's as if the whole sanctimonious-aesthete-in-tinsel-land scene bombed out ten years ago, and he's the only one who's noticed, or who's cared.

He's been assembling a repertory company of Santas for this picture, and it's their movie. They're knockouts. These squalid duffers're the sexiest men in pictures right now. Redford doesn't have their gutter appeal; neither does Newman, who's a fop, or Burt Reynolds, who's a mincing synthetic stud. There's always been something tony and fake about screen actors' erotic energy; women've sensed they were somehow playing a part. The Santas are a jazzy gang of tacky geezers, the kind of men who'd really paw you, not just your ordinary oversalaried, swanked-up stars. They're joke stars. It's as if they're wacked out on some cinema festival they'd gone to with discount oldsters' tickets. Altman didn't pay them anything. He didn't pay technical people, either; he let me cut the picture. Paramount's not willing to release it in time for Christmas. They're not unaware; they sense that if *St. Pete's* ever shown, Altman'll've sent moviemaking as we've known it down the tubes.

Roger Angell, the *New Yorker*'s fiction editor, loved the piece and called my sister up, thus beginning their relationship as writer/editor. Ron had just broken up with Rick Hertzberg, who was at that time the editor of the *New Republic*. Like most of Ronnie's romances, it had been a frustrating affair, she waiting supportively and patiently for Hertzberg to dump his girlfriend, which he did, only to be baffled and betrayed when he then went and married someone else. They remained friends, but friendship, as we all know, is the booby prize in romance, although I suppose it beats the hell out of getting your head caved in with a claw hammer.

I didn't see much of the *New York Review of Books* while I was locked up in Nassau County Jail or while I was in Daytop. I wasn't really an avid fan of Pauline Kael, nor had I read her famous review of Robert Altman's *Nashville*, so even if I had seen my sister's parody it would've gone over my head. You'd think I'd have followed Ron's writing, but I never read any of her stories until they were collected much later in a book. It's not just that I was antiliterate—I was reading Marvel comic books at the time and the *New Yorker* was something I thought of in terms of clever cartoons and dentists' waiting rooms—but Ron never encouraged me to read her stuff, or even let me know in which issue I could find her work. Maybe she didn't think me capable of appreciating what she was doing. We didn't communicate much, so for all I know she was disappointed

I didn't show any interest in her writing. But she'd worked her ass off to get away from our crazy family, and I felt like she didn't want me sticking my nose in her business in any way, shape, or form.

My own career as a booster was also taking an upward swing, and just in time. Mom was gone, Dad had pretty much written me off, and my sister had never bought into the sympathy bit. Life is like that—only when there was nobody left to lean on was I willing to pull myself up by my bootstraps and become a really good thief. One night at an East Village thieves' den, I ran into a guy known around upper Broadway as Nicky P (the "P" stood for pimp, an occupation that no longer suited his life as a married man), who'd come downtown to the Village to dodge his uptown police profile. Nick was fishing for a new hustle.

He was a stocky Armenian guy from the Bronx, with bushy black eyebrows and a scowling face. He'd just gotten out of Atlanta Federal Penitentiary for counterfeiting and was on parole, so he was wary of throwing any big bricks. In the old days Nick had swaggered around Midtown with a hatchet in a shoulder holster. The idea of driving a shoplifter around the country in order to hit greener turf looked to him like a perfect low-risk endeavor, and I was only too happy to expand my hustle out of the New York/New Jersey area where I was developing a profile of my own.

Nick was not a drug addict or an alcoholic and never touched the stuff. His only vices seemed to be chain-smoking Pall Malls and making fast money. He bought a heavy-duty van with the proceeds of our first few scores and stocked it with the kinds of promotional flyers and paraphernalia that a record distributor would carry—a legitimate front if we were stopped by cops with a van full of records. He bought detailed maps for each area we intended to work, with chamber of commerce overlays that depicted every shopping center. He plotted out the routes that brought us to the maximum amount of stores with the minimum amount of driving time, always staying underneath the felony radar. He showed me where to acquire phony ID cards that could be filled out with a local address for the state where we'd be working. (You're considered a bail risk if you're out of state.) My criminal career was moving up a notch or two.

We split 60–40, with me taking the lion's share since I was doing the boosting and most of the fences were my connections. I made so much money with Nick he would've been worth more than 40 percent, but he never pushed me for more. Once we got out on the road, Nick filled in the long hours of driving by recanting stories of the old days when he hung around the Ham 'n' Eggs on upper Broadway.

"So me and Red goes over this guy's hotel room, collect the vig. You understand vig?"

"Yeah."

"Vigorish."

"Yeah. The vig."

"That's right. Little lightweight loan-sharking, okay?"

"Yeah."

"No big deal. So he's standing there. His belly, his ass hanging out his panties like a fruitcake, ironing his clothes. So he tells me and Red, get this, Go fuck yourself for the money!"

"No way."

"Yeah. Can you believe it? So I picks up the iron and moosh his face in with it, you follow me?"

"Yeah."

"Never seen nothin' like it," Nick said, slapping the steering wheel. "His eyebrows stick to the hot iron and his face puffs up like a balloon. Then he runs out into the street in his panties, screaming his head off. Heh-heh. Red laughed so hard I had to carry him out to the car."

It wouldn't take much, I thought to myself, for this guy to get out of control. What was I getting into? But Nick stuck to our agreement about the 60–40 split, and took care of me like a protective older brother, although he continually pushed up the prices to the distributors and retailers who bought our records by playing one off against the other.

"Stack 'em over in the corner, Nick," said Max, as we wheeled box after box of records into his storefront on a dolly. Max was our best fence for hot albums. "How many pieces you got here?"

"Three thousand pieces, Max," said Nick. "But we got to make this the last load. Guy over in the Village giving up three and a quarter apiece." Max had been giving us three.

Max sneered. "Yeah, but he's retail. He won't take everything you bring like I do."

Nick shrugged. "I don't know, Max. He *says* he wants everything we can bring him. So maybe he eats a few. Maybe he lays off to the other re-tailers. All I know is his money's good. End of story."

"Fuck him," said Max. "I can go three and a quarter."

Then we'd go over to the guy in the East Village and Nick would tell him, "This is gonna be the last load. Guy uptown giving us three-fifty."

Sometimes we'd get tested. A fence would throw up his hands, cry about the high cost of doing business, and we'd have to pack up all our records, tow them back into the van, and take them all across town to "the other guy." I argued with Nick about these heavy-handed tactics. After three full days of shoplifting, from ten in the morning when the first stores open, then racing to hit the last K-Mart that closed at ten at night, plus the days of driving back and forth across the country, I was always in a hurry to get it over with, get the cash, and get busy with the fun of spending it.

"C'mon, Nick. Let's take the three and a quarter. I don't want to be driving all over town with a load of swag."

"Leave the business to me. It's what you're paying me for. You want to go get high here's a couple hundred. I'll meet you later after I take care of this."

"But what's the big deal? We got nine large here. Why break balls about a couple hundred?"

"Fuck are you, insane? You think like a junky, go out there put your freedom on the line, what, thirty, forty times a day, then ask me what's the big deal? Man, you don't know what the big deal is, maybe you should find another way to make a living."

When I'd been a booster on the street I had sold records like hot-cakes for two dollars a pop and thought I was doing good. Rock and roll was a mania back in the late sixties, and it continued to be so through the next decade. Nick knew a good thing when he saw it, and he meant to wring every penny he could out of it while it lasted. He was right, too, be-cause the eighties would bring an end to the vinyl era with the advent of the cassette and the compact disc.

During the ten years I worked on and off with Nick, all through the seventies, he never once let me sit in jail when I got pinched, no matter if it was in Cleveland, where my bail was fifty large—"I was in the Delta, Your Honor," I said pleading my case, "with the Ninth Infantry Division and caught some shrapnel. Haven't been quite right since. Look, I still got the hole in my head." "Young man," said the judge, "I have a son who was in the Ninth, and they're in Korea, not the Mekong Delta. Bail is set at fifty thousand dollars!"—or in Cranston, Rhode Island, where an old probation violation from Florida popped up and made bail a near impossibility. He always showed up, and he always found a way to get around the legal system no matter how complicated. In Cranston, Nick found a lawyer, a prospect for mayor and a very popular guy with local political clout. When this lawyer walked into the police station and asked to see me, the cops all got the blues. Next day I was out.

Nick did not like me to carry drugs or drug paraphernalia on the road, although he put up with most anything that helped me get the job done, the walking in and out of twenty to thirty stores a day, past newer and more insidious security devices. The whole point of this hustle was to go for quantity but still remain small-time. A pinch for shoplifting was usually broken down to a class-B misdemeanor, but getting busted with drugs and paraphernalia jacked the stakes way up. I agreed to compromise by using methadone, which could be carried inconspicuously and required only one dose a day. Finally I got away from heroin altogether, and since methadone was dispensed free at many clinics around New York at the time, the cash began to pile up. I had a safety deposit box crammed with hundred-dollar bills.

But fast money or no, there were more and more occasions where I'd find myself standing in a huge shopping mall, somewhere in middle America, watching families and other young men and women about my own age, shopping, buying gifts for their children, going about their normal lives. I'd watch them in wonder. How the hell did they *do* that? It was a total mystery to me. At those times I often thought of my sister, who also seemed to have stumbled upon that missing manual for living that I'd never had. It was a form of self-pity that I could not afford as a shoplifter. When those feelings came over me I'd hide out in a mall movie theater with a pint of booze for an hour. When I got back to the car, I'd tell Nick I'd gotten busted in one of the stores and had bullshitted my way out of an arrest. The outlaw romance of fast money was fading. Stealing was becoming a routine grind.

Nick occasionally got caught up in larcenous enterprises of his own that had nothing to do with me, including a massage parlor-cum-whorehouse joint he ran briefly in Chelsea, and so was unavailable for weeks at a time. Other times he'd have to chill when under scrutiny by some legal agency, like the parole board, or when the feds started dropping by his house to say hello. I'd drum up other characters that had access to a car to drive me around. These guys were usually addicts like myself and not as trustworthy or dependable as Nick. I was therefore less willing to let some store dick clap the cuffs on me and then have to rely on my partner to bail me out. I was more apt to make a desperate attempt to flee. This mind-set often resulted in madcap chases.

I was working Connecticut with a guy named Eddy one day, coming out of a discount department store. I glanced back over my shoulder through the plate-glass windows of the store and noticed two store detectives hustling past the line of checkout counters in hot pursuit. I looked around frantically for the car, but in my panic I forgot where we'd parked. I let the records slide out of my belt in back and the first guy that came hurtling out of the store slipped on the shiny packaging and sat down hard on his fanny. The second guy was on me in a flash. When he started to drag me back into the store, where I knew it would be all over, I turned and saw Eddy pull up about ten yards away. He leaned over the front seat and opened the door to the passenger's side. Freedom beckoned. I twisted away and lunged for the car, but the store dick was tenacious. He hurled himself onto my back and I dragged him with me half into the front seat. When I reached over to push him away so I could close the door, he snapped a set of handcuffs on my wrist, then tried to snap the other cuff around his own wrist. A furious struggle ensued. It was do or die—if the guy got the other end of the cuffs attached to his wrist we'd have to drag him all the way back to New York with us.

Eddy was screaming, "Get this crazy fucker out of my car," as though he was an innocent bystander.

Just when the dick was about to snap the cuff to his wrist, I leaned in and sank my teeth into his hand and he let go. I slammed the door and Eddy gunned the car toward the exit of the parking lot.

"Steve!" he screamed. "Make like you're strangling me, like a hostage. They got my plate number." Then he leaned out the window and started yelling, "Help, help!"

There was a hot pursuit on foot for a few moments, but when we got out of the parking lot no vehicles came after us.

Half an hour later we stopped at a Dunkin' Donuts on the turnpike. I had to let Eddy go get me coffee since I still had handcuffs dangling off my arm. Back in the city we drove around until we found an old jailhouse friend of Eddy's who jimmied them open with a bobby pin, but I couldn't forgive Eddy his "Make like you're strangling me" routine. This hoople would've gotten me knocked on a kidnapping just 'cause they got his plate number. What a knucklehead.

Several weeks later I found a reason to forgive Eddy. I was getting chased through a parking lot by a store dick, and just as he was about to catch me, Eddy pulled the car out of his parking spot right in front of the guy and cut him off.

"Hey," Eddy yelled at the guy through the window, "did that guy steal something?"

"Yeah," said the store dick.

"Goddamn thieves! Don't worry. I'll catch the sonofabitch."

The store dick stood there and watched as Eddy peeled out, roared through the parking lot, and screeched to a stop beside me. I got in the car and we drove off.

Another time I was sitting in a department store security office, already pinched but unable to summon the stoic patience needed to go through yet another miserable lockup, fingerprinting, questioning, and then endless hours of waiting and hoping for bail. I was still uncuffed and acting resigned, so when the store dick went to call for a local squad car to come pick me up, I just bolted out of the security office. I sprinted through the busy store, knocking over displays and discount tables full of ladies' wear, and out into the huge parking lot of a suburban mall. Since my running was unexpected, pursuit took a few minutes to get going. I had a good head start. But, again, I totally forgot where we were parked.

It was a hundred-yard dash to the end of the parking lot and I still hadn't spotted the car, so I ducked around a building, which turned out to be one of those steak and brew joints. Gasping for breath I walked in the front door. The place was doing a slow lunchtime business and nobody noticed me. I slipped into the walk-in coatroom and hunkered down in a corner behind several topcoats. Through an open window came the voices of the store dicks.

"I think he went around the other side, but check in there."

This wouldn't do. Pretty soon the local cops would be on the scene doing a more thorough search. I peeked through the topcoats just as a waitress stopped by the coatroom and caught my eye. She went away immediately and I knew I'd have to move. I took off my coat, snatched one of the topcoats, threw it over my shoulder, and made my way down the aisle that ran along beside the dining room to the restrooms. No one noticed.

As I entered the restroom I heard the waitress somewhere behind me say, "I could've sworn I saw him in there."

The restroom had a long row of stalls but no urinals. Must be the ladies' room. Good. I entered a stall near the back, left the door slightly ajar, and hunkered with my feet on the toilet seat so I couldn't be seen under the door. The restroom door squeaked open and someone came in. Footsteps approached. A voice said, "Nobody in here." Footsteps retreated and I heard the door close. I felt a momentary thrill of reprieve, but I knew I had to get out of the building or I was trapped. I cautiously stepped out of the stall and glanced in a mirror, my mind racing for ways to change my appearance. I set down the topcoat, took off my shirt, and wrapped it around my head like a turban. When I pulled on the topcoat, I saw that it was a woman's coat with fur trimming on the collar. I looked like Phyllis Diller on a bad day.

When I got up the nerve to finally step out of the restroom, there in the aisle were the store dick and his partner, grinning from ear to ear, both of them in matching red blazers like Tweedledum and Tweedledee. The waitress peered over their shoulders.

"Don't you love it when they run?" says the first dick.

"Oh yeah," says his partner. "I love it when they run."

chapter 12

T hieves often come off glib and brag about their profession, but most of the ones I knew eventually developed a secret longing to go legit. Which includes yours truly. One day in 1976, Sean, a junky-shoplifter friend of mine, told me about his aunt who was a partner in a Village saloon down on Seventh Avenue South. She'd lost her co-owner and needed to borrow a few thousand dollars to help get through the rough first year. Thinking of all those hundred-dollar bills in that safety deposit box, I went over to the West Village to take a look at the joint and see if it was worthy of my magnanimous attention.

It was a late summer morning in the midseventies, the sun getting hotter by the minute, when I walked in off Seventh Avenue into Stella's. Immediately the crisp air-conditioning hit me, enhanced by the cool, light gray walls and mauve clay tiles on the floor. Clapton's version of "Little Wing" was playing on a jukebox to my left. The place was dark except for track lights along the ceiling that made the black enamel surfaces of the bar top and tabletops gleam. A woman was slicing up lemons behind the bar and she shot me a warm smile as I came in.

"Howdy stranger. We really don't open till noon," she said, "but the kitchen's up and running and I never turn a thirsty customer away."

I walked over to the bar and pulled up a stool. The bar itself was a substantial vintage one of old polished oak with a shiny brass rail.

"Gimme a Heineken. You must be Stella."

She put the lemons aside, wiped the knife on a clean bar rag, and extracted a beer from the depths of an ice machine behind the bar. Her long, jet black hair fell over her shoulders as she leaned down, and through the unbuttoned top of her cotton blouse I got a glimpse of ample breasts. Tight Levi's were stretched over a nice ass and thighs. She poured the beer into a frosted glass with a practiced poise that made my mouth water, set it on a coaster, and looked me over.

"Don't tell me. You're Sean's friend Steve."

I nodded.

"Well, for God's sake then, why don't you take a table and let me get you something to eat. Any friend of Sean's is a friend of mine."

She plucked a cigarette holder with a smoldering Pall Mall in it out of an ashtray and squashed it out before she came out from behind the bar, then proceeded to set me up with silverware and a bread basket. As she worked she filled me in on the difficulties of running a saloon single-handedly—cooking, serving food, tending the bar, keeping the books, and ordering food and liquor. Obviously she needed more than a few bucks. She needed professional help.

"Don't you have waitresses, bartenders, and cooks?" I asked.

"Sure, there's no shortage of waitresses. They'll work for ten bucks a shift and tips. But I can't afford bartenders yet, and a cook worth hiring is hard to find, not to mention out of my budget. Got a guy in the kitchen right now washing spinach and keeping an eye on the soups, but he couldn't make a good quiche if his life depended on it. Which reminds me, how 'bout one for lunch? If you don't think my spinach and bacon quiche is the best thing you ever tasted, I'll give you double your money back."

Saloons had never been my thing, but this place was a hedonist's dream. Stella brought me a chicken-avocado salad (big chunks in the chicken salad, not the stringy commercial kind, set inside half an avocado on a bed of spinach) and a freshly made quiche with the most delicate crust and sweetest egg-custard filling I've ever had. The best thing about the place, though, was her cleavage, which seemed to radiate heat each time she put a plate of food in front of me. She was a sexy, knock-around Village broad who loved Rémy with her coffee and really knew her way around a bistro. After working and drinking in Village saloons for years, Stella had hit on a tasty formula that combined salad-and-quiche-type cuisine with the reliable pot roast, a hip jukebox, and cool ambience that smacked of potential success.

Not only did I lend Stella several thousand dollars, I moved in with her and became her under-the-table partner, taking promissory notes for the money I started pumping into the joint. Not the brightest move, but the money wasn't doing me much good. I probably would've blown it on drugs. Being in my thirties, the wear and tear of boosting was taking its toll, and I was happy to finally be involved in a legitimate enterprise. In actuality there was no way I could have my name on a liquor license, not with a criminal record, but in my mind, Stella's was my first opportunity to go legit. I wanted it so badly I was more than susceptible to self-delusion.

At Stella's, I got an education in the fine art of drinking alcohol. We'd wake up in the apartment over the saloon and come downstairs for Bloody Marys. Then followed beer with the first arrivals when we opened at noon, white wine with lunch, aperitifs before dinner, wine with the food, brandy and coffee afterward, and brandies with soda-backs until we closed at four in the morning. Then we went to after-hours clubs with the other saloonkeepers, waitresses, and bartenders, and switched to brandy stingers, maybe a little bump of coke to stay awake and drink more. When I started getting headaches I figured it was the brandy, so I switched to vodka. It only got worse.

After a year of drinking around the clock, I became a full-blown alcoholic. A Jekyll and Hyde personality emerged—I would drink *at* people who pissed me off, then fly into rages. At the drop of a hat I could turn into one of those crazed, bite-your-nose-off barroom brawlers, and Stella changed right along with me.

I tended bar while she ran the kitchen. When we closed, we'd stagger upstairs to our apartment for a couple hours of sex before we passed out, then wake up the next morning and do it all over again. She'd catch me flirting with some chick at the bar, walk up beside me after a few shots of booze, and try to clock me with a left hook. Hey, I figured it was all part of the business to flirt with the women who came in and spent their money. But her obstinacy when jealous or challenged made her fearless, and, after a few drinks, she was incapable of being reasoned with or intimidated.

Once we had a terrible fight, Stella and I, in a saloon full of customers. The fight had been instigated by a couple of women bartenders from Kelly's, a dyke joint down the street from us, who were good customers of ours and always sent their patrons over to our place to eat. I'd taken a ride home with their amusing gay bartender one night, and these girls, bless their treacherous little hearts, told Stella that I was sleeping with him. It was nonsense, but Stella was enraged. She was pushing me toward the exit, raking my face with her nails as I backpedaled away from her out the door and into the street. An angry thought flashed through my head: Who does this crazy bimbo think she is, shamelessly using me to keep her saloon going and then pushing me out the door? My foot hit the sidewalk as we burst through the doors and my fist came up in a reflexive punch that she stepped right into—and knocked her out cold. I rode with her in the ambulance over to St. Vincent's, and when she came to in the hospital she picked up raving at me as though she hadn't missed a beat.

It seemed like I'd grown blinders, unable to see where this side of my personality came from. I was a guy who usually charmed his way out of trouble, but here I was, turning into a violent drunk. And worse, I was fighting with a woman! Maybe my old hustling mentor had been right, that some women liked it when you showed them your teeth, because after a fight Stella and I would make up and have passionate sex. But the farther down this road we traveled, the more sex and booze we needed. Business problems became so entangled with our personal resentments and jealousies that they seemed unsolvable.

But there were nice times as well. One day I came back to the saloon on a clear summer day and saw Robert De Niro and Diahnne Abbott sitting at the little table we'd set up outside. Another time Debbie Harry came by to apply for a waitress job. She'd not yet become Blondie and she knew me from when I went out with one of the girls in her band, the Stilettos. But Stella took one look at the way I grinned at Debbie and put the kibosh on that deal.

A small jazz club called St. James Infirmary opened up briefly across Seventh Avenue, and we'd catch Chet Baker playing there on a regular basis. For years Chet had lived as an expatriate in Europe after losing his cabaret card for drug arrests, and he'd finally gotten it back—maybe a little too late. He looked god-awful lonely up on that tiny bandstand, like he'd really been through the mill. His face was sunken in like a toothless old lady's and the best years of his career seemed behind him. But he still had the magic. Hearing his soft voice on vocals and the sweet, familiar tone of his horn gave me that old feeling. But it was sad too, seeing Chet so withered and old in that sparsely attended little basement of a club. Tears would come to my eyes and I'd have to leave.

There was more life down the street at Stella's. The regulars were a diverse crew of aging beatniks, artists, and musicians like Robbie Robertson, who were all part of the Village saloon crowd. There were waiters and bartenders from other saloons and neighborhood wannabe wiseguys—most of them looking for the biggest bang for their buck and every third one on the house. There was a crazy Chinese guy named Joe who'd come in and play "Kodachrome" by Paul Simon on the jukebox about twenty times in a row. When he'd pass out on the bar with his head on his arms, Stella would point him out and say, "Joe is what you call a satisfied customer, Steve. That's what we aim for here—serenity." Another guy, who'd recently married the daughter of a local mafioso, would order a drink, look around nervously, and say, "Don't let me get outta line with the broads here, Steve. Christ, my father-in-law can put more soldiers on the street than LBJ."

Money ran through Stella's like water through a sieve. I'd quickly depleted my own stash and was still going out on the road with Nick, just to keep up with the high rent and liquor bills—so much for being legit. But we'd still run out of cash. One week I had to borrow a grand from a fence so we could pay Ottomanelli's, the butcher, who had put Stella's on a cash-only basis until we paid our back bills. Nick picked up the cash for me from one of our fences and dropped it off during the busy lunch business. I felt a rush of pride standing behind the bar as Nick, looking like the hard-nosed character he was, came in and plopped down a shoe box full of tens and twenties on the bar. Several local tough guys and friends of Stella's were standing at the bar, duly impressed. One of them turned to Nick.

"Let me buy you a drink."

Nick looked at him like he was crazy. "I don't touch that shit. Strictly for suckers." Nick gave me a wave and headed out the door. He enjoyed the bad-guy image, tossing that pile of cash on the bar, but he had no time for the West Village saloon crowd that Stella was so much a part of. To Nick, selling booze was no different than selling any other drug, and legality had nothing to do with it. You want to make money, you don't use the product.

Financial troubles at the saloon were quickly resolved by my ability to make fast cash, but boosting was becoming more and more difficult in the late seventies. Stores were putting magnetic stickers on the albums, and if I didn't make sure I'd stripped them all off I could trigger an alarm going out. This drastically raised the risks, because the time spent stripping the buzzers gave security and other personnel more time to get a read on you and remember your face. One time I was out on the road with Nick. We were settling down for a night's rest in a cheap, fly-by-night motel and I made the following proposition.

"Hey, Nick. Why don't we open our own retail joint, or even a distributorship? We could undersell everybody else and really go legit."

"Listen," said Nick. "Being legit ain't all it's cracked up to be. Yeah, right now you worry about getting busted, but when you go legit the IRS becomes the Man. Then you got all kinds of headaches trying to make inflated overhead—rent, booze, food, salary, city tax, state tax, federal tax, not to mention bribes to city inspectors, accountant's fees, unemployment compensation for employees. Everybody wants a piece of you. Guy comes in, ten thousand swizzle sticks in a box. You whip out a calculator and go, How much for one swizzle stick? Guy goes, maybe point-o-five cents, you dig? Even if it tallies up you gotta tell this guy, Take your swizzle sticks and jam 'em up your ass, I got a guy does point-o-four. Kind of shit you're running into at Stella's. You got no idea how lucky you are doing what we're doing right now. The fuck *any*body would want to go legit is beyond me."

Nick got up, lit a Pall Mall, went to the window, and pulled back the curtain.

"What's the matter?" I asked him.

"Just checking the car. Lotta thieves out there."

Stella and I were sitting at the bar one night, polishing off a bottle of Martel Cordon Bleu cognac and trying to figure out where all the money was going. We were well into our first year in business and still more money was going out than was coming in.

"I don't know, Steve," she said as she tossed the empty bottle in the trash and opened another one. "Maybe the cook is stealing. You're my man. What do you think I should do? Let him go?"

"Yeah," I agreed, gratefully holding out my snifter for a refill. "Maybe we should let him go. Fuck 'em. Do it ourselves like when we started."

"Yeah, fuck 'em all," said Stella, holding her brandy aloft. "Here's to the good ol' days." She tossed off her drink, popped a smoldering butt out of her cigarette holder into an ashtray, and stuck in a fresh Pall Mall. She was a tough lady, which is what I loved about her. She was as protective of her saloon as a mother of her child.

"To the Mom 'n' Pop saloons," I rejoined, quaffing my brandy with relish and relieved to have found the solution to our problems—firing the cook. Neither of us noticed, or cared, that we were drinking our most expensive cognac like it was going out of style. My real suspicion was that the cook she'd hired and trained couldn't possibly make food taste the way she could—maybe nobody could—so why pay somebody to turn out an inferior product?

But I wasn't about to tell her to go back to the kitchen and stay there. No way was Stella going to stay in the kitchen once the bar started jumping, even though it was her personal magic touch that made the food so wonderful. She loved the action too much. This was her dream, being Stella of Stella's. Why even bother if she couldn't stroll around the bar and accept the adulation and drinks that were showered on her by customers, saloonkeepers, and bartenders she'd worked with over the years?

At one point in my career as a Greenwich Village saloonkeeper, I called Ron and she came for dinner with her friend Ruth, who also owned a bistro. Ruth Adams Bronze, or Miss Ruby as my sister and her friends called her (after the name of her Tex-Mex bistro on Eighth Avenue), was another of my sister's dear chums. If Veronica had bad luck with guys, her women pals were tremendously loyal. Ruth's zaftig figure seemed testimony to her enthusiasm not only for good food but for everything in life, and her warmth and great good humor were infectious. She and Ronnie loved our food, the great jukebox, and the hip interior design. When Veronica saw that I was involved in what appeared to be a legitimate enterprise, she jumped into my corner and wrote a press release for Stella's. Somehow it got passed along to a restaurant reviewer and was published in a local paper under the byline of that reviewer.

The weekend after my sister's press release appeared, people from all over the boroughs and New Jersey lined up along Seventh Avenue to get in. Here was the power of my sister's writing in action, but it didn't really help our cause. We were set up to operate like a neighborhood bistro and were ill-equipped to deal with reservations and a sudden, huge influx of customers. People who'd driven all the way from Jersey were hopping mad that they had to stand in line, especially when they'd called to make reservations. We had a local following of steady, hard-drinking, good-tipping customers, so the waitress gave them tables that were supposedly reserved. I went outside and tried to calm everybody down.

"Would you like to come in?" I asked the first couple in line. "Come on in and have a drink at the bar."

"Are you crazy? We had dinner reservations for seven o'clock. It's now eight. Where the hell are we going to get another reservation this late?" The guy was dressed in a seersucker suit, the rumpled jacket slung over his shoulder. He was perspiring heavily and his wife, who was wilting in a linen cocktail dress and straw hat, wasn't making it any easier for him.

"What kind of creep joint are you people running here?" she said to me. "We drove all the way up from Short Hills, New Jersey. If we wanted to drink at a fucking bar we could've fucking stayed in fucking Jersey."

I was embarrassed and felt sorry for them. I went back into the bar and proceeded to get drunk, the only reliable solution to any problem.

Predictably, Stella's went down the tubes. I found out one day that she'd set up a business meeting to sell the place to some local entrepreneurs, without even mentioning it to me. I'll be damned, I thought, if I'll let her cut me out of the picture, after all the money I pumped into the place. I crashed the meeting with all my promissory notes and declared that the only way anybody was buying or selling this joint was to first compensate me for the fifty large I spent keeping it going. The potential buyers quickly lost interest and Stella never forgave me.

One day about six months later she came over to my apartment, offering to make amends for her treachery, and slipped an overdose of Valium in the coffee she made me. When I passed out, she poured lighter fluid over me and all my belongings, and torched me. I came to on my bed, surrounded by flames. I thought it was the afterlife and I was in a pipeline to Hell. Luckily I escaped that love affair with only the scarring of a patch of skin on my neck. Women it seemed, at least the ones I'd known, were just too volatile and unpredictable. Why the hell couldn't I meet a woman as trustworthy as Nick or as level-headed as my sister?

The only clue to Veronica's life during this time, aside from her literary success, is a one-sentence paragraph I found years later in "A Lot in Common":

> I don't remember much about my birthdays through the 1970's, but probably they had something to do with sex.

This revelation came as a worrisome surprise to me. I preferred to think of my sister living in her ivory tower on the Upper East Side, way up on the fifth floor, basking in the praise of her great wit. She was writing laugh-out-loud-funny stories for the *New Yorker*, goofing on everything from baseball to politics, often seeming to confuse the two, like in "Kemp, Dent in Reagan Plans," where George Steinbrenner trades Bucky Dent to the Republicans for Jack Kemp. She was able to lash out at all the things she loathed, make people laugh, and make money all at the same time. In "Buon Giorno, Big Shot" a reporter interviews a "fascist hyena," named Signor X, but it sounded to me like a vicious swipe at Dad. She also did parodies of people she loved, writers like Henry James, Raymond Chandler, James M. Cain, and even Donald Barthelme. She was enjoying a creative and productive existence that I could only fantasize about.

Little did I know that she was becoming increasingly bitter about romance. She endured frustrating affairs with other writers at the *New Yorker*, Frederick Barthelme and Mark Singer to name a few. She suffered from her own form of the Franny and Zooey Effect—she was too bright for her own good. She'd become righteous about her convictions and not a lot of men will put up with being intellectually bullied by a woman. It made them uneasy and drove them away. She, in turn, blamed it on her lack of sexiness.

There were a few rare, tearful occasions when she'd let down her controlled exterior and confide in me about her romantic troubles.

"I don't know, Steve," she said to me once in despair. "I feel like I missed the boat on sex appeal. Guys are turned on by women that seem helpless, or not-too-bright, and I just don't come off like that."

My associates were mostly thieves at the time, so I didn't know any suitable guys to match her with, but I helped her as best I could.

"Listen, Ron. Forget helpless. You ever seen Marilyn Monroe looking helpless? What makes you sexy is confidence, kinda broad walks around like she's got Fort Knox between her legs." I then walked back and forth in her apartment trying to demonstrate what this looks like to a guy. My sister laughed till tears came to her eyes.

Unfortunately for her, she was so good at covering up the chinks in her armor with sharp humor and testiness that no one saw the simple truth about her that was so obvious to me: She wanted what every girl or woman wants, what we all want, to be loved and held, to have someone wrap his arms around you and say, *Don't worry, baby. Everything's gonna be alright*. And then treat you like you've got Fort Knox between your legs.

I would hear rumors from her women friends that she'd jumped in the sack with everybody from Arnold Schwarzenegger (she'd interviewed him when the book *Pumping Iron* came out) to every writer she'd ever worked with. God bless her, I hoped that it wasn't all just sweating over a typewriter, but I listened to the gossip with skepticism. She usually kept me in the dark about her men troubles, but I knew well what a clever actress she was, and how frightened of the intimacy she longed for. On the other hand, I felt a deep rage that these jag-offs might've treated my sister like an easy shot, passing her around and taking advantage of her weaknesses.

chapter 13

My partner Nick, impatient with my attempts to go legit, got arrested in some larcenous swindle that I knew nothing about. He was out on bail, trying to keep a low profile and reluctant to go out on the road. I kept boosting on my own and got pinched in a record store in Queens. I called Nick and he sent a lawyer to help me make bail—as crime partners go, they didn't come much better than Nick—but before I reached court, the feds showed up with a warrant for Unlawful Flight to Avoid Prosecution, or UFAP. All those times Nick had bailed me out under an alias I'd always gotten fingerprinted, and eventually my prints had uncovered my arrest record in all the other cities. There were warrants out in my name from three or four states, and eventually the feds had issued a warrant for Unlawful (interstate) Flight. I anticipated getting shuttled from state to state, doing a year here and a year there, on and on into a grim-looking future.

When I got processed into the federal lockup—MCC, Manhattan Correctional Center—they gave me one of those orange jumpsuits like they give to guys like John Gotti and Sammy the Bull. I sat around for a month or so with people who were getting indicted on serious federal charges—terrorists, kidnappers, counterfeiters, bank robbers, Mafia. I felt flattered, being just a booster, but the feds, once they were notified by several states, were compelled to respond to the federal charge of Unlawful Flight to Avoid Prosecution.

I was put on a floor with two tiers of single cells, one tier above the other with a big dayroom in the center. Many of the inmates who'd been there awhile had a radio or a tiny television in their cells, and when we were locked in at night, there was a muted cacophony of noise from all the radios and televisions tuned to different stations. Although the physical side effects of drug withdrawal were always minimal for me, going through the mental anxiety in a jail cell was like being in a sensory deprivation tank. After a few weeks of long, sleepless nights, lying in the dark, worrying about my future, and staring at steel walls, the appalling dearth of information would send my anxiety-ridden mind out into the ether, scrambling for any kind of input. One night I zeroed in on a radio station where they were interviewing my sister and all my friends—about me!

"Is it true, Veronica, that your brother is a habitual criminal who's wanted in half a dozen states?"

"Please, I have no idea what my brother is up to. You seem to know more about this than I do, so why don't you just go ask him?"

Good for you, Ron! I thought with an irrational wave of affection. Next I heard the interviewer with some of my cronies over on Cooper Square right outside the methadone clinic.

Victor Ortez, a notorious burglar, said, "Record Steve is the best booster I ever knew."

"That's right," chimed in Victor's old lady, Sandy. "We're all rooting for him out here."

Midtown Charlie, who I envisioned looking particularly treacherous in a porkpie hat, said, "Hang in there, Rec. We aim to have a sit-down on the courthouse steps till y'all cut his ass loose."

Christ, I thought with rising horror, these people are gonna get me crucified. Frantic, I begged the hack to let me make a phone call.

"Hey, Nick," I ranted into the phone. "What are you people doing out there?"

"What?"

"Jesus Christ, haven't you been listening to the radio? I can't believe you people are doing this to me."

"The fuck are you talking about?"

When I managed to explain to Nick what I'd heard, he got pissed off and told me never to call him again with some crazy bullshit like that. Turns out I was having audio hallucinations. I went back to my cell, somewhat mollified, but still worried that the clever feds had contrived the radio broadcast as a sinister brainwashing or surveillance technique, aimed at making me crack and "spill the beans."

In the end, the feds weren't really interested in prosecuting me, let alone inventing cryptic radio broadcasts. The states that had warrants out for my arrest also passed on the opportunity to extradite me—who wants to go to the expense of an extradition to prosecute a mere shoplifter? I just wasn't all that damned important. The warrants got vacated, the charges dropped, and I got cut loose after a month.

The federal warrant officers who'd originally picked me up, the guys who'd escorted me through my lockup and subsequent court hearings, were instructed by the judge to release me into the custody of a local family member. My sister was the only one around. They volunteered to drop me off at her office at the *New Yorker.* Perhaps they wanted to see if I was bullshitting, or maybe they were just bored stiff, but they were very solicitous. I had an eerie feeling that my life had changed, turned a corner, and I couldn't go back to what I'd been doing. It was one of the many instances where I felt that benign forces, The Powers That Be, were offering me a fragile window of opportunity to move my life forward.

The two cops, totally out of character, offered me tips on how to straighten myself out and stay away from drugs.

"Hey, Steve," said the driver. "How far did you go in school?"

"Listen," I pleaded as they steered their faceless sedan through West Village neighborhoods where I knew plenty of bars to drink in and plenty of places to score drugs. "Couldn't you guys just drop me off around here? I kicked a junk habit while I was locked up in there and I need some candy bars before I flip out."

"Let me ask you something," said the big, heavyset guy who was riding shotgun, blandly ignoring my protestations. "Have you ever thought about going into the health food business? I mean, you're no dummy, and addicts all seem to have a fascination for body chemistry. It'd be a positive way to do the same thing. You know, maybe work on healthy carbohydrates instead of candy bars."

I groaned with impatience as his hatchet-faced partner turned onto Tenth Avenue and headed uptown.

I'd never visited my sister at her workplace before, and now that I was finally getting around to it I was arriving with an FBI escort. My head was swimming with a mixture of pride, embarrassment, and shame as these feds took me up on the elevator to the offices of the *New Yorker*, which were then on Forty-third Street. My sister, who'd been notified by phone earlier and was expecting us, came out and met us in the lobby, thanked my escorts with a strained look of forbearance, and then took me into her office. I was struck once again by how great she looked in her wool skirt and cashmere sweater. I cringed under my own clothes that were filthy and rumpled after being crammed into a property locker for weeks.

"Well," she said to me, after I explained the sad saga of my boosting career. "What do you plan on doing now?"

"Jeez, Ron. I don't know. I really don't know anything except stealing and getting loaded."

"Alright, listen. I've been getting a lot of weird phone calls from Daddy."

"What do you mean, weird?"

"I don't know. Crazy stuff about hurricanes. I can't even explain it, but the point is that he's getting senile. Either one of us goes down there to live with him or we put him in a nursing home."

"Do I have a choice? Or do we flip for it?"

She lit a cigarette and looked at her watch. I looked around at the bustling offices of the *New Yorker.*

"Okay," I said. "I get it. You can't get away from work."

"That's right. I can't get away from work to go down there."

Those were still the days of William Shawn's regime as editor in chief, and Ron was thriving under his cherished leadership. Wild horses couldn't have torn her out of that place. She'd been freelancing with them for a while but had finally become an editor in their fiction department. When Ron first told me about Mr. Shawn, her description made me think of Daddy Pitman back in Philly and her longing for a life far removed from our family. Now it seemed like she couldn't wait to be rid of her troublesome brother so she could get back to her own life and her new family of wits and sophisticates.

"Let me get this straight. You want me to go down there and take care of Daddy?"

"You don't have to take *care* of him. Just go down there and *be* with him so he doesn't freak out. For God's sake, you can at least get away from your troubles here, and maybe it'll be good for you. He lives right on the beach now in a house that Helen left him when she died. I've been there and it's really beautiful."

I'd been so out of touch with my family that I had totally missed this period in our father's life. A year or so after Mom died, Dad had gotten married to a widow named Helen who owned a bungalow on Clearwater Beach. I never met the woman. Ronnie told me she was really sweet, but then she died and left Dad her little house on the Gulf of Mexico.

Sitting in Ronnie's office at the *New Yorker,* every cell in my body was screaming for a drink, and my mind raced to find the hidden flaw in her proposition. In the end, the idea of escaping all my troubles in New York to loaf around the beaches of Florida won out.

part five

the prodigal son—
and then what?

chapter 14

I stood in the shade on the front porch of my father's house on Clear-water Beach and watched the taxi drive away. My three-quarter-length boosting coat was totally inappropriate for Florida. I could feel sweat dripping down the small of my back as a mailman in Bermuda shorts and a safari helmet went by on a tricycle and waved at me. It was 1980, and I had absolutely nothing to show for my thirty-seven years on this planet. My arm felt like it weighed a hundred pounds as I reached out to ring the doorbell. Dad was in his mideighties by then, and the last time I'd seen him was ten years before.

The door opened a few inches and a shriveled old face peered out at me.

"Is that you, bud? I didn't think you'd get here so fast. What'd you do, fly?"

"Yeah."

He opened the door a little more and looked around for my suitcase.

"Where the hell are your things?"

I was wearing everything I owned, and I didn't feel like explaining that I'd just gotten out of jail, and that when you get busted, the cops don't necessarily give you time to go back to your hotel, get your things, and put them in storage. So I did what I always did. I lied. "My bag got lost on the flight."

The tainted aroma of mildew and a vague sense of paranoia emanated from the darkness behind my father as he peeked out at me.

"Jesus Christ, I told Ronnie not to let you fly. You could really get your tit in a wringer you get on a goddamn airplane these days. Why the hell can't you kids listen to reason?"

My whole life I'd had an antagonistic relationship with this man, to put it mildly. I figured he hated me and so the hell with him. The prospect of having to live with him and put up with his recriminations was not something I was looking forward to. Riding the Beach Taxi from Tampa International Airport, across the Courtney Campbell Causeway that spanned Tampa Bay, I thought of all the times I called him from New York to ask for a couple hundred bucks, supposedly to come home for a visit. I'd rarely bought a plane ticket with that money. I'd gone out and gotten stoned. When I'd call him again he'd complain and ask where the hell I was, but he often came through with the dough. It all came back to me as I stood there on his porch, totally defenseless.

"It's okay, Dad. I had a good flight. I'm just tired." I was still suffering the side effects of methadone and alcohol withdrawal—sleeplessness, fatigue, and irritability. Even the month I was locked up by the feds, they gave us tiny doses of Dolophine (another name for methadone) every day, and Ron had put me on a plane so fast I hadn't had time to go score.

"Well, what're you standing out there for? C'mon in and take a load off," he said.

He turned in the doorway, stepped back, and watched me stumble through the door. A huge television just inside was tuned to a tennis match. The whispered comments of the play-by-play announcer were punctuated by the *pok* of the ball hitting the racket. A feisty young John McEnroe was giving Björn Borg fits.

"Boy, am I glad to see you," he said. "This is terrific. I was getting lonely as hell here all by myself." Then he started banging the front door against the door frame half a dozen times until it finally stayed shut. "Goddamn salt air warps everything around here."

An atmosphere of neglect struck me the minute I walked inside. Dentures rested on a metal TV table in front of a raggedy armchair, and there were greasy stains on the faded old carpet. The windows of the dining area at the back of the house were so smeared that I could barely discern the shiny expanse of the Gulf of Mexico stretching to the horizon. My father looked so small and fragile, I was glad that he turned just then and went into the kitchen to get me a soda. I didn't want him to see the tears welling up in my eyes.

It broke my heart to see him this way, all withered and old, but he was happy to see me! It floored me. Here was this guy I thought I hated and vice versa, and in an instant I realized that I loved him. I couldn't remember the last time he or anybody else had been glad to see me—except maybe when one of my street associates needed money, a drink, or some drugs. Usually whenever my father saw me he knew it was going to cost him money and heartache. Yet here he was, making me dinner, helping me fix up the spare bedroom, phoning the neighbors to brag about his son from New York who'd come down to stay with him.

"Don't worry, bud," he reassured me. "Just relax and take it easy. I got plenty of money and plenty of food."

He proudly opened the kitchen cabinets to show me shelves stacked with cans of Dinty Moore Beef Stew, which we ate for dinner that night off of our fold-up TV tables while we watched *Jeopardy* and *Password*. We both had second helpings of the stew, which tasted like filet mignon to me.

"Tomorrow I'll show you around the beach."

When I finally went to bed that night, I found the stacks of detective novels that my sister had left behind, which made the next month of sleeplessness, my standard detox symptom, bearable. I took lots of hot baths and hiked up and down the surf along the Gulf of Mexico. Occasionally Dad would knock softly at my bedroom door and bring me a mug of hot chocolate. He instinctively knew that I was suffering in some way, although we never talked about it. During the day we strolled around Clearwater Beach, watched television, or went shopping at the supermarket over on Island Estates. Something deep down inside me began to shift, a tiny spark that I'd never quite been able to snuff out, a faint glimmer of possibility that maybe I wasn't doomed.

The second night I was there, we walked up to the Pelican Grill on Mandalay Avenue, the main drag on Clearwater Beach. I was still shaky and weak as a kitten from withdrawal, squinting at the painfully bright colors cast by the setting sun, but my father's frail, hesitant gait filled me with a protective strength. Our waitress knew the Colonel and was very solicitous. Dad bought me the biggest steak they had. At one point I caught him glancing around nervously and stuffing crackers into his pockets. He literally emptied the huge bread basket full of saltines and oyster crackers into the pockets of his jacket and pants, eyes darting around to make sure nobody was watching.

"Hey, Dad. What are you acting so sneaky for? These people don't care if you steal the crackers. They put them on the table for free."

"Awferchrissake," he shot back at me. "What're you talking? Nobody's stealing anything here."

Again I felt a huge wave of affection for him, a fellow thief. I scooped the bread basket from a nearby table and helped myself to a few handfuls of oyster crackers, jamming them into the pockets of my warm-up jacket. Dad looked over at me and winked. It was a good meal, sitting there like a couple of beach bums, thick as thieves.

Several weeks later I took my father to play golf at a par-3 course he used to frequent back in the days when my mother was still alive. The last hole of the front nine was a ninety-yard chip shot over a lake onto the green, which was right in front of the clubhouse. Dad hit two balls into the lake before he made a shot with his six-iron that rolled past the clubhouse and onto the practice green where you practiced putting. I lofted a towering nine-iron shot that dribbled in for a hole in one. Pure luck. Dad strutted into the clubhouse.

"You see that hole in one? That was my son," he said, beaming.

When I checked our scorecard, I noticed that he didn't count the balls that he'd hit into the lake. A few holes back I caught him kicking his ball up the freeway while I searched for my own ball in the rough, but I never mentioned that I caught him cheating, even though it burned my ass. When I couldn't find my ball, he charged me two strokes to lay one on the freeway.

"Christ, you'd a never got out of that mess in one."

A couple old duffers pulled me aside in the clubhouse and asked me, "Was that the Colonel we saw you with out there?"

"Yeah," I said. "I'm his son."

"Well, I'll be damned. Never thought I'd see the Colonel out here again. If that don't beat all!"

*　*　*

The first job I got in Clearwater was driving a cab for Beach Taxi. The other drivers knew the Colonel well. They'd been doing everything for him, picking him up to go shopping, or even going to the store *for* him if he only needed cigars and beer. They didn't have time to go through a supermarket with a shopping list, but some of those cabdrivers, a guy named Pete in particular, were the closest thing to family and friends that my father enjoyed in this town. The only downside to the job was my father's omnipresence. The radio in the cab would squawk to life.

"Base to ten. Base to ten."

Calls for Beach Taxi were handled by a dispatcher and relayed to the drivers on the radios in their cabs. Ten was my call number.

"Ten here. What do you got, Al?"

"I got Mrs. Goldstein at Island Estates going to bingo at the Elks Club, then the Colonel wants you to pick up a six-pack of beer, some beef stew, and a pack of cigarillos on the way home. You Roger that, ten?"

"Yo, on my way."

"Yo is not proper radio procedure, ten. Roger is the correct response. And the Colonel says the Hava Tampas, not the Robert Burns. You copy?"

"Copy, Roger, over and out." An hour later he'd call and tell me the Colonel wanted some ice cream and said to tell me there was a hurricane in Texas.

I accepted these taxi troubles gladly—light stuff compared to those bigger problems in New York. Where to score drugs in Florida these days was a mystery, so the old yen seemed to have been lifted simply through lack of access. Nor had I forgotten my fear of getting busted again in Florida. But booze was everywhere. I tried hard to stay away from drinking. I felt like I'd caused my father enough trouble over the years and I didn't want him to see me go off the deep end again, but I just couldn't stop. I took the Beach Taxi across the causeway to Tampa one night with a fare to the airport and afterward went drinking in lap-dance joints on Dale Mabry. Then I drove home in a blackout, waking up at the first stoplight in Clearwater, the engine idling and my heart racing with terror, wondering how the hell I'd navigated that two-lane causeway with the surf licking at the rocks on either side.

When I wasn't drinking and driving for Beach Taxi, I sat around with Dad, eating Dinty Moore Beef Stew and watching sit-coms.

"Hey, Dad," I proposed one night. "You keep the air conditioner on full blast all day and the heat on all night. Why don't you just open the windows? Then you'd be warm in the day, and cool at night, instead of vice versa, which is the way you have it? Plus," I added logically, "then you would get fresh air."

"Aw, what're you talking? The air conditioner's on the roof."

"What's that supposed to mean?"

"That's fresh air."

"It's *conditioned* air."

"The hell you know about fresh air? Christ, you been living in New York for twenty years."

Irritated, I went over to the windows and started to crank them open. "It's suffocating in here and I'm opening these windows."

Dad leaped out of his chair and hurled himself onto my back. "You stay away from those goddamned windows!"

When I felt how little my father weighed, all the steam went out of me. He was light as a child and slid off my back, banging his hands painfully when he hit the floor. I closed the window and held my hand out to help him up.

"Fine," I said. "We'll leave the windows shut."

"Christ," he said, disdaining the proffered hand and massaging his wrist. "You play rough."

"I'm sorry, Dad. Hell, it's your house."

He sat there for a few moments, getting some mileage out of the injured wrist. Finally he allowed me to help him up.

"Your mother *never* opened those windows. She knew better than to let the salt air in here."

It threw me when he said that. Mom never lived in this house. She died years before he remarried and moved here, but I let it slide. The poor guy's memory was probably deserting him and he didn't need me to rub it in his face. Besides, he was right—what did I know about fresh air?

Ron came down for a brief visit. Her appearance was just what I needed, diverting the tension with Dad and lifting the urge to get drunk. She immediately reacted to the signs of neglect and poor housekeeping and swept through the house like Mr. Clean, vacuuming the carpet, snapping on rubber gloves to do the dishes piled up in the sink, and after she went over every inch of the kitchen with disinfectant she started on the bathroom.

Dad was thrilled to have her around too, and he kept saying stuff like, "Christ, why don't you leave all that and sit down and relax?"

Ron laughed. "I don't mind, really. But you two might want to think about hiring a maid."

"Aw, that's the silliest thing I ever heard. Me and Steve were doing just fine, and I don't know why the hell you want to go back to New York. You could get a terrific job down here writing for the *Clearwater Sun.*"

Ron didn't say anything to that, but she shot me a wry look like, *Neither of you have a clue about what I'm doing, so don't even start.* And she was right. Ron was developing into a great editor at the *New Yorker*, championing writers like Ian Frazier, Jamaica Kincaid, and George Trow. But of course she never talked about any of that to Dad and me, and we wouldn't have recognized those names if she had. She'd reviewed movies for the *Soho Weekly News* during the late seventies and was selling one story after another to the *New Yorker*. Her following of readers was growing, and I felt guilty that I wasn't one of them.

"Ron, I always meant to read your stories, but I never knew which issues they'd be in or—"

"Don't worry about it, Steve," she said. "They're all just goofy pieces of satire and parody. It's not worth troubling yourself or running around combing through newsstands and spending money you don't have, for God's sake. I should have thought to send you some of them, but I was never sure where you'd be until now. When I get back to New York I'll definitely send you some."

I had a sneaking suspicion she never would, so I changed the topic. "Hey, want to go to a movie? There's this Vietnam flick called *Apocalypse Now* that just opened and I heard it's pretty good."

Ron's face lit up. "Steve, you've got to see it. It's an incredible movie. I just saw an early screening of it in New York, and hell yes, I'd love to see it again with you."

"C'mon, Dad," I said. "Want to go to the movies?"

Dad declined, content to go back to his cable television now that his two kids were buzzing around his house. He'd probably given up hope long ago of ever seeing that happen again.

Ron and I hopped in the Beach Taxi, zipped over to a little neighborhood theater, and hunkered down in the dark with a huge bucket of popcorn. Soon the ominous sounds of helicopters filled the air and the next two hours were pure joy.

Ron was confused at first, then delighted to see me convulsed in laughter over scenes that she'd taken seriously when she'd seen the movie in New York. She knew that I'd been in the army during 'Nam, and after my unexplained, fugazy discharge, she sensed that my take on that war was probably more cynical than the filmmaker's. Another thing about the movie was that, no matter how hard I tried, I could not take Martin Sheen seriously. The more crazed and dangerous he acted, the more I guffawed. When the final scenes with Hopper and Brando doing their over-the-top shtick rolled around, we were both convulsed in laughter. We had such a good time at that movie that the other theatergoers—local retirees and snowbirds—were all looking at us like we were nuts as we filed out onto the street.

Sometime later I found a review of *Apocalypse Now* by my sister in the *New Yorker*. She was filling in for Pauline Kael, and Veronica seemed to support my reaction to the movie in the following two sentences from that review:

> Both times I saw the movie, there were nervous titters, more or less respectfully suppressed, every time it moved into a surprising tone. I reacted this way the first time through, and now think I was wrong to mistrust my laughter.

For a couple of days Ron seemed relatively content in Florida, stretching out in a beach chair on the sea wall behind the house, working on her tan. I drove her to a local bookstore where she casually strolled the aisles, me tagging along but watching very intently, hoping to pick up a clue to a good novel or some insight into her taste. But she never bought anything or even picked up a book to read the dust jacket. She was much more fascinated with the free newspapers stacked up by the door. I picked up a big, hardcover collection of three Ross Macdonald novels and plopped it down in front of the cashier.

Ron shot me a look. "What are you buying that for?"

"I love his stories."

"Well, so do I, but why would you want to spend all that money? We've got a bunch of his paperbacks in the garage, and those will be out in paperback in another month."

Fuck her, I thought. I'm not letting her bully me out of buying a book. Later I realized that I'd been making an unconscious attempt to atone for all the books I'd stolen. Ron picked up a handful of freebee newspapers and we went back home, where she pored delightedly over the latest issues of the *Belleair Bee* and the *Beach Beacon* and I guiltily followed the latest adventures of Lew Archer.

Ron spent some time jotting notes on manuscripts and tidying up behind Dad and me. Nor did she mind cooking for us—she took one look at Dad's reserve of canned beef stew and immediately went to the supermarket and stocked up on broccoli and chicken cutlets. But her testiness with Dad had not diminished over time, and Dad—who the hell knew what kind of sad, bitter trip he was on, having endured estrangement from his children for years while he sat alone in front of a television. He could not, would not, abide her aloofness. Sooner or later he'd find a way to get under her skin.

Sure enough, one day Ron had preempted the television and was watching a memorial to Martin Luther King Jr on PBS. Dad made one of his cracks about shipping 'em all back to Africa.

Ron flew into a rage. "I can't believe you said that. Martin Luther King was only one of the greatest, most heroic, brilliant men this country's ever known and you sit around . . ." She could barely talk she was so pissed.

"Aw, why don't you calm down, smarty-pants," Dad said with a laugh. Seeing Ron upset was much preferable, as far as he was concerned, to her controlled hauteur.

"That's it," Ron said. "I'm out of here." She went out to the little Florida room where she'd been sleeping and started packing her things.

"C'mon, Ron," I said as I watched her pack. "You know he only kids around like that to get your goat."

"Kids around? That's what you call that?" she snapped at me, letting me feel the full force of her fury.

"Hey, take it easy. What did I do?"

Then she backed off. "I'm sorry, Steve," she said, fumbling for a cigarette and trying to hold back the tears. "I was really just curious to see if you were alright and I never should've come down here in the first place, knowing damned well what a pain in the ass Daddy can be. I don't know how you can put up with him. You should definitely stay here, though, because you seem to be thriving on whatever's going on. But really, there's only so much of his arrogance I can endure, and if I stay any longer it'll only get worse."

Once Ron made up her mind, there was no talking her out of it. The next day she caught a cab to the airport while I was out on another taxi call.

Dad suffered a bout of moodiness after Ron's departure, mumbling to himself about how ungrateful kids are these days. I wanted to tell him, Hey, Dad, I'm still here! But the only thing that snapped his despondency was spending a lot of time on the phone with his bookie, making complicated bets on the dog races at Tampa Greyhound Track. One morning the phone rang, and when Dad picked it up, his voice went low the way it always did when he made bets with his bookie.

When he got off the phone I asked him if that was his bookie.

"Yeah," he said with a sly look. "He called to see do I want any action on today's races."

"What? You mean this guy don't have enough action he's gotta call *you* up? What kind of a bookie is that? Sounds like he's got you pegged for a sucker."

"Aw, whatta you know about it?"

"Dad, look. Using a bookie is a sucker's bet, 'cause if you win they take a percentage, so in the long run, even if you win you lose. Tell you what—either I could drive you over to the dog track in the Beach Taxi or I'll take your bets myself."

It was pretty dumb of me. I of all people should've recognized the Damon Runyonesque kick he got by using a bookie on the down low, but the idea that anybody was playing my father for a sucker riled the hell out of me. In the end he just laughed at me and went out to watch television and make notations on his scratch sheet.

I started going out with one of the lap-dance girls in Tampa who turned out to be a junky—my old Achilles' heel popping up at the worst possible time. One night I went to a wedding party on Indian Rocks Beach, where my new girlfriend had a little cottage. I was in some kind of a jealous rage and drank a bottle of vodka before I got out of my car. Several hours later I woke up in a cage in the middle of a small-town police station, foaming at the mouth and hurling obscenities at the cops. I had no idea how I'd gotten there or any recollection of what had happened at the wedding party. Then they read me the police report. I'd gone so violently out of control they'd had to call the cops to subdue me. Luckily nobody pressed charges. I knew that if I got locked up again in Florida they would throw the keys away. Things were getting scary.

One night I was sitting with Dad, watching television. He'd dozed off in his armchair and I was just considering waking him gently so he could go to bed when a public service announcement came on television for some local rehab for drug addicts and alcoholics. It showed young men and women who looked like teenagers to me, washing cars in some car wash that was part of the rehab. They were all smiling and laughing while they sudsed up the cars and sprayed them with water, the sun reflecting off the polished fenders. A telephone number appeared on the screen accompanied by a friendly voice-over.

"If you have a drug or alcohol problem, or know somebody who does, please call this number."

I was desperate, so I jotted the number down, then went into the kitchen and dialed it. What did I have to lose? It was not something I would've normally done; normally I would've sneered at the idea. Hell, I'd already been to Daytop, though that was only at the urging of the courts. What could this rinky-dink rehab do for me? The woman who answered had a distinctly Brooklyn accent. She listened to me for a few moments, then briefly outlined her own drinking and drugging history. I could tell immediately that she was a thoroughbred, that she'd been out there like me.

"Listen," she said. "I don't know if you need the kind of long-term treatment this place offers." (This rehab was one of those behavioral places for youngsters, very much like Daytop Village.) "Why don't you try going to a twelve-step meeting?"

I didn't want to hang up the phone. In the space of a few moments, I felt a strange connection with this woman. I decided to take her advice, if only to see her again.

The next day I found myself at a clubhouse in downtown Clearwater called "The Serenity Club," an old wooden A-frame building with huge screened windows that ran around the entire main room. Comfortable armchairs were arranged horseshoe fashion around conference tables. There was a small kitchen with those big commercial pots of hot coffee and several smaller rooms, one with a pool table, and another for smaller, more intimate meetings.

The denizens, at least at the noon meeting I went to for the next year or so, were mostly old guys living on Social Security—a rough-looking crew, with few teeth and more hair in their ears than on their heads. Most of them looked like they'd been drinking cleaning products and sleeping under bridges. The younger people in the local community called this place "The Senility Club."

"Forty years ago," some old guy growled as the meeting began, "I put the plug in the jug, goddamnit. And I never been s'damned happy!"

Whereupon an elderly lady raised her hand and said, "You fellas that say you're happy, joyous, and free? I wish you would please notify your face."

The entire room howled with laughter. These people were having a good time and they weren't drinking!

I raised my hand and said, "Hi, I'm Steve and I'm an addict and an alcoholic."

They all turned and looked at me. You could hear a pin drop in that place. A few smiled at me encouragingly so I went on a bit.

"This is my first time at a meeting, and so far I haven't had a drink today."

They all burst into applause. I felt this huge wave of empathy and attention. After the meeting, people gave me their phone numbers and I began to go out for coffee and lunch with them at the local diners. That night after my first meeting, I was up all night thinking about what I was going to say to these guys the next day.

chapter 15

I began an immediate love affair with this twelve-step fellowship in Clearwater. I was in relatively good health since living with Dad and so didn't suffer from shakes or sweats or weeks of sleeplessness, nor was I under any pressure to make money to survive. The camaraderie in this fellowship seemed to have lifted the obsession with booze right out of me, and, along with it, the fear of Dad seeing me go over the edge again. But I'd been down this road before. My emotions were like exposed nerves and I knew from painful experience that it wouldn't take much to set me off in the other direction. What I didn't understand, though, was the insistence of these people at meetings that I needed some Higher Power to believe in if I was ever going to lick the problem of alcoholism.

It was baffling, so I asked these grizzled old characters to run it down to me.

One guy would say, "Your Higher Power can be anything, long as it ain't *you*. Hell, it could be a doorknob."

Then another guy would bristle and say, "Look here. Someday the only thing between you and a drink is gonna be your Higher Power, so what good is a goddamn *door*knob going to do you? I'm telling you, brother, you need to get *Jesus* in your soul."

I went to work with one of these guys—the taxi was getting me in too much trouble—steam-cleaning carpets for folks who lived in mobile homes. He was a big, blond, redneck guy named Don and he always went to a meeting at twelve o'clock sharp every day, no matter what we were doing on the job.

"Hey, Don," I asked him one day as he steered his panel truck full of cleaning gear to the local meeting, "you go to a meeting every day?"

"Yup. I drank ever day, so I need to go to a meeting ever day to get the program."

I couldn't argue with that logic, so I asked him, "What about this God stuff?"

He looked over at me as he shifted gears and grinned. "That *God* stuff? Hell, that *is* the program, son."

Still confused, I decided to call my sister and ask her what she thought. Veronica knew everything, and if she didn't, then she knew how to find out. So I called and explained to her this principle of the twelve steps. When I finished, she told me that she knew a wonderful writer who attended those meetings. She really admired this guy and said she'd ask him what he used for a Higher Power. The next day she called me back. Ron said that her friend told her that his Higher Power was *Art*.

This sounds like a silly twelve-step anecdote, but I was floored that my sister, who as far as I knew had thrown God and religion out the window along with Santa Claus and the Easter Bunny, responded to this whole Higher Power business with earnest enthusiasm.

I started praying, at the prompting of these old-timers, in the morning when I woke up and before I went to sleep at night. The results were immediate—my day had a beginning and an end, a simple sense of order that I'd never known. I was used to passing out at night and coming to in the morning desperate for a drink and worrying about bail money. Some old guy named Henry, who'd been a merchant marine, took me to a Buddhist temple where a Vietnamese monk taught me the rudiments of meditation. Cool. I'd seen enough Bruce Lee flicks to delight in the posture, and I could sense the power inherent in stillness. I began to experience some small sense of well-being.

My father was not enthusiastic about this "going to meetings" business. It took me away from him and he resented it. One day I brought a woman home with me. We'd been playing tennis and she wanted to change out of her sweaty clothes.

When she went into the bathroom to change, Dad said to me, "Where the hell did you meet this blimp?"

"I met her at those meetings I go to, Dad."

"Christ, you mean she's an alco*holi*c?"

"Yeah."

"Well then, why the hell didn't you offer her a drink?"

He just didn't get it and it frustrated me. One day I was complaining to my Buddhist friend Henry about my father's inability to fathom what I was going through.

"Why don't you try understanding *him* for a change?" said Henry. "The guy probably don't have much time left, and if you don't show him some love now you could miss your only chance."

When I got home that night I asked Dad to tell me about his father, who was a complete mystery to me.

"What's there to tell?" he said "We all hated the sonofabitch." Then some memory made him go on with a wry look. "The old man would tell me, Chick, I want you should go to the store, get me a canna beedz. So I run to the store and come back with a can of peas. He goes, The hell you bringa me peas? I said beeeeedz. Beeeeedz. So I run out and come back with a can of beets. What the hell izza *this*? he says. I tell him, You said beets, right? He goes through the roof. *Beeeeedz!* How much time I gotta tell you? Beeeeeeeedz! Beeeeeeeedz!"

"So what was it he wanted?"

"Maybe a can of beans, who the hell knows? The sonofabitch was crazy."

Suddenly we were both laughing.

I decided to take Henry's suggestion a little further. Next day I was driving Dad over to see his doctor. He was wearing his funky little fishing hat that I remembered him wearing when he visited me in jail all those times. I turned to him in the front seat and said, "Hey, Dad. I love you."

His eyes bulged and his hand shot out and slammed into the dashboard as though to brace himself for a collision. "Jesus Christ," he said, "watch where you're going. Didn't you see the goddamn speed limit? It's only thirty miles an hour on Clearwater Beach. Where the hell did you get a driver's license anyway, Sears and Roebuck?"

At one point I called my sister to ask her advice on what to do about our father's growing health problems. I told her how I'd take Dad to see his doctor, but then he'd tell the doctor that he felt fine. When I insisted that he wasn't fine, the doctor would slough it off as a pulmonary problem. Tell him to stop smoking, the doctor told me. I suspected it was something worse. My sister was amazed at my concern.

"I can't believe," she said to me, "that you're so worried about this guy after what he did to us."

Maybe she was talking about him calling me a bum, or the way he'd devastated her self-esteem as a child on a daily basis. Who knows—maybe she thought he'd killed Stubby. That all seemed like such a lifetime ago to me, but I could still hear the resentment in her reaction, and it saddened me. When I tried to press her about what she meant, she got evasive and finally hung up.

Dad wasn't the only one Ron was tough on. Later I would learn that she was turning into a hellion at the *New Yorker*. She'd become unbending with her editor Roger Angell, arguing furiously over the tiniest editorial comment. There'd be something he wanted her to open up on, or that seemed indecipherable, and he'd point out a particular sentence to her and say, "Now Veronica, this one sentence here on page seven, now just listen, there's one thing . . ." And she'd go off on him. "Oh I *knew* you would say that! *No, no, no! Not that!*" Ron was damned touchy about this thing that was closest to her heart.

Roger Angell claimed my sister was the toughest writer he ever worked with, but he hung in there because she was so brilliant and he loved the enthusiasm she brought to her work.

Charles "Chip" McGrath and Dan Menaker also edited my sister's stuff for a while when Roger sort of stepped back and Chip became head of the fiction department. Ron's relationship with McGrath had always been distant, but once he started editing her he quickly discovered how difficult she could be. Chip, though, was always amused at Ron's stubbornness as a writer; he noticed that as soon as she put on her editor's hat she was suddenly trying to get other writers to fix their stuff and not *be* so stubborn, complaining about guys like George Trow who just *didn't get it*, and how you just couldn't edit this guy. Which was, of course, what Roger and Chip were saying about *her*.

At least Chip didn't get the door-slamming and shouting that Ron subjected his pal Dan Menaker to. In fact, Chip was such a huge fan of

Ron that he was even jealous of her friends like Mark Singer, Sandy Frazier, and Jim Downey, a writer from *Saturday Night Live*, who'd come in
and hang around her office. He'd watch them from his office, next door to
hers, watching them laugh and laugh, Chip really wanting to be more of a
pal. They were all being so brilliant and so funny, and there he was, just
being a drone and doing his stuff.

Too bad I didn't know Chip McGrath. I could've told him how much I
related to his predicament, jealously observing Ron and her brilliant friends
hobnobbing in a Village bar, or standing at her front door while Donald
Barthelme made himself comfortable on her couch. I could've told Chip of
all the times I'd said something stupid and she'd get this distant look on her
face and get up to go to the bathroom or to hail a cab. For Veronica, there
was no time to be wasted on inane people, other than making them the butt
of her sarcastic wit. On the other hand, I relished the idea of Ronnie storm-
ing around the offices of the *New Yorker*, slamming doors and yelling, "You
people must be insane!" either because they didn't want to buy a story she
loved or because they'd bought a story that she thought was a piece of shit.
But both Chip and Roger loved the passion that she brought to a magazine
that sorely needed an infusion of such energy.

What I needed down in Clearwater was not feistiness or passion, but a
little peace of mind. My emotions were still painfully raw, and in brief
moments of anger, loneliness, and longing, I sensed the specter of my past
dogging my steps, waiting for a moment of weakness.

I got a job in the sun doing grounds work at a local tennis club, resurfacing and maintaining the clay courts and helping the pro give lessons
and clinics. He often had me fill in as a fourth in doubles, and after a few
months of his patient instruction I began to rise up the competitive lad-
ders at several other clubs. The physical labor and healthy exercise soon
burned off my need for kinky sex joints in Tampa, and I settled down into
an honest routine for the first time in my life.

But after a while of going to meetings, working all day in the hot sun,
and then taking care of Dad in my spare time, life started to feel a little
grim. I needed to have some fun, and I didn't want to hang out in bars trying to pick up women.

One day I was walking through downtown Clearwater and stopped in
front of a small movie house, The Carib, which had been turned into a

space for community theater. Young, attractive people were filing in, and a notice on the door announced auditions for *A Funny Thing Happened on the Way to the Forum*. I walked up to a guy with a clipboard and asked him if I could go in and watch.

"I'm the stage manager," he said, "and no, you most certainly can*not* go in unless you want to audition."

"What do I have to do to audition?"

"Hel*lo*," he said, pointing at the notice on the door. "*Forum*? As in musical comedy? How about a song and a few lines from the script?"

"Okay," I said, feeling glib. "I'll audition."

"You need *sheet* music, mister. You can't just prance in there la-di-da. They want to see you sing with accompaniment."

I must've looked brokenhearted, so the stage manager said, "Tell you what. I know they have the sheet music to the score, so why don't you just do one of the songs from the show?"

"I don't know this show or any of the songs from it."

By now the guy had either taken a shine to me or seen in me some great potential for the stage, because he proceeded to teach me there and then the chorus, "Something familiar, something peculiar, something for everyone a comedy tonight." Ten minutes later I was sitting in one of the plush red seats in the darkened old movie house, surrounded by whispering, energetic young actors and actresses waiting to audition. I started rubbernecking around at everybody to dispell the anticipation creeping up my spine. Again, as with my twelve-step meetings, it was an immediate love affair, even though I was terrified when I suddenly heard my name called out.

My singing voice quavered with nervousness and tension and the piano player cut me off after one pass through the chorus. When they called me onstage to read I didn't do much better. I had no idea who the character was supposed to be, and having just seen *Raging Bull* the day before, everything came out sounding like Jake La Motta on a bad day. When I finally sat down in my seat I was flushed with embarrassment. A girl sitting behind me leaned forward and spoke into my ear.

"You don't want to be in this production, Steve. We're having auditions for *Romeo and Juliet* over at the civic center and we really need guys. Why don't you come over there with me?"

The girl was a doll, and when we got to the civic center my glibness saved the day.

"Can you do a cockney accent?" the director wanted to know.

"Kin aw do cook-nay? Gow wawn, luv!"

They cast me as Samson, one of Capulet's ruffians who swaggers out in the first scene with all those sarcastic plays on words and instigates a sword fight.

The production was for only one performance to be held in the auditorium on the Clearwater campus of St. Petersburg Junior College. My father insisted on coming to the show, although at the time he was eighty-seven years old and in a lot of physical discomfort. But he came and he sat there on one of those wooden fold-up chairs in that auditorium for almost four hours' worth of one of the worst productions of a Shakespearean play that's ever been staged.

The night of the production I was so nervous I smoked a million cigarettes and the overdose of nicotine gave me flulike symptoms. I started sucking on chewable vitamin C tablets to counter the flu, which then gave me acid reflux. Just before I had to walk out onstage, I realized I'd lost my voice. I tapped my scene partner on the shoulder as we huddled behind the curtain, just before our opening scene.

"Listen, man," I croaked. "I can't talk. I can't go out there." My voice was so far gone I had to mime the words in order to be understood.

"It's just stage fright," he said. "Go on out there and you'll be fine."

He was right. As soon as I walked out onstage, I stuck my boot in the rear end of an actress who was doing her Italian bag lady stage business and sent her sprawling. It was an ad-lib and the girl shot me a look from the stage floor full of venom. My scene partner broke up laughing, the fear vanished, and Capulet's two bullyboys proceeded to build the tension for the first big scene in *Romeo and Juliet.*

"Draw if you be men!" I loved snarling that line as I whipped out my sword, and my glee was an irresistible appeal to the berserker in every actor onstage. The guy who'd choreographed the fight scene had told us he wanted *A Clockwork Orange* sort of feel, so we had all these weird spiked maces and ball and chains, and the ensuing sword fight erupted with such wild enthusiasm that nobody noticed or could even hear the prince when he walked out onstage and commanded us to stop. He was standing there screaming, "Drop your swords!" for several minutes when a sudden lull occurred in the battle, everybody pausing at once to catch their breath, and the prince, his voice strained all out of proportion, shrieked into the silence, "I said drop your fucking swords!"

When it was finally over, I washed off my mascara, stripped off my purple tights and velvet knickers, tossed my sword into the prop box, pulled on my street clothes, and walked out the back door of the auditorium. I found my father waiting with not a trace of the four agonizing hours on that hard little auditorium chair.

"Hey, bud," he said with a strange, soft reverence. "You were terrific."

This from a guy who never approved of a single thing I ever tried to do. I've never been quite so disarmed. I decided at that moment that come hell or high water, I was going to pursue a career in acting, which I did.

Funny Girl with the same community theater company came next. (I had a nice little song and dance number with Fanny.) Then I got cast in a dinner theater production of *The Music Man* (I was getting *paid* to do this!) in which I did a broad caricature of Charlie Cowell, the anvil salesman, tugging at my mustache and cackling through my lines like Snidely Whiplash.

At one point during that production, I came down with a bad case of shingles, erupting like the measles around the nerve center at the small of my back, and finally spreading very briefly to one side of my face. The doctor told me that shingles were common in people my age who'd had chicken pox, particularly in times of stress. No big deal. I applied a thick layer of pancake makeup for performances, and a few weeks later when the shingles went away I forgot about it.

Around this time I fell in love with Laura, a girl I met at a twelve-step meeting who, believe it or not, sang in the choir at a Southern Baptist church. She was quite beautiful, by anybody's standard, with brown eyes and a mane of dirty-blond locks. And though in her late twenties and divorced, she possessed an irresistible mixture of Southern elegance, Baptist innocence, and unabashed naughtiness. We were coming out of a meeting with a lot of other people one night and I offered her a ride home. Up to that point we'd hardly exchanged a prolonged conversation.

She stopped walking, gave me a sort of mocking smile, and said, "I don't need a ride home, Steve. What ah need is a kiss." She tilted her head up, eyes shut, and, impervious to everyone milling around us, presented her closed but enticing mouth.

As our lips touched ever so lightly, a thrill of sweetness shot through me like an electric current, rearranging my brain cells and altering my perceptions. The surrounding room and people were blotted out by details of her nearness: the tip of an ear peeking through her hair, the length of her eyelashes, the aroma of whatever she'd washed her hair with, the forward tilt of her shoulders as she leaned slightly into the kiss. People were shooting us curious looks. I backed off and walked her outside.

"Lord o'mercy, chile," she said, laughing (she loved to parody Southern dialect), "some folks got nothin' better to do than stare at a body all night."

From that moment on I thought I'd never want to kiss any other woman, in any other way. We started spending as much time together as we could, going to movies and dances, chatting in the parking lot after meetings. During a brief hurricane that knocked out everybody's electricity, we found each other at a mutual friend's house and spent the day happily playing Trivial Pursuit. I went to her church one Sunday to hear her sing a solo. She blew me away, and afterward, when I raved about her voice and begged her to sing for me, she laughed and conceded to sing one song, so I'd better pick a favorite—it was the only time Jiminy Cricket's been outdone on "When You Wish Upon a Star." Laura's Southern speech patterns increasingly made my head spin, but despite my most charming efforts, she refused to take me seriously.

"Steve, how can ah introduce you to my family? Hey, Mom, this is my new boyfriend. He worships Buddha. Chile, they'll just flip right out."

I joined a Baptist church—not hers, that would've been too obvious. I got interviewed first by the pastor, a charismatic guy who looked like Henry Fonda. When I told him I'd been raised Catholic and now prayed at a Buddhist temple, he asked me why I wanted to join Calvary Baptist Church.

"To tell the truth," I said, surprised at my own reluctance to tell an easy lie, "I'm in love with a girl who's a Southern Baptist, but she won't have anything to do with me because I'm not Christian."

He looked at me for a long minute in dead silence. I felt like jumping up and running out of his office. Suddenly he threw back his head and started laughing.

"Let me tell you, son," he said. "People don't come to Christ for theological or idealistic reasons. No, people come to Christ because they're desperate, because they want something real bad. Son, I'd be happy to have you as a member of my congregation anytime you like."

I got dunked in the baptismal trough one morning in front of the entire congregation, wading out into the waist-high water in nothing but a cotton smock. The pastor (wearing what looked like rubber fishing overalls over his suit and tie) used one hand to support my back and the other to pinch my nose while he leaned me over backward until I was entirely submerged. The moment my face broke the surface again I looked around the church and studied the faces of my fellows, searching for some slight change in perception. Part of me really hoped that I'd be cleansed and free of the demons that haunted me. But another part of me smiled and thought, C'mon, man. You know you're only doing this for the girl.

I attended Bible studies and started singing in the church choir. My relationship with Laura was the first I'd ever had that wasn't just about wild sex and getting stoned. There was such a sweet innocence about being with her, just feeling her hair brush my cheek made my head giddy and my knees weak. Sometimes I'd try to tell her how I felt and my tongue would cleave to the roof of my mouth. Unable to contain the feelings, I'd gush about her to my twelve-step buddies. But they warned me that my heightened emotions were a result of "early sobriety," emerging for the first time from the fog of booze and drugs. I was acting like an adolescent, they said, and if I didn't slow down I'd get drunk. I figured they were just jealous. "Hey, get a life!" I'd tell 'em. On the rare, precious occasions that we slept together, our faces nearly touching on a pillow, inhaling her sweet breath was like oxygen for my ravaged spirit. God had sent me an angel. I was convinced that this girl could save my soul.

Laura was happy that I was now a Christian, but I still couldn't get her to take me seriously.

"C'mon, Steve," she'd say, lightly laughing off my persistent proposals. "Ah've *been* married, but you have no idea what you're talking about."

She'd applied to a Christian college and had her heart set on moving back to her hometown in the Bible Belt. But my hopes that I could somehow change her mind persisted. Long past my old resentments toward Christianity, I enjoyed good times with the local Baptist crowd. They were always inviting me out to diners for breakfast after church, like the twelve-step crowd. We'd sit in a classroom at Bible studies where the walls were adorned with maps depicting the geography of biblical times. I'd follow along (in the Bible Laura had given me) as we read stories from the Old Testament, entertaining fantasies of striding through the desert like Charlton Heston in the epic movie *The Ten Commandments*. Singing four-part harmony in the choir was like blending my voice in a street corner doo-wop group. But I suspected that it would all vanish if I lost Laura.

* * *

During this time, I got cast as Nathan Detroit in *Guys and Dolls,* my all-time favorite musical comedy, at the same dinner theater where I'd done *The Music Man.* I would've paid *them* to do this one. As one of the leads I had to do some complicated song-and-dance routines, so I took modern dance lessons.

Doing Nathan in *Guys and Dolls* was the most fun I ever had as an actor and the highlight of my acting career. Here again I couldn't get De Niro's performance in *Raging Bull* out of my head, but this time it worked. The crowds, half lit after dinner and drinks, howled with laughter eight shows a week at the way I did Nathan. The reviews in the local papers were raves. My romance with Laura mirrored the one in that wonderful Damon Runyon story, where the gambler Sky Masterson falls hopelessly in love with Sergeant Sarah Brown from the Salvation Army. Laura sat through the show several times and visited me in my dressing room, which provoked the ire of the actress playing Nathan's sweetheart, Adelaide.

On closing night Laura and her friends got about thirty people from her church and local twelve-step community to come. After the show they crowded outside the dressing rooms to congratulate me. If I'd died right then I'd have died content.

Dad never got a chance to meet Laura or to see me in any plays after *Romeo and Juliet.* Several months after that first production I came home from work and found him bent over in his armchair choking.

"Steve," he managed to say through gasps for air. "I can't breathe."

I carried him in my arms into the car and into the hospital. I was afraid if I waited for the ambulance he would die, and I'd be damned if I'd let this guy die now that I had him back in my life. Turns out he had Lou Gehrig's disease. He had it in the swallowing muscles of his throat or esophagus, so food and liquid were getting into his lungs. That's why he'd been having trouble breathing, and I was furious thinking of all the times I'd taken him to his doctors, who'd never been able to diagnose the poor guy correctly—*Tell him to stop smoking.* The doctors at the hospital told me they could cut a hole in his stomach so he could feed himself with a plastic syringe, like you baste a turkey with.

I tried to cheer him up. "Hey, Dad," I said, "don't worry, they can fix this." But he just looked at me and shook his head. One thing he'd always asked me was to please not put him in a nursing home—to let him die in his own home with a little goddamned dignity.

I stayed with him that first day at the hospital, making sure the nurses were giving him what he needed. I found a huge television sitting unused in the hallway. With the instincts of a thief, I took advantage of the empty corridor to wheel it into Dad's room and hooked it up. When the nurses looked askance at the television, I said my father had asked to have it put on his bill. Nobody argued. At one point Dad waved me over closer to his bedside. I bent down to hear what he was saying, and as I did so, he fumbled in his pockets for his wallet. Then he pulled out a twenty-dollar bill and handed it to me.

"Don't spend it all in one place," he said. It was the last thing he ever said to me, doling out a twenty to the kid who'd never grown up. Even in his dying breath he could hit me where it hurt.

I woke up at home to the phone ringing. My father's EEG had flat-lined. I rushed back to the hospital. The horrific picture of my father lying on that gurney, his brittle old body lurching with each spasmodic gasp of air, has been burned into my memory for all time.

"He's been brain-dead for quite a while now and his breathing is just reflex," the doctor advised me. "But we can keep him hooked up to these machines and keep him going. We need your permission to pull the plug."

It never occurred to me to call my sister. It was a decision I had to make right then and probably live with the rest of my life. But I instinctively knew what he would've wanted, and it wasn't to live like a vegetable, brain-dead and hooked up to life support.

"Do it." It was a no-brainer.

That night I went out and got roaring drunk. It didn't help. I was lonelier than ever with Dad gone, so I went right back to meetings where all my new friends were, waiting to console me. I was whining to my friend Henry about Dad's last, painful words—"Don't spend it all in one place"—and Henry burst out laughing. Between spasms he managed to say, "Yeah, but you took the goddamned twenty, didn't you?" That's when it hit me, how perfect it was, how *exactly* like Dad to be "kidding around" right to the end. In his last moments, with me at his side, he'd been completely himself. Pretty soon Henry and I had the whole meeting full of people laughing about it.

And so life went on. I had a mission now. I would be an actor.

chapter 16

The biggest wrench that life threw my way came at about two years sober. I was hearing a lot of news about this thing called AIDS that many of my old junky friends were dying of back in New York. I was so in love with Laura that I wanted to marry her, but I knew that if I were ever going to have a long-term relationship with any woman, I'd better get myself checked out. There was a local doctor who apparently knew how to conduct blood tests for AIDS, and I spent a few weeks in dreadful anxiety about the results—he had to send to California for the tests.

They came back positive. This was during the early eighties when it was considered a death sentence, so I was loath to talk to anybody about it. People with AIDS back then were treated like they had leprosy or the plague. Even in the twelve-step community that embraced the lowest of the low, people's faces grew grim when the topic came up. Their eyes shifted sideways and I sensed their fear.

One young guy from local meetings died very quickly after he was diagnosed. He was a sweet, handsome kid, a gym-rat who'd always looked buff in his cut-off T-shirts. I listened closely to the remarks about his death, sentences of sympathy tailing off into shrugs of hopelessness. *He seemed like such a nice guy. Who'd have thought . . . ?* I knew I never wanted anybody to talk about me like that. My own reaction to his death was less than admirable. I could detect nothing in his aspect even remotely similar to the street junkies I'd known who got infected through shared needles. So I judged him a closet queen, attempting to mislead us all by strutting around with his cute girlfriend and acting like a man. I knew my feelings were born out of fear. I wanted to go visit him in the hospital because I'd admired him until that point, but I was afraid of my reactions to seeing him wasting away. I'd spent too much time watching my father die and didn't think I could handle any more tragedy.

My romance was suddenly out the window. Immediately upon being diagnosed I insisted that Laura get tested and tortured myself about what she might find out. The time spent waiting for her test results were worse than the anxiety about my own. Thank God, she turned up negative. She handled the whole thing with great good humor, patience, and compassion. I suspected that her calm in the face of such danger owed much to her Baptist upbringing and her trust in God. I couldn't comprehend the idea of life without her now, and feared I'd lose my mind if I lost her. But I could hardly ask her to stick around just to watch me die.

Without the drugs and booze to push this heartbreak down into that hidden, inner landscape, my feelings zigzagged uncontrollably from one end of the emotional spectrum to the other, and my behavior became increasingly erratic. On Monday I'd feel in such good health that I'd suspect the blood tests were wrong or that a cure was just around the corner. My hopes would rise and I'd cherish Laura's affection and support. Then the next day I'd feel doomed and treat her coldly, feeling like I had to drive her out of my life for her own good. I couldn't shake the guilt I felt for putting her in the position where she had to get tested in the first place.

On any given day I'd wake up seized with terror about what would happen to me, now that I felt relegated once again to the role of outcast. But something, some life force, or my old ability not to let anything get me down, kicked into gear. I swallowed my anxieties and focused on my acting ambitions with a hard-bitten desperation to succeed, and succeed in a hurry. So don't get in my way. I joined an acting workshop in Tampa. The woman running it, impressed with my work, put me in contact with an agent she knew in Miami. I took Laura down there with me for moral support. Leaving her at a Holiday Inn on Biscayne Boulevard, I drove over to meet what I hoped would be my future. (Actually, I couldn't tear myself away from her so she finally pushed me out the door—"G'wawn now!"— and locked it.)

The Ada Gordon Talent Agency was nestled in a strip mall in a tacky neighborhood just off Dixie Highway in North Miami Beach. When I walked into Ada's office she took my headshot and résumé, leaned back in her chair against some filing cabinets, and fanned her face with it. She was a wizened, tough old bird with bleached, lacquered hair, a glen-plaid pantsuit, and reading glasses that hung from her neck on a chain. I liked her instantly.

"I've heard some good things about you," she said. After a long pause, she added, "Well, don't just sit there. Let me see you do something."

I jumped out of my chair and launched into a stylized monologue from a Sam Shepard play. As often happened when I found myself on the spot, it came out sounding like De Niro's Jake. Ada stopped fanning and her eyes widened. Just when I was really getting warmed up the phone started ringing—and she answered it! My heart leaped into my throat. Christ, this was my shot! Couldn't she understand that? Determined, I plunged on with increasing fury—way too much for that enclosed little office.

Ada, warily keeping her eyes on me, snapped into the phone, "I gotta guy in here," then hung up.

By the time I finished, she had her glasses on and was reading my ré-sumé. "Been over to Dee Miller's yet?"

When I told her I had no idea who Dee Miller was, Ada laughed and said, "They're casting for *Miami Vice* and they're always looking for lu-natics like you. I want you to get yourself over there immediately! And don't accept any nonspeaking or extra work. I don't want them to see you as just another interesting face."

When I got back to the Holiday Inn I took Laura out for a steak din-ner to celebrate.

"So, did they hire you? Did you get cast in anything?"

"Not yet, but I met a real agent, and the casting people seemed inter-ested. Said they'd call me in a week or two and asked me how fast I could get down to Miami from Clearwater if they did call."

"See, ah *knew* it," she said, laughing softly. "You're gonna be famous, Steve, and never even remember ol' Laura."

By the time she left Clearwater for Christian college I still hadn't heard from *Miami Vice*. I decided it was all just pie in the sky, and the Miami trip an unkind thing to have done to Laura, prolonging a painful relationship that we both knew had to end. Although she'd laughed at my proposals of marriage, she proved herself a loyal friend and continued to take my calls after she moved back to the Bible Belt. I went out with a few other women after she left, but there was no known treatment for AIDS, and I could not bear the thought of infecting someone or having to confess my dread secret. Relationships remained brief and superficial from that point on.

After Dad died, Ron called a few times and sounded really sympathetic about how it happened. She was sorry I'd had to deal with it alone, and disarmed at how much I'd cared for him at the end. Who knows—maybe she was even a little jealous. But she was far from sentimental and became adamant about selling the house. He'd left it to both of us, and Ron was not the least bit interested in being co-owner of anything with her unreliable brother.

The *idea* of selling the place was appealing. I was champing at the bit to go to Miami and pursue my acting career, and the money we could get for the house would enable me to do it. But I was reluctant to pick up just then and leave that place that was so full of memories of my romance with Laura and my first joys as an actor. It was the one place where I'd been close to my father and where, for a brief while, we'd been happy together. I was scared too, knowing I had a disease that might end my life shortly. That house was a safe place I could always come back to if I needed a final refuge. There was no way, though, that I'd tell my sister about my illness. No way I was telling *any*body about that.

My reluctance to sell the house must've sounded irrational to Ron. She seemed relieved to finally be rid of Dad once and for all, and when I tried to explain my feelings about it to her we ended up having a terrible argument.

"This is ridiculous," she said, shortly before she hung up. "What're you—snorting cocaine or something? You sound like you're still getting high."

My sister's career had taken a big step when she published her first book, *Partners*, a collection of all the satire and humor she'd written up to that point. It was the mideighties. The Newhouse family had just bought the *New Yorker,* and William Shawn was soon replaced by Robert Gottlieb as editor in chief. For Veronica, this was much worse than losing her blood father. Gottlieb, who'd run Knopf, brought to the *New Yorker* a much-lauded literary tradition. He'd even edited some of *my* favorite writers, like Len Deighton and John le Carré. But nobody could have been less like the eccentric, one-of-a-kind Mr. Shawn.

Where Shawn was distant and remote, Gottlieb was quick-witted and in-your-face. He and Ronnie had a sort of intellectual flirtation at first, but she resisted the transition. She couldn't get over the loss of the one man who'd made her feel special and protected. The magazine continued to buy and publish her stories, but her inability to be flexible with people, particularly with her new editor in chief, was the beginning of her undoing. She slowly began to drift away from her work as an editor in the magazine's fiction department, the home that had become more of a family to her than her real one.

Eventually I found some potential buyers for the house, and Ron came down to help me settle up Dad's will and nail down the real estate deal. During the weeks we spent making those arrangements, my sister and I began to recapture some of the closeness we'd shared as children in Philly. I wasn't drinking or using drugs and was slowly learning to take care of myself without stealing. (My inheritance from Dad went a long way toward solving that problem.) So perhaps because she didn't have to worry about me, Ronnie loosened up. I began to notice how her take on life and the world around her was constantly feeding her muse. She always carried a little notebook with her, and every so often she'd start snickering to herself, pull out the notebook, and start scribbling in it.

"Steve," she said to me when I remarked on it. "If you don't write an inspiration down, it will disappear like a rabbit down a hole."

We were driving around Clearwater one day, trying to find a coin shop that might buy a collection of old coins that our father had accumulated. As I pulled up to an intersection, I pointed at the traffic lights suspended over the street on cables that swayed in the wind.

"Last year after the hurricane," I said, "those traffic lights were hanging by a thread."

Ronnie burst out laughing and out came the notebook and pencil. I had no idea what struck her so funny.

We pulled into a strip mall with a Krispy Kreme doughnut shop. Ron shot me a look, like—What are we stopping here for?

"Let's go get some doughnuts," I said.

"You're not serious?"

" 'Course I am. Hey, you gotta keep your strength up." Again, out came the pad and pencil.

Later we were having lunch in some diner or cafeteria. Over at a corner table sat an elderly couple, still as stones underneath a ceiling fan that circled precariously just above their heads. Ronnie took one look at them and almost choked on her coffee. Out came the notebook. To me they looked like typical Florida retirees—glassy-eyed under their sun visors. I started to ask her what was so funny, but as I watched the huge ceiling fan whirling and wobbling almost out of control (hanging by a thread) just above those immobile heads, it hit my funny bone as well. My sister's quirky perspective was infectious, but fleeting—you had to write it down. Veronica explained to me how Sandy Frazier and other writers she knew kept all kinds of lists and notes about seemingly meaningless trivia. This was not information I thought I'd ever need, nor did I feel that Ron was nudging me to try writing. But it was the first time she'd privileged me with inside information into her world and let me glimpse intimate details about her greatest love—the written word.

Finally we sold the house and divvied up the money. One morning while my sister made preparations to fly back to New York, the phone rang in our father's house. When I picked it up some guy asked me if he could speak to Veronica. When I asked whom should I say is calling, he said, "Tell her Andrew Wylie."

My sister once told me about her agent, Andrew, back when I'd first started getting sober, as an example of someone with a checkered past who had managed to pull himself together, probably to inspire me to do the same. I'd been honored by her confiding in me, and had indeed gotten sober, while Wylie had become one of the most successful and powerful agents on the planet, with an awesome list of major clients. It wasn't power or success, though, but some quirky quality in Wylie that appealed to my sister, and when she loved somebody she went all the way. No one would ever get her to indulge in backbiting gossip about Andrew Wylie.

I'd been impressed, and as I stood there with the phone to my ear, I said, "Hey, Andrew. I heard about you. I'm Steve, Veronica's brother."

"Yeah," he said affably. "I thought it might be you."

I felt my face flush, figuring that maybe he'd heard a bit about me too. The silence on the line grew. Finally I put the phone down and went and got my sister.

That was the last time I remember the phone ringing in that house, and when Dad's service was turned off I got a beeper—there was still an outside chance the Miami talent agent would call. With the house sold there was nothing to keep me from moving to Miami to pursue my acting career. I packed up my things in a U-Haul trailer, hooked it up to the back of my sturdy Buick station wagon, and checked the oil and coolant. It was a long drive through the sweltering Florida Everglades.

As I pulled out of the driveway onto Eldorado Avenue, I stopped to take one last look at that old bungalow. There'd been a little storm damage after the recent hurricane and the paint was peeling near the roof. Weeds were growing up through the concrete driveway and little chameleons were dashing across the pebbles that had replaced the lawn—Dad's idea, to cut down on maintenance. The new owners planned to knock down the place. They were interested in a much more elaborate structure that would show off their beachfront property. The old landscape of small beachfront bungalows was vanishing, and I knew I'd never see that place again.

chapter 17

Once again The Powers That Be opened a window and threw me a line. Nothing, not life-threatening illness, memories of Dad, or losing Laura, could dampen my excitement as I drove south through Florida—*I had an upcoming audition for* Miami Vice*!* The first time I checked my new beeper it was Ada telling me to call her and get my ass down to Miami. Hurtling across Alligator Alley through the Okefenokee Swamp, I rehearsed audition monologues and guzzled coffee. Vultures were silhouetted against the sky as they circled slowly above the gnarled trees and shimmering heat, but they'd have to wait for my carcass. The game wasn't over yet.

When I hit Miami I transferred my belongings from the U-Haul to a motel room and proceeded over to the Alexander Hotel where Dee Miller, *Vice*'s casting director, had told me to meet her. Bonnie Timmerman was casting the New York actors, but Dee handled the local talent. Dee was another interesting lady—tall, dark, and haunted. She was one of the few women I've known who could simultaneously do languid and hyper, as though lolling comfortably on the edge of a nervous breakdown. The elegant lobby and carpeted hallways of the Alexander Hotel, rising up from the strip of Collins Avenue called Millionaire's Row, gave me my first flush of anticipated success. I wished Ron could've seen this—Gatsby might've waltzed through this lobby or skipped jauntily down that winding staircase. Dee grinned at my gawking. She'd been there a hundred times with a hundred other new actors. She patted my arm as we rode up in a gilt-edged elevator.

We entered a gigantic suite where half a dozen men in suits sat behind a long conference table. I was so self-conscious when Dee introduced me to the producers and directors, I remembered only that Don Johnson was among them. Surprisingly, Don wore none of the flashy clothes that the show was famous for. He was laid-back in Levi's and slouched in a chair, but he had that glow about him. When our eyes locked briefly, I felt a crackle of alpha-dog tension.

They had me read a few lines from a script and ad-lib pulling out a pistol and barking stuff like "Freeze! Keep your hands where I can see 'em!" They watched me closely, but revealed nothing by way of their murmured remarks to one another. Before I was dismissed, Dee winked at me and gave me a thumbs-up. Soon I was signing my first Screen Actors Guild contract.

The first scene I did on *Miami Vice* was being shot in one of those beautiful old art deco hotels down on South Beach—but in the basement, where it looked like a dayroom in a psych ward. I can't even remember the clothes they'd given me to wear in the scene, something institutional like Dickies workpants under a bathrobe. I was supposed to be one of a half dozen screwballs in a veterans' hospital where Crockett (played by Don) and a reporter named Stone (Bob Balaban) had come to investigate the smuggling of heroin from Vietnam. I had one line, and it was a good one. No problem.

I was still the same hammy kid, though, who'd done Johnnie Ray on our front porch in Philly, but I got a lesson in "less is more" on my first shoot. It was my first-ever bit on film so I was revved up and going for broke. Don Johnson was also directing the episode, and he stopped the entire production in the middle of my big scene.

"Cut! Cut! Okay, set up for a medium shot over there, but first I want a close-up right here." Don put his arm around my shoulders and walked me slightly out of earshot as the camera crew dollied the camera around, changed lenses, checked light meters, and slipped gels over the lights.

"Look, Steve," he whispered softly, putting his mouth near my ear but never taking his eyes off the camera crew. "This guy Stone [Balaban] is not a very big guy, right?"

"Right, Don."

"So you don't need to be real big to intimidate him, right?"

"Yeah. That's right, Don." I'd been poking my finger and barking at Balaban like a pissed-off cabdriver.

"And that's just how I want you to do that line," Don whispered. "Just like I'm talking to you right now—soft, flat, no inflection. Got it?"

"Yeah, Don. I got it."

I was so excited I would've hurled myself through a plate-glass window if he'd asked me to. When they shot the close-up I whispered the line, "If you look too hard for your story you're liable to become part of it," just as Don directed, only staring with deranged intensity over the top of Balaban's head, nostrils flared, one eye twitching, and directly into the camera. When the episode aired, my big scene had hit the cutting-room floor.

Next time I got cast I strolled on the set like an old pro, this time as a homicide cop. Don took one look at me and went through the roof.

"Christ," he complained, "this guy was playing a psycho only a couple weeks ago. How the hell is he gonna come back and be a cop now?"

This show was Don's baby, and it had such an obsessive following that continuity was intensely scrutinized. But the director laughed and said, "Don't worry, Don. His scene got cut so nobody'll recognize him."

What a joy to work on a show that was shot with such careful attention to detail, and with the full production values of a major motion picture. I'd turn up for wardrobe at the elegant Alexander Hotel, where the production offices took up one entire floor. The wardrobe mistress would lead me down aisle after aisle of the latest fashions from Paris and Italy, listening with close attention to my interpretation of the character I'd be playing as she held up jackets and shirts under my chin. Though a "day player" and auditioning for each episode, as a "principle" I'd get my own little trailer with my character's name on it. Catering served up stuff like broiled grouper and asparagus vinaigrette for lunch. My head swelled dizzily with quick success and I entertained visions of stardom. This was more intoxicating than coming off the road boosting with Nick and cramming a couple grand in hundreds into my pocket—this was legit!

I spent a few months in motels and flophouses in North Miami Beach (to be near my agent and Dee's casting office) and roamed around neighborhoods like Coral Gables and Coconut Grove, going to meetings and trying to get a feel for the city. The twelve-step crowd in Miami was much more diverse and exciting than in Clearwater, and with an abundance of beautiful women. But I couldn't get over losing Laura. I thought of her constantly and ran up huge phone bills calling her. She was still friendly, and her soft Southern voice tore my heart as I clung to the phone.

Thankfully, there was no shortage of work for actors in Miami, if you didn't mind scrounging around. I played criminals in episodes of *America's Most Wanted* and in something called *Psychic Detectives*, plus half a dozen local TV commercials. I had parts in movies that were shot in English, dubbed into Spanish, and went straight to foreign markets. Who knows— maybe I was a star somewhere in Santo Domingo. It kept me busy but wasn't really going anywhere. After living around North Miami Beach for almost a year, and making a ton of money doing a few national TV commercials, I decided it was time to quit crying the blues. I bought a Mazda RX-7 and settled into a studio apartment on Ocean Drive and Seventh Street, in the deco district of South Beach. Might as well enjoy my new-found success.

In the mideighties this neighborhood was going through a cathartic transformation. It was the tail end of the dangerous years following the Mariel boatlifts, when the popularity of cocaine had attracted violent Cuban criminals who'd washed ashore in Florida after Castro emptied out his jails—the Marielitos. As the crime wave escalated, video surveillance cameras were installed over the intersections along Washington Avenue; elderly retirees were shuttled back and forth from supermarkets in paddy wagons. Because of the danger, local Miami residents were reluctant to venture south of Arthur Godfrey Road, and the stores in Lincoln Mall were going out of business.

By the time I arrived, those *Scarface* days were past. The locals, though, still hadn't gotten over their dread. South Beach was dead as a doornail. The upside was that a studio apartment on Ocean Drive overlooking the Atlantic Ocean could be had for as little as three hundred bucks a month.

With enough money, the texture of any neighborhood can be transformed. Real estate investors and developers saw the potential and were snapping up and renovating those old art deco hotels along the waterfront. One big catalyst for change was, of course, the smash-hit TV show *Miami Vice*. My timing as an aspiring actor had been impeccable.

When I arrived in 1985, during the second season of the show, the neighborhood was still in transition. The hotels along Ocean Drive and their patio cafés had been renovated and spruced up and the pink, lime, and mauve exteriors given a new coat of paint. But they were still deserted. Miamians had long memories. I found myself sitting all alone on the patio of the Edison, looking out across the beach as the sun came up out of the ocean, ordering my breakfast from a bored waitress, and reading over my latest "sides" from a *Miami Vice* script. I'd roll out of bed at the crack of dawn, pull on my swimming trunks, and stagger across Ocean Drive to the deserted beach and jump in the ocean for a swim. Then I'd sit on the sand to meditate and let the breeze dry me off. The only other people around at that time of day back then were an occasional wino or crackhead, catching a nap on the benches along Lummus Park that ran between Ocean Drive and the beach.

A busy crack house flourished just around the corner on Seventh Street. I'd wake up to loud, violent disputes between crackheads and tranny hustlers and their pimps. Glass from broken windows of vandalized cars and shattered wine bottles covered the streets, crunching underfoot like hail from Hell. I got a vicarious thrill out of watching it all, savoring memories of my old love of sleaze, but when I actually considered jumping into the fray it turned my stomach. Someone or something was looking out for me.

One night I woke to an ominous, rhythmic thumping on the street. I went out onto my balcony and in the predawn light I saw a ribbon of black-clad bodies, about five abreast, jogging in formation up Ocean Drive. They all wore black shorts, black T-shirts, and black sneakers. The officer in charge jogged near the head of the column and barked out the rhythm, the words indistinct but reminiscent of basic training.

> Yo left, yo left.
> We don't care if it's day or night.
> We don't care if you're black or white.
> Yo left, yo left.

Several weeks later I was looking out the side window of my apartment onto Seventh Street. A black van pulled up outside the crack house and half a dozen nightstick-wielding guys in ski masks jumped out and rushed into the place. Moments later they dragged the denizens cuffed and kicking out into the paddy wagon and whisked them off to the hoosegow. You'd think I'd have felt compassion for my old street brothers, but instead I applauded the hard-nosed-cop tactics. Those pathetic creatures would've been crawling over my balcony and ripping off my television in a heartbeat if the cops hadn't swept them off the street.

With that kind of concerted effort, it didn't take the cops long to clean up and restore a little safety to the neighborhood. Within a year, the popular News Café had opened on the ground floor of the building where I lived. Nightclubs like the China Club and Woody's, a Pepto-Bismol pink joint opened by Rolling Stones guitarist Ron Wood, had them lining up in the streets. Suddenly I was having a hard time getting the waitress's attention on the patio at the Cordova. Practically every actor and bullshit artist in Miami had a Screen Actors Guild card.

I still couldn't resist calling Laura to tell her how good things were going. Unawares, I'd been clinging to a wild hope that success, fame, and wealth would eclipse my having AIDS, or that they'd find a cure, and we'd somehow wind up back together. But as time went on she had less and less to say. One day she confessed that she'd dropped out of Christian college and had met a guy she really liked. I sensed impending betrayal—why the hell had she led me on, taking my calls, telling me how much she still cared for me, if only to blow me off for some other guy? Besides, I thought she'd gone back to the Bible Belt to become a sunbeam for Jesus, not fool around with men. For the next few months I threw myself into auditioning and working out with renewed vigor and determination. Whoever this small-town guy was that she'd met, by God, I'd make sure he paled next to my beauty and fame. But the next time I called Laura she said she was considering marrying her new boyfriend and went on about what a great guy he was.

Panic lit me up like a pinball machine. Hadn't she been listening to my success stories? I was healthier than I'd ever been. Who knows, maybe God had healed me, so there was no need for us to be apart. I was suddenly consumed with urgency to stop poor Laura from making a drastic mistake.

At that point sanity fled.

There was a scrambled rush for a flight to Virginia. A fire-engine-red Firebird was the only Avis rental available at the airport. I took it, then roared down the highway toward Laura's hometown. My mind was filled with a white noise that precluded the entrance of rational thought.

After a few phone calls, I tracked Laura down at her job and caught her coming out of her office into a grassy quadrangle between buildings.

She greeted me with amused warmth and surprising composure—she had no idea I was going to show up. She invited me over to her house for lunch. We watched a rerun of *Mayberry RFD*. I have no idea what we talked about. Afterward I drove around strange, deserted neighborhoods, squinting at street signs. I found myself standing in 7-Eleven parking lots, wondering what I'd stopped for. I don't remember eating. My hands trembled on the steering wheel and my heart pounded so hard in my chest I thought I was having a stroke. There were blank spots about whether I got a motel room or slept in the rental car.

The next day I found her again at a local meeting. Her boyfriend was with her and they held hands and nuzzled, while I considered methods of bodily harm.

I called her later and she again invited me to her house. It was night. She was alone. Desperately, I following her into her kitchen and tried to persuade her to give me another chance.

"But Steve, ah already told you I love this guy. I can't just jump up now and start in with you again." She was wearing a big gold ring on a chain around her neck, obviously a man's ring.

"What happened to the ring I gave you?" I asked, pointing at her bare hand. It was an elegant estate piece I'd bought at a jeweler's auction. I was really coming unglued. Treachery lurked in every nuance.

"It's at the jeweler's. I dropped it and the stone fell out."

What did she think I was—an idiot? "You traded in a priceless family heirloom for that vulgar bauble?"

Okay, so maybe I exaggerated the piece's pedigree, but her dubious explanation sounded smarmy and hollow. I couldn't believe this was the same girl I'd envisioned saving my soul, who'd sung so angelically from the choir at her church. My angel was slipping away into some humdrum existence where her beautiful voice would be wasted screaming at kids over a pot of boiling potatoes.

"C'mon, Laura, please," I begged cajolingly. When that got no response, I snapped at her, "Will you wake the hell up!" Which is what she should've been yelling at me. As my hopes evaporated, the room tilted and I thought I was going to pass out.

I tried to grab her, maybe to try and shake some sense into her, but she skipped out of my grasp and over to the stove, handily snatching up a huge iron skillet. We stood watching each other warily. I've never understood the dynamic that makes people lash out when they feel rejection. Perhaps I wanted to end it once and for all, do something so unforgivable that I'd never be tempted to call her or see her again. As I stepped toward her, she hefted the frying pan above her shoulder like a baseball bat, her lovely face a grim mask of courage, and it hit me how scary I must've looked. It was so ludicrous that we both almost laughed. My heart broke in that instant, realizing that she'd never be mine. The sound of doors slamming nearby gave me a moment of panic. Maybe her boyfriend had pulled up, or the neighbors had heard my antics and called the cops. I got in my car and hauled ass out of town. I was so distraught that later I couldn't remember if I drove all the way back to Miami or caught the plane.

Sometime later I called Laura's number a few times and unscrewed the mouthpiece so my presence on the line would be undetectable. And that was our last contact, me trembling with the phone pressed to my ear, and her voice softly repeating, in that lovely accent of hers, "Hello? Is anybody there?"

Fortunately, having a scary aspect of unpredictability was a bonus as an actor, and I continued to get cast in episodes of *Miami Vice*. Lori Wyman, once Dee Miller's assistant, took over casting the Miami people herself. Which was great for me, since Lori and I had become friends at an acting workshop. She was a blue-eyed, blond, younger version of my sister and familiar with my mercurial style from scene study and making passes at her. Lori would call me in for anything and the hell with continuity. Once I came on the set as a bearded CIA agent in a wheelchair, and Don said, "Christ, is this guy the only actor in Miami?" Sometimes I'd be a burned-out cop and sometimes a deranged criminal. Then I'd call my sister and let her know when those episodes would air so she could watch my rise to fame. My agent had forbid me to accept nonspeaking roles and, as a result, all the scenes I did were with the leads, Crockett (played by Don) and Tubbs (Philip Michael Thomas).

When I didn't have a TV or film gig lined up, I did theater around town and made the rounds of local acting workshops, staying loose and trying to keep my name in the game. I did some Brecht plays in a black-box theater in Coral Gables and joined a comedy-improv group called Mental Floss.

In spite of my fears, I remained in good health, working out and swimming every day, and occasionally doubted the validity of the blood tests I'd taken. But the terror was still there, hidden in the dark places inside me, keeping me ever more isolated, and even prompting me to seek out arcane healing techniques. I sat in a huge hall with Guru Maya and a hundred yogis when they blew into town, chanting, praying, and following my breath. I went to Buddhist temples and patronized macrobiotic restaurants, tried vitamin C overdoses, acupuncture, herbal remedies, visualization tapes, subliminal and self-hypnosis tapes (*"Do not listen to this tape while driving a car"*). Marlon Hoffman, an actor friend of mine, took me to something called "A Course in Miracles." After a guided meditation, we'd anonymously write our most dire fears on slips of paper or list people we wanted the group to pray for, then fold them up and pop them into a hat. The brother leading the meeting would then pick them out and read them aloud. There were strange and beautiful Haitian women who attended "Miracles" and gave it a voodoo texture that I liked, so I went back a few times. I also attended twelve-step meetings nearly every day. But I wasn't worried about relapse. I was going to meetings to flirt with the women and assuage the loss of Laura.

I recall that time in my life as being difficult, or tough, only in retrospect. Back then I was so caught up in the competitive acting scene, and had so much fun with all those healing techniques, walking around like some new-age guru (a persona that attracted troubled women), that I had little time to worry. There was much beauty—watching a fiery sun rear up out of the Atlantic Ocean in the morning, and then a gigantic, cheesy moon loom up from the same spot at night, gleaming postcardlike over the pastel buildings as I returned from a late-night swim.

Toward the end of the eighties I got cast in a movie called *Miami Blues*. It was based on a Charles Willeford cop thriller that Ron and I both loved. In the scene I did, my character is trying to rob the Big Fish restaurant on the Miami River (an actual popular spot) when an unhinged ex-con (played by Alec Baldwin) walks in and shoots me in the leg. In the credits I was listed as the Big Fish Robber. When we rehearsed the moment where I get shot, Baldwin, seeing my uncertainty, pulled me aside.

"Hey, Steve. Let me just throw this out there for you. Now, I myself have never been shot, so I have no idea what that feels like. But my father's been shot, and he told me what it feels like and how he reacted. Stop me if you don't want to hear this," he said and laughed.

Tak Fujimoto, the DP and famous cinematographer, walked up and aimed a light meter at my face. *Miami Vice* was one thing, but this Jonathan Demme coproduction was feature filmmaking on a whole other level.

"No, please," I told him. "Run it down." Baldwin was a rising star, so much so that the script (and later the editing) had been redone to make his deranged character the main focus of the movie rather than Hoke (played by Fred Ward), who was the cop hero in all the books. (Ron, when I told her about it, thought the casting was excellent.)

When we wrapped for the day, I thanked Alec for passing along the anecdote about his father's experience.

"Hey, what can I tell you?" he said, his voice a soft contrast to the loopy character he'd been playing all day. "Everything I've ever done as an actor has been driven by my feelings for my father."

I knew what he meant. If I thought of my father for two minutes, I'd either be angry, laughing, or in tears. Fathers, it seemed, leave their indelible marks on us all. One night I went to the Miami City Ballet production of *The Prodigal Son* choreographed by Edward Villela, once George Balanchine's favorite male dancer. The father-son dynamic was so moving I wept through the whole thing. I felt sorry for my sister that she hadn't appreciated how much Dad had loved her, how much like him she was, and how much of her goofy wit sprang from his army lingo and cornball tirades.

About a month later I flew up to New York to dub some dialogue I'd done in that movie—they had to clean up the language for a network TV release. After I left the sound studio I met Ron at the café in front of the public library on Fifth Avenue and Forty-second Street. We had lunch and, by way of apologizing for that time her jewelry got ripped off by my junky friends, I gave her a set of silver earrings. She immediately lit a cigarette and waved her hand, dismissing the lost items as inconsequential and forgotten. Then she started laughing and crying at the same time.

She wiped her eyes and, holding the earrings up to the sunlight, said, "These are the most beautiful things I've ever seen."

It was a precious moment but hardly scratched the surface of my regret.

Back in Miami, I got a call from Veronica asking me if I knew Donna Rice, the actress whose affair with Gary Hart was ruining his political career. Donna was, in fact, a member of one of the local acting workshops I attended on a regular basis—PAAF, which stood for Professional Actors

Association of Florida. I started right in telling my sister about it, happy that I could be helpful to her in some way.

"Ronnie, I can't believe you're asking me that. I was just in an acting workshop several nights ago where Donna Rice goes and—"

My sister cut me off. "Steve, do you mind if I record this?"

"No, of course not." She clicked her answering machine on RECORD and I proceeded to go on for about ten or fifteen minutes of gossipy, acting bullshit, interspersed now and then by a question from Veronica— What does PAAF stand for? What is AFTRA?

Several weeks later I got a call from a fact-check editor at the *New Yorker* who wanted to know if he could call the people I mentioned during that phone call to my sister and see if it was alright to use their names in an article. Sure, why not? The next week, in the May 18, 1987, issue, right after a "Notes and Comment" piece about the Iran-Contra hearings, the following article appeared in "The Talk of the Town" section, which in those days did not give the writers a byline.

PAAF

Politics and theatre: are they converging? This issue—the issue of the President as actor, the Iran-Contra hearings as divertissement, the campaign trail as sex-farce avenue (limited runs only)—is being widely debated in terms of its implications for politics. But what about the implications for theatre? Last week, one of our staff members placed a long-distance telephone call to Miami Beach, Florida, to her brother Steve, an actor, who has appeared on "Miami Vice." She asked him if he happened to know Donna Rice, the Miami actress who knows Gary Hart. Steve's answer may restore some balance to the debate:

"I can't believe you're asking me that. She's in my workshop. It's just amazing that you asked me that. I was just thinking about her on the way home. She's in a workshop with me. It's a PAAF workshop. PAAF is Professional Actors Association of Florida or something like that. It's one of those organizations that help protect the Florida actor and help encourage more business—you know, promoting producers of commercials to shoot down here. Like for example, they're talking about having a motion going down to rescind some proposed five-per-cent sales tax on productions in Florida, 'cause the reason people shoot so much here now is 'cause it's cheap. So anyway, PAAF does a lot of stuff like that—they're political, you know. . . . So this girl is a member of PAAF. You can become a member of PAAF only after you've done three principal characters a year in a SAG production or, I don't know, maybe AFTRA, too, which is American Federation of Television and Radio something or other, and so . . ."

And on and on I went for another fifteen minutes about local bullshit that had little or nothing to do with Donna Rice, other than the fact that nobody in the workshop knew who the hell she was, except Antony, who was supposed to do a scene with her for a showcase and was pissed off when she didn't show up. Reading this goofy "Talk" article by my sister now, seventeen years later, it seems even funnier, and I'm struck not just by her wit, but also by my own single-minded obsession with that whole acting scene.

"But anyway, nobody had any idea that she was politically motivated and interested in a candidate's campaign or whatever. And so this Monday night when we went to the workshop, it was like news to all of us—and it's funny, this woman Susan, who runs the workshop like a PTA meeting or something, started off with this long, gossipy tale about Oh, well, one of our members has really made it big, she's on national TV now. And everybody's saying, Who's she talking about? 'Cause at the time I don't think in the news it identified yet who this girl was who went to see Hart, you know. So everybody said, Oh, wow, somebody made it in a—At first I thought she was talking about my friend Richard, who just did a movie. Nobody knew who the hell she was talking about. So this woman went on about Donna being the one they're talking about in the news, and so finally everybody said O.K., enough already, you know, terrific, so the girl is getting fame, you know, fine, let's get on with the workshop, we've got scenes prepared, there's a showcase coming up. . . ."

And that pretty much summed it up—I didn't have time to worry about politics. The final paragraph in my sister's "Talk" article went like this:

"And Antony wanted to do this scene from 'The Woolgatherer' for this showcase. Now the girl isn't there this Monday night. So he comes in late and I'm filling him in on what happened to Donna. See, he'd lent me this scene from 'The Woolgatherer' 'cause he thought I would be good, too, as this wise-guy sort of character, and anyway I'd lost the scene, I misplaced it somewhere, so Antony was telling me, 'See, Steve, if you'd brought that scene last week to the workshop, the girl would still be here.' Anyway, and I've seen her on several commercial auditions, like at Dee Miller's. Dee's a casting director. She's the one who casts for 'Vice.' But they also cast commercials and stuff, and movies. Dee's one of the biggest casting directors in the area. So that's about all I can think of."

There are no plans to cancel the PAAF showcase.

Somewhere during the late eighties, my sister flew down to Miami to do a promotional reading from her new book, *Love Trouble Is My Business,* along with several other writers—Jay McInerney, who wrote *Bright Lights, Big City*, was one of them. The reading was held in some kind of outdoor stage in a shopping mall and I was awed by the huge, enthusiastic ovation when it came Veronica's turn to read. The stories in this second book of hers were possessed of a depth that some of the earlier ones lacked. Chip McGrath would one day say to me, "Her later stories were so brilliant that they went beyond humor and became . . . something else." But best of all in this new book were the short journal sketches that followed each story, describing how she came to write each one and the events and people that inspired her.

One piece, for example, titled "Remorse," was a goof on Major League Baseball's attempt to conduct urinalysis tests after the Keith Hernandez exposé about his cocaine use.

> Thanks to advances made in recent years by medical research surveys and major corporate personnel departments, we now know that the primary cause of human mistakes is a lack of self-respect, in turn caused by an impersonal society in which no one has cared enough to monitor our body chemistries on an individual, one-to-one level in a scientific setting.

In the journal passage afterward she wrote: "One problem I couldn't sidestep was submitting urinalysis jokes to the *New Yorker*. The idea was to show that the drug testing was just punitive and symbolic; but I initially got carried away and had urine samples being delivered to Commissioner Ueberroth at dinner. A note about the manuscript, from William Shawn, said 'No urine delivered to table.' It was always tempting to try changing material Mr. Shawn found objectionable to something *even worse* but worded in a way that he couldn't possibly object to; usually that would force solutions more creative than the original crudeness."

I could picture her sitting at her typewriter and cackling over that. There was nothing that she and Sandy Frazier enjoyed more than slipping something inappropriate, or even senseless, past the editors and seeing it in print. I could see why they missed Shawn—he'd been the father figure to defy, the standard against which they sharpened their edge.

I can't remember which story she read in Miami that day. All I remember was shuffling around the outskirts of the crowd, mostly women, with tears running down my face, so proud of my sister's courage to get up in front of such an audience. I bumped into my friend Marlon, who asked me what I looked so sad about. I should be happy and proud for my sister, he said.

When I finally caught up to her I gushed, "Jeez, Ron, I can't believe it, the way you pulled off that reading in front of all those people. You were terrific and the crowd loved it. I'm a little awestruck."

"Oh, please," she said. "I hate doing those kinds of promotional readings. I only agreed to do this as an excuse to come down to Miami and see you in a play. I'm starving, so let's get the hell out of here. I want to see South Beach where you live and maybe get a hotel over there. James is coming down for a couple days, so it's got to be a place with a television."

Ron had told me about her boyfriend James Hamilton, a photographer for the *Village Voice*. But it struck me as odd—a guy comes to Miami to shack up with his girlfriend on the most romantic beachfront in the United States and he's worried about a television? I shrugged it off. What did I know about relationships anyway?

"No problem. C'mon, I got my car here." I'd wrecked the Mazda by then and was driving a vintage Plymouth Valiant that I'd bought in pristine condition from some old lady.

We walked a ways in silence, jostling through the crowd, and I kept sneaking looks at her. She carried a small travel bag over her shoulder and looked radiant one moment, then all business and slightly troubled the next, probably about the hotel room accommodations. Passing clouds briefly blotted out the sun. A voice in my head said, *Hey, Ron, I think I'm dying of AIDS.* Then I quickly snuffed it out. How could I lay that on her at a time like this? It was a gorgeous Miami afternoon, heightened by the romance of strutting through the crowd with my successful big sister. We were both at the top of our games and it was a moment that I would cherish for many years.

Later that night she came to see me in *American Buffalo*, which Marlon,

Larry Silverberg, and I were doing in a theater in downtown Miami that got me my Actors Equity card. She made a much bigger fuss over my accomplishment than I ever did over hers. Larry and I took Ron out to dinner after the play, and Larry, who I'd been studying the Meisner Technique with at the Coconut Grove Playhouse, got her so interested in those acting exercises that she took a couple classes in New York. She then went around the *New Yorker* trying to get guys like Philip Roth to do them with her. The interest that my sister took in my life and acting then was incredibly dear to me—she'd certainly never been much impressed with Record Steve's shoplifting expertise.

I'd given Ronnie a set of keys to my apartment on Ocean Drive in case she needed anything, and when I came home the next day I found her sitting on my couch, bent over and her shoulders shaking as she listened to a tape recording I'd made for her. She'd been asked to submit a story for a collection of humor, the topic being something like "summer vacations from college." She'd called me from New York and asked if I remembered anything from her vacations from Penn. I told her I'd think about it, then rode around Miami from casting to casting, ad-libbing bits of zany dialogue I remembered between me, her, and Dad into a little handheld tape recorder. When she first arrived in Miami I'd given her the recording, and when she looked up at me as I walked into my apartment, I noticed tears running down her face.

"Hey, Ron. What's the matter?"

She just shook her head and I could see that she was laughing mostly, but crying too in little fits and starts. "This is the funniest thing I've ever heard," she managed to say, and then gave me the strangest, pleading look. "Steve, you've got to let me use this for a story."

Of course I agreed, happy that she'd found it helpful. She later typed out the dialogue word for word like a play, and sold it not only to the humor collection but to the *New Yorker* as well.

STEVE: Hey, Dad, didn't we use to have a couple bowling balls?

DAD: What do you want with bowling balls in this heat?

RONNIE: Maybe they're in the garage.

DAD: Don't go in the garage now. What do you want bowling balls for at this time of night?

STEVE: Ronnie has to bowl.

DAD: Aw, what are you talking about?

RONNIE: We're just going bowling.

DAD: What do you mean, bowling? Do you know what time it is?

STEVE: It's only nine o'clock.

DAD: Nine o'—Jesus, what's the matter with you? Your mother's already asleep.

RONNIE: Gee, then I guess we can't bowl in the house. We'll have to go to the bowling alley.

DAD: Nine o'clock at night people don't go bowling. Look at it, it's dark out.

RONNIE: I thought the car had headlights.

DAD: You don't even have bowling shoes. What are you gonna do, bowl in those? You can't bowl in sneakers, you gotta have shoes.

STEVE: Look, Dad, they rent the shoes.

DAD: *Rent?* What, you're gonna wear somebody else's shoes? . . . What do you want to go bowling for? All of a sudden you've got this big interest in bowling now all of a sudden.

STEVE: Dad, look—Ronnie couldn't pass her grades in college because of her phys ed credit, so now she has to bowl because she didn't want to go in the water and swim.

DAD: Jesus Christ, do you know how much a bowling ball weighs? How is Ronnie gonna go bowling? She looks like a good meal of corned beef and cabbage would stand her on her feet.

RONNIE: Look, all I want to do is graduate from college.

STEVE: Dad, leave her alone. She's upset enough that she doesn't want to put her head under water.

DAD: What's that got to do with anything?

STEVE: You know, it's a swimming credit she couldn't get.

DAD: Swimming—all swimming is is relaxing. In the water. That's all it is. Swimming is relaxing. You put your head in, you relax, that's it. Otherwise you sink like a stone. Tense up in the water and you can forget about it.

RONNIE: Oh, so, Dad, wait a minute, when's the last time I saw you swimming? You go out there and wade.

STEVE: Come on, Ronnie, don't pick on him.

RONNIE: You *wade* in there, in your shorts—

DAD: Get out of here. You're gonna tell me about swimming? You've been in college too long, that's what your problem is. Then you come here and tell me about bowling and swimming.

RONNIE: This is just really upsetting me. If I don't fulfill this credit—Oh, forget
    it. Forget about it. I'm not graduating from college. Just forget about it.
    We're not going bowling.

DAD: Oh, you're not graduating from college now, huh? Now it's my fault
    you're not graduating from college because you don't have bowling shoes.

When that piece was published she split the money she made with
me. She said she tried to get my name on the byline with hers but was told
by her editors that it would be too confusing. I could've cared less at that
point about a writing credit or even the money. It was just gratifying to see
the things I told her in print, and it helped to lift my sorrow about how I'd
treated her.

On the other hand, she used everyone around her, even her boyfriends, as grist for her pieces, and I didn't like sharing the spotlight. I was
having lunch with Ronnie one day in a South Beach diner and she showed
me some photographs that Hamilton had done. I had to admit, the guy
was good. But Ron expressed impatience with his seeming reluctance to
try to move beyond a staff position at the *Village Voice*, and I was startled
at the frustration in her voice. When Hamilton finally arrived in Miami, I
began to understand why they got on so well. He was so laid-back and de-
void of affect that he seemed a perfect counterpoint to my sister's control-
ling and opinionated personality. Here was a guy she wasn't likely to drive
out of her life. For some reason, though, I never felt comfortable about
James Hamilton, but I dismissed it. Their relationship had been the fuel
for some of the funniest stories in my sister's new book, and I was jealous.
When Ron and James went back to New York, I was relieved to see them
go. It was hard enough trying to get close to my elusive sister, but with her
equally baffling boyfriend around and the way they communicated on
some unspoken level, it was impossible.

Though I found Ron's boyfriend mysterious, I had good reason to be
deceptive myself. One night after Ron had gone back to New York, I
walked into a twelve-step meeting and encountered a guy who was dying
of AIDS. He had that wasted, haunted, hollow-eyed look and clearly
didn't have long to go. There was a swath of empty tables and seats all
around him. Everyone acted like he was invisible, while he sat there weeping. After the meeting I took him out to coffee but didn't tell him what we

had in common. No way was I exposing myself to that kind of treatment. Later, one of my friends from the meeting came up to me.

"Hey, Steve. You don't want to be hanging out with that guy. People will start thinking *you* got the monster."

It was the late eighties, and there was a mounting hysteria and ignorance about AIDS that was spreading faster than the disease. Many suspected the virus was airborne and could be transmitted by being in close proximity to someone infected, or that you could catch it from physical contact, like shaking hands. Later it was shown that the virus needs a point of entry into the bloodstream, like a transfusion, sharing needles, or unprotected rough sex that causes bleeding, in order to be transmitted. But that was only after years of research, and in the meantime thousands suffered needlessly as they faded away. Silence, staying fit, and avoiding intimacy seemed my best defenses. I'd lived a life of deception before and felt confident that my robust health would stand up under casual scrutiny.

My longing for physical affection, though, was overwhelming, and there were a few times, despite the terror of anyone finding out that I was infected, or the danger of my infecting them, that I gave in to it. Afterward I'd be ravaged by remorse at having endangered those women in spite of the precautions we took.

Somewhere around 1990, I was invited to take part in a play, a rehash of Sam Shepard's *The Tooth of Crime*, that my friend Marlon was hot to do. The production started in a South Carolina playhouse and somehow got booked for a month or so in the basement theater of a Greenwich Village bistro. Miami Beach was getting too crowded—by this point you had to crawl over coaxial cables and production crews on a commercial shoot to get from Ocean Drive to the beach—and I was eager to see what it would feel like to be back in the big city. My sister was excited when she heard that I was coming to New York in a play. She said she'd be staying all summer in the Catskills, but that she'd come down to the city and see the play, hang out with me, and catch up with the latest developments in my rise to fame.

I jumped through that window with both feet.

part six

scrapple in the apple

chapter 18

"**G**et this," Marlon said to me as we drove north through Virginia. "One day Lee sends me out for coffee and I bump into Pacino coming in the front door of The Actors Studio. Hey, Al, I said. I'm Marlon Hoffman, big fan of yours. He jumped back like I'd scared the hell out of him, scuttled past me with his eyes smoldering and shit. Haw! Whatta goof. The dude was *in*tense. But those dogs have had their day. Wait'll they get a load a you and me."

It was 1990 and Marlon and I were driving from Miami to New York in his Volkswagen camper, almost identical to the one Dad once gave me. We'd enjoyed packed houses at a South Carolina playhouse doing the Shepard play. But now we'd be playing the West Village in front of a much hipper audience, and smack dab in the middle of my old stomping grounds. As we drove, Marlon related amusing anecdotes from when he'd been a caretaker at The Actors Studio in the days of Lee Strasberg, bumping into stars like Pacino. Eventually he got around to his father, whom he mimicked with the same stentorian tones as he did Strasberg.

"He drives me out to this construction site of a shopping mall. I'm maybe five years old. We get outta the car and he starts waving his arms around and goes, 'Alright, how many square feet you got there?' I'm looking at this huge empty field. 'Damnit, I asked you a question, boy. I said how many square feet? And stop blubbering. Use the brains God gave you. Don't you realize what this is? You're looking at your future—real estate!' "

No wonder Marlon was an actor.

On the last leg of the journey up the Jersey Turnpike, the familiar skyline of Manhattan hove into view. Memories of the old days flitted through my head: approaching the tunnels into the city with Nick after five days boosting on the road; unloading and counting the records at Max's and jamming fistfuls of hundred-dollar bills into our pockets; next stop, Sonny St. Claire's crib or wherever my connection happened to be; and finally nodding out in a hotel room to *The Late Late Show* or listening to Chet Baker with a cigarette burning through my fingers. My selective memory always glossed over the turmoil, and my life back then seemed as predictable as Swiss clockwork.

But when we came out of the Holland Tunnel onto Canal Street there was none of the glitzy sheen of my erstwhile life, when I'd viewed the traffic lights and neon business signs through a prism of anticipation—the dependable rush of a shot of smack. Now the streets looked dingy and flat, the future tainted with uncertainty. Homeless men lurked in the shadows. My new actor's persona was a thin disguise, and the squeegee guy who wiped off our windshield leered at me with a knowing glint in his eyes— Welcome back, babe.

The rheumy-eyed aspect of these squeegee guys brought me back to my obsession with HIV. I'd been hearing a lot of new information. I realized now that the attack of shingles I'd suffered during that dinner-theater production of *The Music Man* was an indication of a disrupted immune system. If my health fell apart and cut short my acting career, I could end up out there with a squeegee and a cardboard box—or worse.

"Hey, Marlon," I said, pointing out a greasy dim sum diner on Mott Street. "See that place over there? I once scored for some Chinese rocks in there off a guy named Petey Delaw."

"Petey what?"

"De-law. He got the moniker 'cause he looked like an undercover narc in his sunglasses and dated wardrobe. So I go home and cook up the Chinese rocks. Never had this stuff before but the smell was awful familiar."

"Did it get you high?"

"When I geezed it, it made my ears buzz so loud I couldn't be sure, so I went back a couple hours later and scored some more. Turns out it was kitty litter."

Marlon laughed. "Whoa!" But his laughter was uneasy, and he shot me a look, like—Who the hell *is* this dude?

The entire cast of our play was quartered in a railroad flat in Hell's Kitchen. After we dumped our belongings on a couple mattresses on the floor, I went out for coffee and doughnuts at a Roy Rogers or Krispy Kreme I knew was right around the corner. It was a place where I used to score for Dilaudids, an opiate derivative that had risen to popularity during the junk panic in the seventies: Brother Fats would steer me over there after we'd cruised Tiffany's and Baccarat's for cut-glass figurines and other negotiable objects; then west through the diamond district where we sold them to bearded guys with yarmulkes on their heads and a jeweler's loupe in one eye; and once we got the cash we'd kept going west into Hell's Kitchen to score—bing bang boom, a nice orderly routine.

At first I couldn't find the doughnut shop but then discovered it had been renovated by another fast food chain. None of the old crowd was in evidence. I picked up some sandwiches and headed back to the railroad flat.

The play we were doing was booked to run for several weeks in the basement of a bistro in the West Village. Shepard's *The Tooth of Crime* has an allegorical thru-line—new versus old—like Westerns where the tired old gunslinger faces down the eager young hotshot in the final shoot-out. Only in *Tooth* it's done musically—old blues singer dukes it out with punk rocker or gangsta-rapper. Actually, I loved the play, which can be a compelling and entertaining piece of theater but a tough gig to pull off under any circumstances. Rarely have I seen it attempted. Ours turned out to be a less-than-happy production. I was embarrassed to be a part of it and was glad it was hidden down in a basement where hardly anybody came.

Of course, one reason the production was so bad was that Marlon and I, competitive as actors anyway, got out of control, and we didn't have a strong director to rein us in. One night Marlon (in the punk-rocker antagonist's role) started bringing a gun onstage with him and waving it around. I strongly objected to this and the next time he did it I tore my shirt off in the middle of a scene and screamed at him.

"So shoot me! Gaw head, just fucking shoot me!"

Marlon looked sadly at his prop gun, shrugged his shoulders, and walked offstage. As he stepped to the wings, he turned to the audience and said, "I'll be back when Cheyenne calms down."

But the night my sister and two of her friends came, they guffawed loudly at just the right times. Every time I went onstage, I kept sneaking glimpses into the audience. A tall blond woman with soulful blue eyes (must be Brooke, who Ron had told me was an actress) turned to my sister during one of my scenes and went, Wow! My sister smirked and laughed. Good ol' Ron. To me she was the toast of the town and her presence was tremendously reassuring. When I was offstage I'd peek through the curtains and spy on her. Hamilton was with them, and Ron looked so at ease she might've been sitting on the couch in her apartment. She was almost fifty but still had that lean, laid-back, college girl physicality. It gave me a warm feeling of familiarity to watch her toss her head back when she laughed, and I could hardly wait for the damn play to be over so I could go talk to her.

After the show we walked down Greenwich Avenue searching for a place to eat, and I kept peeking at my reflection in store windows, wondering at the too-eager chump who looked back. Ron and Brooke were going on about which scenes and performances they liked best (mine, of course). Brooke, who was a pro, knew how desperately actors hungered for praise, but it didn't help. It only increased my feelings of being a bumpkin in a bad play and my envy of these savvy New Yorkers. James, thankfully, was more reserved and kept trying to turn the focus to where we were going to eat. I hated to admit it, but at times I genuinely admired the guy—he was unflappable, and I could see why Ron loved him.

At one point I turned to my sister and said, "Hey, Ron, those white dinner jackets we wore in that doo-wop number? That was my idea. I bought them at a thrift shop called Cheap Jacks." Brooke and Veronica had agreed that that was their favorite scene.

James came to a sudden stop, the way street conversationalists stop suddenly to emphasize a point, which caused the rest of us to stop and look at him.

"*Ron?*" he said to my sister. "Your brother calls you *Ron?*" He laughed, a short bark of disbelief.

My sister just shrugged and nodded in assent, and we all continued walking down Greenwich Avenue. At one point my sister wanted to know if such and such a Mexican restaurant would be too crowded.

"It shouldn't be, Ron," said James. "Not on a—"

My sister cut him off. "No, James. Only my brother can call me that."

Immediately I felt like the savviest person on the block. Veronica could do that for me sometimes.

Sitting in that Mexican restaurant on Greenwich Avenue with Veronica, Brooke, and James, I was getting a peek at this new family my sister had gathered around her over the years. Although I'd met Hamilton briefly in Miami, I didn't really know what to make of him. His style was typical urban-ninja-photographer—black boots, black jeans, and black polo shirts—and he was quick on the uptake. Like any brother, I was highly critical of guys who might be boffing my sister, but I kept my mouth shut. I was certainly no genius about relationships.

Brooke was splendid, a big-boned gal with blond curls and a warm face that changed expression abruptly. She gave me her phone number and offered to introduce me to her theatrical agent as well as her commercial agent, which I later took her up on. She said she could introduce me to casting directors for different TV shows.

By the time the waiter brought us our food, I'd come to the decision to stay in New York after the play rather than move back to Miami. In a burst of magnanimity, my sister volunteered to let me stay in her apartment. She said she'd be at her place in the Catskills all summer anyway, a house that she'd bought with the money we made from selling our father's house in Florida.

Starting in on my burrito, I made a conscious effort to eat with only my right hand and keep the left one under the table. The fingernails on my left hand were getting overrun with a crusty fungal infection. Like my brief case of shingles, it was another clue that my immune system was breaking down and no longer capable of fighting off such things. I pushed it out of my mind.

When the play closed, Brooke's agents kept me busy running around town on auditions, and Ronnie's cozy apartment was in an ideal location. I found a whole slew of twelve-step meetings in the neighborhood, and a stroll through Central Park brought me in easy walking distance of castings. A little of the old cockiness returned and put the cut back in my strut. The meetings in New York were often full of celebrities from the show-biz world and I'd scan the room for casting directors and people who could move my career forward. Record Steve was history. I scored a casting for an industrial film for Bell Telephone Company that got me a few days' work. I was on my way.

Ronnie came back from the Catskills for a few days to meet with her agent.

"Hey, Ron," I asked her. "Isn't he the guy you told me about when I first got sober?"

"Yeah. Want to meet him? I told him I might bring you along."

I wasn't disappointed. Wylie was lean as a hound and seemed an old-school New Yorker in his dark suit, crisp white shirt, and blond hair brushed back off a receding hairline. His relaxed posture as he slouched behind his desk couldn't hide his quickness—this guy didn't miss much. We were sitting there chatting in his office when something he said—comments about clients he'd worked with, like William Burroughs, and a book of photographs he showed me by his friend Larry Clark, homoerotic shots of speed freaks in Tulsa—struck a familiar chord in me.

"Hey, Andrew," I said. "I used to hang out with characters like that back in the sixties and seventies. Guys like Rotten Rita, Billy Buffalo, and the Turtle—guys who were so far out there they made *me* look like a citizen."

Andrew laughed. "I don't believe it! You know the Turtle?"

Ron's jaw dropped.

"He was just here in my office a couple of months ago," Andrew went on, "trying to borrow money to go to Israel."

"No shit."

"Yeah. The cops were after him and I said, Stanley, you can't be calling me, I'm straight. But I put him in a limousine and sent him off to JFK and he went to Israel."

The Turtle, a charming but often cranky little guy, was an East Village character and an artist who might've done more with his talent had he not also been a dedicated junky and speed freak. His apartment on East Second Street had been a hangout during the seventies for nefarious charac-

ters that had spun off of Andy Warhol's crew, and Wylie, apparently, had
been among them.

When my sister and I finally left, she couldn't believe that Andrew
had sat there for a half hour chatting about those wacky characters.

"Christ," she said. "People have a hard time getting Andrew's attention
for five minutes, and he sat around bullshitting with you for a half hour."

"I'm sorry. I wasn't even thinking that you two probably had business
to talk about."

"You've got to be kidding me. What could be more important than
Rotten Rita and the Turtle? I wouldn't have missed that conversation for
anything in the world."

I enjoyed the quips and picked up on the amusement behind her
feigned annoyance. Walking down Fifty-seventh Street with her I felt the
same closeness we'd had walking up Nedro Avenue on the way to the
public school yard—even as kids there was something romantic about
hanging out with Ron. Now she was letting me into her world in a way
that she'd never done before, not with anybody in our family. I prayed
that I wouldn't disappoint her—she needed people around her just then that
she could trust.

Hidden underneath my sister's cavalier attitude, work troubles
loomed. Her increasing estrangement from the *New Yorker*, which I knew
nothing about then, might have made her more available, but those problems were much too complicated and she much too proud to be dumping
them on her younger brother. Right about this time, something happened
that made my sister feel that her original editor and mentor, Roger Angell,
had betrayed her. The way the process for selecting pieces for the magazine apparently worked was this: A submitted manuscript would circulate
around and the editors would type out a little note expressing their opin-
ions of it (all off-the-record, mind you) before it went up to the editor in
chief. Roger had typed out a comment about a piece by Ron, something
like—What are we going to do with Veronica's piece, I mean, is it worth it
to us to go through this, to take the heat? Roger was not her editor at that
point. He'd addressed his comments to Chip McGrath, who was her editor, and felt secure in the tradition of comments being off-the-record. The
piece went up to Bob Gottlieb and they bought it. But then Bob showed
her Roger's opinion! Ron had nothing but ice for Roger after that, and

Roger was furious at Gottlieb for doing things that went totally against the rules. He tried to make it up to Ron, but she didn't easily forgive or forget—just ask Dad.

Christ, what a pack of screwballs. I wish I'd known about all this. I could've told Ron how clearly self-defeating her reactions were. And since my sister had made her colleagues at the *New Yorker* her new family, it was no surprise at all that she'd get cranky—that sort of intimate dynamic always drove Ron up the wall. Being rejected by a magazine is one thing, but to be rejected by your family is infinitely worse. And if Bob Gottlieb had transgressed "the rules" it hadn't bothered Ron's writing. He apparently possessed the same love of the subversive that Ron did, and under his regime she was writing her best stuff. Perhaps I couldn't apply such wisdom to my own predicaments, but other people's problems seemed like utter foolishness.

When Ronnie used her wit as a weapon she was at her best, but her uncompromising attitude was working against her. She'd begun to hole up in her apartment or her house in the Catskills, always one to cherish privacy, and devoured everything in print, writing and editing only as the mood suited her. And so it also seemed to suit her mood to have me around, with my irreverent naïveté about that whole literary scene.

Rehashing the old days with Wylie had tweaked my curiosity—whatever had become of those characters I'd known? It was now the nineties and decades since I'd seen any of them. I wondered what they were up to, what they looked like now, or even if they'd survived. I took a subway down to the East Village one day, curious just to see what the old neighborhood looked like. I could scarcely believe the change.

The stretch of Second Avenue between St. Marks Place and Fifth Street had once been a hip stroll for artists, druggies, and punk rockers. I remembered the New York Dolls clowning around for their fans on a photo shoot in front of Gem Spa candy store on the corner; jumping in a cab with Dolls' guitarist Johnny Thunders in search of a connection; and a brief fling with a sexy black girl who sang in Debbie Harry's old girl group, the Stilettos. I'd been a fixture, watching with a fond eye as the crowd went from long hair and bell-bottoms to buzz cuts and skin-tight jeans, from Jimi Hendrix to the Talking Heads.

I'd been broke, flush, hungry, nodded out, and chased by Hell's Angels on this piece of real estate, and it was as familiar to me as an old lover's caress.

Now it had turned into a beggar's market, like a slum in Calcutta. Homeless characters laid out a vast array of rubble for sale on moth-eaten blankets—everything from piles of coat hangers and doorknobs to pieces of electrical wiring, worn-out shoes, and piles of moldy, dog-eared magazines. You literally had to step over and around this rubbish to move down the block.

A thrill of anticipation ran through me as I strolled east toward old junk neighborhoods around Alphabet City. My jaw dropped when I saw Tompkins Square Park looking like a camping ground for the homeless. Makeshift tents made out of blankets and pieces of old clothing covered the grassy sections from corner to corner. Electricity was wired into some of the more elaborate hootches from power sources at the bottom of streetlamps—winos sipped pints of Thunderbird and watched soap operas on discarded televisions. These characters were dug in deep. A self-respecting hipster from the old days wouldn't be caught dead in such a scene. Gone were the young, aspiring musicians, practicing Eric Dolphy riffs on a flute early in the morning. Instead, bottom-feeding crackheads and penny-ante dealers scuttled from hootch to hootch like cockroaches. Bleeding-heart social service workers trucked in hot meals, and the riffraff lined up like depression-era soup lines. Carelessly discarded disposable syringes, wine bottles, and crack pipes littered the ground. There was a stench of human waste, and even the squirrels seemed to have moved out. Whoever still remained of my old crowd had gone underground in the face of the crack epidemic that was now in full swing.

I recognized a guy on First Avenue from the old days whose handle was Black Bobby. He was wearing a raincoat and carrying a stack of LPs under his arm. This guy had once tried to take me off at knifepoint, and he was reluctant to get within arm's reach. When I got him calmed down, he started filling me in on who had survived, and who hadn't. Black Bobby knew them all.

Sonny St. Claire had died in Bellevue some years back of AIDS complications, with no friends or family to mourn his passing. Jimmy Porter, one of the most notorious burglars on the Lower East Side, purposely took an overdose in a Midtown hotel one night after he found out he was

HIV positive. Victor Ortez, another old thoroughbred, seemed to whither of old age right before everybody's eyes. Turned out he'd had AIDS too.

I remembered the night at Sonny's place when Victor told us about being locked up in the Tombs with Chet Baker. The hacks had let Baker bring his mouthpiece to his cell, up on the seventh floor where they put all the dope fiends. At night, Vic told us, Chet would have the whole tier in tears, playing so sweet with only his hands cupped around that mouthpiece that Dizzy Gillespie had given him on their first gig together.

Far as Black Bobby knew, the Turtle was still around. Liz, one of our old connections, was over on East Sixth Street but had stopped dealing since the feds busted her old man. BJ the Queen of Crime was still killin' 'em in bookstores, keeping the street-vendors' tables up and down St. Marks Place stocked with art books, and Shoppin' Bag Billy had vanished, maybe gone out to the West Coast to try his luck.

God knows where the rest of that crew ended up—Abdul Wadu, Sometime Annie, Rotten Rita, Billy Buffalo, No-Cotton John, Junky George. Some may have survived, but the list of junkies I'd hung out with and who ended their lives in jail, a nuthouse, or an AIDS ward, or were left to die on a rooftop after an overdose, is long and unheralded.

"So, Bobby," I said, pointing at his armful of records. "You pick up my old hustle or what? Figured that was played out by now."

"Nah. I never had the nerve for boosting. I get these a buck apiece, you know, remainders. Sell 'em in bars and shit. Ain't much but it beats a blank. I got off the smack years ago and don't need much to get by. What're you up to these days?"

"Nothin' much. Gotta run, kid."

"Watch out for the bogeyman, Rec. They ain't many of us left."

I flagged a cab and left the neighborhood, feeling somehow disappointed, but relieved to see that there wasn't anything there for me anymore.

chapter 19

Back uptown at my sister's apartment, I found Ronnie sitting on the floor with the phone wedged against her shoulder, mumbling softly into the mouthpiece as she laid out tarot cards, "Yeah, uh-huh, uh-huh, yeah . . ." It was odd. I'd never seen her looking so preoccupied or spaced-out. She was chain-smoking, staring at the cards, and mumbling monosyllables on and on into the phone. I went out for something to eat and when I came back she was still at it. I had an image of my sister as a writer and editor who functioned at an extremely high level, but in the months that I'd been staying at her apartment I hadn't seen her go to work much at all. She was either up at her house in the Catskills or doing this thing on the phone with the tarot cards. It was troubling, but I wasn't sure how to broach the topic.

One day I said to her, "Hey, Ron. My being here isn't keeping you from working is it?"

She laughed it off. "Not at all, Steve. I go to the office from time to time to do some editing. This is really totally okay your being here. I wouldn't have it any other way. It's such a bang for me to see you going out on auditions and stuff. So don't worry. I'm still writing, and the *New*

Yorker still gets first dibs on my stories. By the way, want to go dancing tonight with me and my friend Dita?"

Apparently, Dita was the person on the other end of all those phone conversations and now I'd finally get to meet her. That night, as we walked down the hallway to Dita's apartment after getting buzzed into her building, I saw a cute little blond step out into the light, shielding her eyes.

"Hi, Veronica. Is that your brother?"

"Hi, Dita," my sister said. "Yeah, this is Steve. Steve this is my friend Dita."

We shook hands, and Dita looked me up and down. I was still tan from Florida and I didn't look half bad in my latest thrift-shop find—a gray sharkskin suit with narrow fifties lapels.

"Jesus Christ, Veronica. You didn't tell me he looked like Richard Widmark. No wait, not Widmark, somebody . . . Dan Duryea, maybe. I'll think of it in a minute. But you mean to tell me that you're letting this guy *sleep* at your apartment? I mean, he's *living* with you? What're you, nuts?"

My sister laughed. "Dita, he's my *brother*, for God's sake."

"Yeah, but what about all that stuff you told me?"

"That's ancient history. Now are we going dancing, or are we going to stand here all night and debate my brother's housing arrangements?"

Dita gave me another appraising once-over. "Can you dance?"

I gave my sister a look like—What, is this broad crazy?

"Sure he can dance," my sister said.

"Well, you know," Dita said, tossing her head, cocking one hip, and smirking with great severity, "the salsa bands where we're going tonight are the best in town, and the dancing is done with *huge* enthusiasm."

"Enthusiasms, enthusiasms," I deadpanned from De Niro's monologue in *The Untouchables*. "What are mine. What is that which brings me joy."

My sister could do ten minutes on De Niro monologues. She roared with laughter. I didn't care if they were doing the Watusi where we went that night, I knew we'd have a good time. Dita looked puzzled and a little worried, but she was Veronica's friend. If Veronica was having a good time then what's the diff? She shrugged and grabbed her coat and off we went.

Dita was right about the enthusiasm. If Broadways was a pickup joint or a coke spot, you could not have gotten that impression from the night I was there. Everybody was there to dance and get down with the band, which was one of the best salsa bands I'd heard, and having lived around so many Cubans in Miami I'd heard quite a few. When Ron and Dita made their way past the bar and out onto the dance floor, they were both transformed and it was a delight to see this wild side of my sister emerge. They must have danced with a dozen guys before we left, and I felt completely flat-footed watching the smooth, macho moves these guys made as they took Dita and my sister through their paces. I wandered over to a smaller dance floor by the bar where it wasn't so crowded and tried to study a few guys that were putting on sort of an exhibition, showing off for their friends with a studied deliberateness. I started mimicking one of the guys pretty good, when I found myself surrounded by a small crowd of my own admirers, among them Dita and Veronica. Dita immediately joined me, but she was intimidating as a dance partner and I quickly lost my newfound skills.

In the taxi on the way home, Ronnie and Dita filled me in with stories of salsa trips they'd made, famous Cuban musicians they partied with, and one memorable vacation where they'd hung out with Johnny Ventura in Santo Domingo. Clearly, these two had great affection for each other. And here I thought my sister was so cerebral.

At some point during her last years at the *New Yorker*, my sister had a birthday party at a Mexican restaurant in the Village. I think it was her fiftieth, which would have made me forty-seven and change. She was in a strange mood and drinking more than she usually did, probably due to some romance that wasn't going her way. Whoever was playing the music put on a series of Motown tunes, like the Supremes, that had a good jitterbug beat, so I got Ron to dance with me to see if it would cheer her up. I'd almost forgotten how good she could jitterbug, and as we circled and swung around like in the old days at Heidelberg High, I told her as much.

"Of course I'm good," she quipped. "I mean, we were raised in Philly, for God's sake."

I caught her in my arms after a series of turns and twirls, and for a moment, with her body pressed lightly against mine, I felt a self-conscious burn around my ears that was vaguely incestuous, seeing how much sexier and better looking she'd gotten. What I wouldn't give, I thought, to have a chick like this. I wanted to shake her and tell her to snap out of her sulky mood. Here she was, looking better than she'd ever looked, surrounded by an adoring crowd of friends and loved ones, and she was sulking. I pointed this out to her, but with little effect.

Well, let her mope if that's what pleased her. I was familiar with the pleasures of a good sulk, and happy for the opportunity to see how well loved she was.

Although Brooke's introduction into the local acting scene had helped get me started, my ability to make a living as an actor came to a screeching halt. This was a whole new crowd and I was an unknown entity. The actors who'd paid their dues locally were getting the work, and I was no longer a big fish in a small pond like in Miami.

One day I was sitting in the waiting room of a casting office with some other actors, waiting to be called to audition for a commercial, and the actor Robert Vaughn walked in. He went and sat in the far corner of the room and made an effort to avoid eye contact with anybody. I couldn't believe it. I felt so bad for Robert Vaughn, who I'd loved in movies like *The Magnificent Seven*. His performance as the gunslinger that lost his nerve was riveting and I used to mimic him note for note. Seeing him here was the most depressing thing that had happened to me so far and I hoped that we weren't up for the same job. My early successes in Miami had spoiled me. I thought I was a new, edgy actor, the next John Cassavetes— and here I was competing for TV commercials with the Man from U.N.C.L.E.?

I was gradually running out of money, having squandered much of what we made from the sale of our father's house. I'd been living the high life in Miami, had bought a sports car (which I'd wrecked), and had eaten in expensive sushi joints every night, convinced that I wouldn't live long.

During my first year back in New York I schlepped around from one casting call to the next, mostly for commercials, trying desperately to keep alive the diminishing illusion that salvation, in the form of fame and fortune, lurked just around the corner. My days were spent roaming through office buildings in Midtown searching for the audition room.

On one occasion I found a casting director setting up a video camera to record all the hopeful actors. He glanced briefly at my headshot but never made eye contact.

"Alright, Steve. It is Steve, right?" He had that sound in his voice like, Hey, I'm gonna see another fifty guys after you leave, pal, so do your thing and don't let the door hit you in the ass on the way out.

"Yeah."

"So how do you want to try this?" he asked as he adjusted the camera lens. "You want to, uh, maybe put a Seinfeld sort of spin on it? Maybe a Kramer kinda thing?"

"How about if I just do it as me?"

"*Bor*-ring!"

My cheeks kept getting more and more hollow, my nails on both hands turned into crusts of fungal infections, and my teeth went from off-white to yellow—no wonder I wasn't getting cast. The clock was ticking. Not seeing any alternative, I shrugged off the anxiety and plodded on.

At a casting for a sitcom pilot, I ran into Ron Vawter, who was auditioning for the same role. I'd just seen Vawter the previous week at The Wooster Group's production of *Frank Dell's the Temptation of St. Anthony*, one of the most moving pieces of theater I'd ever seen. The packed house had been in either tears or hysterical laughter, and when the play was over we'd sat there in stunned, reverent silence as the actors filed out for a bow, then stood en masse and broke into wild applause. I walked up Wooster Street in a daze afterward, feeling inspired and reenergized.

The day I came out of the TV casting, I caught Vawter standing outside having a smoke. I'd seen an article in the *Voice* about him where he talked openly about having AIDS. I wanted to tell him how brave I thought he was, but all I could do was mumble something about the play, and how I was going to see it again to try to figure out why I found it so moving.

"Come see it again," he said, laughing, "but don't try to figure it out. I mean, we rehearsed and performed that goddamned thing for a year before we did it here—a luxury that most plays don't have. But do come see us again. I'll look for you."

He was so friendly I wanted to ask him a thing or two about our common health problem, but it didn't seem like the time and place. I did come and see it again and brought Ronnie. She was as moved by the play as I was and became a big Ron Vawter fan. He died of AIDS several years later, at the age of forty-five, but his courage was something that I would not forget.

chapter 20

The first time I read a story by my sister's friend Ian "Sandy" Frazier was back when I was still working as an actor in Miami. Ron had called to tell me about Sandy's piece in the latest issue of the *New Yorker*. It was called "Boswell's Life of Don Johnson," a goof on *Miami Vice* and its star, written in the stilted Old English prose of the famous biographer. Ronnie told me that Sandy was inspired to write it after seeing me on *Miami Vice*. In fact, my sister was so full of encouragement she made it sound as though the entire staff of the *New Yorker* crowded around the television for a *Vice* party at someone's apartment each time I appeared on the show.

Ronnie took me someplace uptown one night where Sandy was doing a reading from a piece of his called "Canal Street," and I finally got to meet him. I'm not sure what I thought Sandy would look like, but his personality was no surprise at all—a wry, deceptively laid-back quality that I knew my sister loved. He might've been a sophisticated *New Yorker* wit, but he also looked like the kinda guy who could recite the screwdriver's credo (lefty-loosy righty-tighty). Ronnie could not stop grinning, and I decided then and there that Sandy Frazier was a much better match for my sister than the affect-less James Hamilton. As the two of them stood there making small talk, I cut in and said, "How come you two aren't involved romantically? I've never seen two people more right for each other. You guys got chemistry."

They both feigned outrage at this preposterous notion, but there was enough tension in their laughter to see I'd struck a sore spot. Apparently, this was another affair that had gone wrong. There'd been many, and not limited to her colleagues like Sandy, Mark Singer, and Rick Hertzberg. Back when I was involved with the saloon, Ron had come down there on several occasions when I was out of town and had seduced Stella's accountant, a dapper West Village type whom I used to see out walking his Irish setter around the neighborhood. But none of her affairs lasted long, aside from the intermittent one with Hamilton.

At least Ron was *having* affairs. I was envious of her entanglements, miscues or not. This was the early nineties and I was still gun-shy after the debacle with Laura. I hadn't been involved with anyone for almost a decade. Ron was lucky that her affairs ended (as far as I knew) somewhat civilly, and fortunate to have the sense not to fall for lunatics like me.

Shooting pool one night with some casting directors, attractive young women friends of Brooke's, I leaned out over the table to take a shot and had to quickly curl my fingers in under the palm of my hand to hide the crust that had replaced my fingernails. My fingertips looked like something out of a zombie flick. The virus was catching hold and I knew I couldn't go on hiding it.

One of the last castings my agent sent me on was for one of those *Bill & Ted's Excellent Adventure* movies. They were casting for a guy to play Death and walk around in a cowl with a huge sickle for a prop—the Grim Reaper. My sister broke up laughing when I told her.

"That's great," she said. "You're perfect, kind of like Max von Sydow."

Ron didn't seem to notice my wincing at the remark, and if she detected any physical deterioration in me she never mentioned it. We both had immense pride, always hiding our troubles from each other. I moved out of her apartment as soon I found somewhere to go.

It was a small place in a rooming house on Eighty-sixth and First Avenue, and I holed up with a portable typewriter to write screenplays. If there was anything I'd learned over my years of reading scripts for auditions, it was that most screenwriting was shoddy at best. Maybe I could do better. Might as well take a last shot at accomplishing something before I croaked.

Again I briefly lost track of my sister, and whenever I called her she sounded more preoccupied than usual. Then one night she called me up and asked me to come over for dinner.

"Hey, Hoss, Hoss!" It was a goof on the Shepard play I'd done when I first got back from Miami, and I could always get a laugh out of Ronnie with it. She was a sucker for off-the-wall delivery.

"Hey, Steve. C'mon in."

I could hear her laughing through the door to her apartment—she always left it open after buzzing me in through the street door. Slightly winded after five flights of stairs, I came in and caught her standing up from her typing table, lighting a cigarette.

"You're just in time to help me with something, Steve. Look, I know you're really good with names and there's a character in this thing I'm writing, a trombone player, and I can't find the right name for him."

She had a lopsided grin on her face and her enthusiasm was palpable, her every movement galvanized by some inner force. No matter what might be going on in her life, writing always snapped her out of it.

"How bout JJ?"

"No. JJ is on-the-nose, too famous [JJ Johnson]. It's gotta be more of a common name, but not one you hear every day, and maybe a little sexy too, okay?"

"This character, does he play valve or slide trombone?"

"Come *on*, Steve. This is serious. Names are maybe the most important thing."

"How 'bout Barry? Barry the 'bone man."

"I love the name Barry, but it makes me think of cute boys."

"Okay, so who's your favorite trombone player . . . Curtis Fuller, right? What about Curtis?" Back when I came to visit her at Penn she'd given me Coltrane's album *Blue Train*, which featured Fuller on trombone, and I could do his solo from the title tune note for note, blowing out the side of my mouth and sound just like a trombone. I could do Lee Morgan's trumpet solo too.

She was stunned for half a beat. "Of course! Curtis is absolutely perfect! Why the hell didn't I think of that? I *knew* you would know."

She went back to her typewriter and pecked out a sentence or two, sat back, plucked her cigarette off an ashtray, and reviewed what she wrote.

"Okay, this is great. Now you have to let me make you dinner and take you to a movie."

Can't beat a deal like that.

Envying and inspired by my sister's drive, I plunged into my screenplay, hoping as well that writing would keep alive my connection with her. Though she grew more remote each time I called her, if I said it was about a writing problem she was all rapt attention and full of helpful suggestions.

A character in the story I was writing was loosely based on her—the hero's sister, a helpful mentor full of encouragement and off-the-cuff advice. Proud of the scene I'd written, I went over to Ron's apartment to show it to her.

"Listen," she said to me when she read the scene. "Stop trying to make me so goddamn *nice* because I'm your sister. Nobody wants to read *nice*." She laughed wryly and added, "In certain circles, I've even been called the Ice Queen."

We both had a laugh at that, Ron seeming much more proud of the slur than hurt by it. I went back to my typewriter and turned her character into a dominatrix who kept her boyfriend handcuffed to the radiator.

I was getting just as obsessive about screenwriting as I'd been about the acting scene in Miami. I drank gallons of coffee and smoked cartons of cigarettes, plunking away at an old manual typewriter and combing the nearby drugstores and stationery stores for ribbons and paper in the middle of the night.

One day the guy who lived in the room directly underneath me came banging on my door. He was a Pakistani who drove a cab for a living and he gesticulated so wildly I thought he was going to attack me.

"*Please!* Theez typing, bang bang all day all night iz make me crazy! *Please* stop theez, I beg you. I work all day and no sleep. I hear more theez clack clack I come up here smash typewriter to bits!"

He was right, of course. The walls in this place were paper thin, the floors uncarpeted wooden planks, and through my window onto the air duct between buildings I could hear every sneeze and telephone conversation. I apologized to the poor guy and stuck some towels under the typewriter to muffle the noise. When I'd get burned out, I'd go over to Carl Shurz Park by the East River and Eighty-sixth Street, sit on a bench overlooking the water, and meditate. Late at night, the section with benches along the river turned into a gay stroll, and occasionally I'd come up out of meditation and find some guy staring at me. I didn't mind. I knew they weren't looking for conversation, and their presence made it safe and less attractive to muggers.

I stopped going to castings, but I continued going to twelve-step meetings in the neighborhood, mostly out of loneliness. Occasionally I'd speak up, longing for attention, and my glib wit would attract guys who were having a hard time.

One night a frazzled-looking guy came up to me outside during the smoke break. His hands shook slightly when he lit the cigarette he bummed off me.

"Hey, Steve," he said. "Could I get your phone number? I'm pretty new and not too good at socializing."

He was shivering in a little windbreaker on this winter night, unshaven and his hair unkempt, and for a moment my heart went out to him. I was familiar with this situation, and memories of my early days in sobriety flashed through my head. The close relationship with guys in Florida like Henry had saved me back then.

"Sure, man. No problem."

I gave him my number but didn't stick around after the meeting was over. I wasn't all that secure in my own sobriety, and in the back of my mind the memory of a shot of heroin stood in reserve as a last resort. Besides, I didn't have time to talk to fools who couldn't stop drinking. I had screenplays to write, careers to pursue. I also had too much to hide and was reluctant to let anyone get close to me.

I tried turning a trick with a hooker now and then. They were meticulously careful about using protection, but New York hookers had a much harder edge than the ones in Pigalle I'd been so fond of.

"Alright, baby. Rub 'n' tug fifty bucks, suck seventy-five, 'round the world is a hundred. Whatta you want—half an hour or an hour?"

Fifteen minutes later she reaches over to the bedside table, lights up a cigarette, and goes, "You through? You finished yet or what?"

Well, maybe they weren't all that different, but my needs and perceptions had changed drastically since my late teens, and the gap between horny and lonely was no longer so easy to bridge. The idea of just going to work at a job never occurred to me. I was accustomed to making fast money and spending it faster. Besides, how could I write screenplays if I had a job? My sister's sense of practicality was a trait that had totally escaped me. For the first time in my life I entertained fantasies of suicide—what would it be like to jump off a bridge into the river? A scene from an old James Baldwin novel kept playing over and over in my head, where the guy jumps off a bridge and feels the wind pull his shoes off as he hurtles to his death. My attraction for the dramatic was taking me to scary places.

Writing screenplays offered some relief. Back in my hovel on Eighty-sixth Street, I could escape for hours into the movie in my head and into the lives of the characters. It didn't matter that their lives mirrored my own, because in the world of the story I could play God—reward them when the whim struck, or even kill them if I wanted to. I could take all the irritating details of my everyday life and thrust them into my story where they were transformed—the dialogue between two old ladies on a bus complaining about their recent surgeries became amusing patter when stuck in the mouths of cops standing over a homicide. "You think that's bad? I went in for an appendectomy and they took out half my colon."

I wasn't sure if I possessed a gift for putting words on paper. Ron was the writer in our family, successful and esteemed, and since that slot was already taken it had never seemed an option for me. But screenplays were a shortcut, a thin skeletal structure that was perfect for my short attention span and flair for the dramatic. I'd close my eyes and imagine My Movie, and then write down the action and dialogue that unfolded on the screen in my head. No big deal once I learned the format, and for a mimic with an ear good enough to remember Coltrane solos the dialogue came easy.

My first attempt was a story called "Legit," about (guess what) a forty-year-old booster, Shoppin' Bag Billy, who goes down to Florida to make amends with his dad. I'd so loved those innocent accents and textures of the South, and missed them dearly. I wrote a scene where the hero, Billy, who's driving for Beach Taxi, goes to hear a girl sing at her Baptist church. I'd named the girl in the story Angie, but she was Laura. I could still picture her so clearly in my mind—the way a lock of her hair fell across her cheek, her slightly pigeon-toed stance—I figured I might as well use the memories.

Angie knocks 'em dead with her solo on "An Old Rugged Cross." The services end and Angie and Billy drift out to the parking lot with the rest of the congregation. They stroll over to Billy's taxi.

Billy: Need a ride?

Angie: The pastor always drives me home. (she looks around) What I
need is a kiss. (tilts her face up to his)

It was that unforgettable moment when I'd first kissed her. When I finally finished the scene I sat back and read it over. Not bad. Laura seemed
to leap off the page. Then I read it again, and over and over until finally I
was weeping. Romance was an innocent part of life that I'd left far behind,
forbidden to me now.

Ron wasn't having much luck with romance either. I went over to her
apartment one night and found her in a tearful state of anxiety. I don't
think I've ever seen her so frantic. Some affair she'd been having had gone
awry, and the guy was leaving a string of weird messages on her answering
machine. She could barely talk about it without bursting into tears. I
wanted so much to comfort her, to be the level-headed, compassionate
character she'd been for me so often (like the time I got smacked with a
claw hammer). But couples' counseling wasn't really my strong suit.

"Hey Ron, I know a few guys who'd be happy to polish the sonofabitch for a couple hundred bucks. Hey, times are tough all over."

She was not amused or comforted by this idea. Totally at a loss as to
how to comfort her, I suggested the old twelve-step gambit of praying for
the guy. At least I got a laugh out of her on that.

She calmed down a bit then and went into the details—turns out the
guy in question was Donald Fagen, the Donald in her story "A Lot in
Common" and the old lead singer for Steely Dan. I wondered how she
could be involved with Fagen when Hamilton was supposed to be her
boyfriend. Apparently James had introduced them in the first place and
Ronnie had gone behind his back and tried to indulge in an affair with little consideration for James. Well, I thought, this is all her own doing, but
something about these crumb-bums that she got involved with really
rubbed me the wrong way, and I regretted that I didn't know some nice,
level-headed sanitation worker I could introduce her to, some big Irish
guy who'd come home all sweaty from wrestling garbage cans around all
day and ball the socks off her. Of course I didn't say any of that.

When I got home I continued to fret over my sister's crisis and wracked my brains for a helpful take on it—okay, what did I know about this Fagen guy? His old band, Steely Dan, had peaked during a soft-rock era when people like Cat Stevens, James Taylor, and Boz Scaggs were selling off the charts and whose albums I could've sold by the vanful back in the day. But Steely Dan was a catalog band, mediocre at best, and I didn't know a record booster worth his salt that would go to the trouble of picking up their albums. If Ronnie had poor taste in men, I at least thought she had good taste in music. I was appalled that my dear sister was in such turmoil over this vanilla cookie. I wished I'd thought of telling her that earlier—an abrupt switch to the totally inappropriate was a surefire way to snap Ron out of a funk.

At some point she called and asked me if I'd go jogging with her around the reservoir in Central Park. I suspected that jogging was something she used to do with the creep who was giving her so much grief at the moment, and who had, in fact, taught her proper jogging technique. But sure, I'd go jogging with her if it helped to cheer her up. It wasn't like I had any pressing engagements.

I showed up the next day wearing combat boots—the only jogging I'd ever done in my life was when I was in basic training at Fort Riley, Kansas. At first Ronnie tried to ignore the boots. After she endured one full circuit of the cinder track, with my clomping and thudding and occasionally turning and jogging backward and throwing jabs in the air like Muhammad Ali, she stopped dead in her tracks. I could tell she was making a tremendous effort to keep herself under control.

"Jesus Christ," she said. "I can't jog with somebody who's stomping and banging their feet down and waving their arms all over the place. What do you think you're doing?"

I was hurt. I thought I'd been doing great.

"Gee, I'm sorry, Ron. That's the way guys jog in the army. You know." I jumped from foot to foot, trying to amuse her. "Gimme yo lef rat lef."

"Well, look around you. This isn't the army. When you jog you're supposed to step smoothly and softly, not jump up and down."

"C'mon," I offered. "Let's go around again and I'll see if I can follow how you do it."

So we started off again, and I did notice that she moved very fluidly, rolling each footstep softly from heel to toe, and swiveling her hips so that she seemed to glide effortlessly right along. I tried to mimic what she was doing but it felt completely unnatural and silly, so I went back to my thumping up and down the way I always jogged. Immediately she stopped and started to walk away.

"That's it," she said. "I'm out of here."

"Awferchrissakes," I heard myself saying. "Does everybody have to jog like a fruitcake to please you?"

"I should have known better," she shot back, "to think I could ever do anything like this with you."

That one really hurt. I can't remember what else we said, except that it wasn't nice and made her cry briefly before she went home. I knew I'd bruised a sore spot, but her reactions were so over the top that it seemed an indication of a deeper disturbance.

The next time I saw her we broke into laughter talking about the whole scene, and she admitted that she just had lousy luck trying to get guys to act civilized. I forgot my earlier concern as I basked in this new-found intimacy with her.

Not long after that incident, Tina Brown came in as editor in chief of the *New Yorker.* Hot from her recent success with *Vanity Fair,* she was going to take this financially fading literary magazine that had become a home for quirky writers and make it over in her image for the future. She'd brought her old friend Rick Hertzberg in as one of her new staff writers, and Hertzberg brought *his* old friend Veronica back into the fold. While everybody else at the magazine was skeptical about what Tina Brown was going to do, Ronnie was suddenly excited again. She started going to work every day with a new energy and could barely stop talking about it.

I went over to my sister's apartment several weeks later and plopped down 120 pages of my completed screenplay on her coffee table. I'll never forget the look of wide-eyed reverence on her face.

"Jesus," she said. "I wouldn't have the nerve to even at*tempt* anything this huge. It's too bad you stopped drinking or I'd run out right now and get a bottle of champagne."

She sat down and started poring over it. After five minutes she said, "Where the hell did you learn to write like this? You've got to let me show this to Pauline [Kael] so I can see how much money we can get for this." My sister was a pro, so she tended to translate words and pages into dollars and cents.

She did show it to Pauline, as well as to her agent and a friend of hers who was reading scripts for Sydney Pollack. Ron later told me that Pauline loved the writing, but wasn't sure how to move it forward. Lindsay Duran, the woman reading for Pollack, said some nice things, but that, in the long run, she found stories about criminals depressing. And Wylie said he was a literary agent and didn't work with the film biz. I don't know what any of those people really thought of the story, but my sister's efforts on my behalf were endearing. She reacted with the same earnest enthusiasm she'd displayed when I told her I was going to twelve-step meetings and asked her advice about Higher Power. Anyone else might've said, "Get real, Steve. Every waiter and bellhop from here to LA has a screenplay he's trying to hustle." But not Ronnie. As long as I was attempting something even remotely legit she was in my corner.

I tried writing a romantic comedy next, but that one didn't go anywhere either. Trying to sell a screenplay, I discovered, is a longer shot than trying to make it as an actor.

One day around the end of 1992, I called up my old partner Nick. I told myself that I needed Nick's expertise and Bronx patter to flesh out the textures in my screenplays—you know, for my *writ*ing.

"Stevie, listen to me. You listenin'?"

"Yeah."

"Okay, look. Records are dead, finished, kaput. The thing now is cassettes and CDs, so records are gone with the buffalo. You follow me?"

"Yeah."

"Okay. Two words—computer software."

"Yeah, but I don't . . . ."

"Just shut up and listen. It's the new craze. They got millions a stores cropping up like hotcakes all over the country. You don't have to know nothin'. I got flyers and brochures comin' out the whazoo. But best of all, I got a fence. Guy'll take as much of it as we can get our hands on. That is, if you ain't lost the touch."

Any professional thief can tell you, and Nick was a pro, that the most important part of a hustle is having a good fence. You don't want to go to all the trouble of stealing something and then have to look all over the place for somebody to buy it. No, first you track down the buyer, pinpoint the need, the market—otherwise you're at the mercy of the buyer because you're the one in need.

Nick and I hooked up again. It wasn't hard to justify. I couldn't even get myself cast as Death these days, and I could hardly count on somebody coming up with a couple million bucks to produce a movie about shoplifters. On the real side, I found that I was a better shoplifter sober than I was when I was getting high. I didn't make so many mistakes and my radar was sharper. The down side was the stress that continued to build every time I had to walk through those electronic security gates when I left a store with a copy of *Lotus 1-2-3* under my belt, and now I didn't have the drugs to sweep the stress under the carpet. Somewhere or other, probably in some public service announcement on the radio, I heard that stress was HIV's favorite food.

Once I was a thief again, shady characters from my past started crawling out of the woodwork, like somebody'd put a wire out on the street— *Word come down from the Don Jeech. Record Steve is back.* One day I came back from a few days of boosting with Nick and I went over to Liz's place on East Sixth Street. I remembered Black Bobby telling me where she lived, and I dropped by to chat with the familiar faces, guys like Smitty and the Turtle who were showing up on a regular basis now that Liz was dealing again. They were happy to see me and, surprisingly, looked none the worse for wear. I decided that I'd had enough. It was 1992. I'd been sober for nine years and was miserable, and if I was going to die anyway, why fight it? I'd stopped going to meetings because I felt hypocritical being in a room with people trying to find a spiritual life, and there I was—a thief. Who was I trying to kid? I was sitting there at Liz's, watching these characters get high, and I felt like a fifth wheel.

"Hey," I said to Liz, "let me get a couple of those."

BJ the Queen of Crime was there that night, and she said to me, "Sure you want to do this, Steve?"

I nodded my head. Barbara looked around the cramped little apartment at Smitty, Liz, Tony, and the Turtle. They all got suddenly really interested in their shoes, but there was a vibe of expectation and BJ smiled.

"Well then," she said, "let me be the one to give you back your wings." She handed Liz a twenty for two bags, and said, "Here, Liz. Record Steve's money is no good here tonight."

Smitty guffawed. "I knew that bullshit wouldn't last. I don't know what took you so long to wake up."

"Don't listen to Smitty," said the Turtle. "He's a fucking idiot."

Then they were all laughing, and I didn't quite get that the joke was on me. Once the drugs got me past a brief moment of trepidation, I felt embraced by the jailhouse repartee. I didn't care that they were a deadbeat, strung-out crew. Their presence was familiar and comforting. Loneliness had burned such a hole in my gut that any crew was better than none. For most of my life I'd chased the elusive, childlike feeling of skating downhill, always postponing the consequences, but now, uncaring, the motion had begun to circle the drain.

The junk turned my stomach at first but I kept after it every day, if only to have some company after my boosting trips on the road. I found myself walking down St. Marks Place one early autumn morning on my way to cop and felt the old, familiar sensations of withdrawal—runny nose, quickened pulse, goose pimples, heightened sense of colors and light, and an eager anticipation of that soothing rush that made the symptoms vanish like magic. I should've been petrified. Instead I felt the warm assurance, the profound relief that, once again, I'd managed to boil all my troubles down to one problem   the next fix.

chapter 21

Ironically, Nick, who'd always pooh-poohed the idea of going legit, had in fact gone legit. He'd become co-owner of a car-service company and only had time to work with me on certain weekdays when business was at a low. I bought a car of my own, an old Grand Marquis with a huge trunk, and hunted up other drivers to work with. These guys, usually junkies like myself, were not as reliable as Nick, so the stress factor continued to build.

An actor I knew who'd moved to Miami called one day and offered to let me take over his apartment in Washington Heights. Boosting again had fleshed out my bankroll so I jumped on it. When I first went back to stealing, I told myself that it was better than a full-time job that would deprive me of valuable time I needed to audition or write screenplays. But I couldn't fool myself anymore. I was back in survival mode, that familiar old tunnel vision where the only concern I bothered about from day to day was how to make myself presentable enough to walk in and out of a store without attracting a SWAT team.

Smitty, one of my old crime partners, came up to Washington Heights and moved in with me. We were like a poor man's version of *The Odd Couple*. Smitty was another Cagney jailhouse type who'd gotten anal retentive about keeping his prison cell clean and his hair cut in a forties-type fade. I made fast money and Smitty kept the place clean, cooked a lot of rice and beans, and knew where to cop. If we ran short of laundry money, Smitty washed his clothes in the bathtub, stirred them around with the toilet plunger, and hung them around the apartment on coat hangers. He liked Jerry Springer, who annoyed the hell out of me, and we'd have fights over the television. We found a reliable Dominican connection, past Yeshiva University, across Broadway and up the hill to Wadsworth Avenue and the noisy bodegas in the Spanish section. If I couldn't get it up to go out and steal, Smitty would go out and make a few bucks as a messenger.

My sister, knowing that I had a car, asked me at one point if I'd drive her to her house upstate. It was in a sleepy little town called Bloomville, about twenty miles west of Woodstock in the Catskill Mountains. Her house was a two-story, modest little country affair made of wood, run-down but comfy. Winter was coming on and she needed to do some seasonal maintenance since the place wasn't winterized, like turn the water off so the pipes wouldn't freeze and burst. It was a beautiful piece of property with woods all around that were turning colors this time of year, and I was happy to spend some time with her. I'd been up there with her once before and we'd had a good time—read books by the fireplace, shopped at Home Depot, drove to the movies in Delhi, and smoked up a carton of her True Blues. This time, though, I had another secret to hide—the fact that I was stealing and using drugs again. No big deal for the master of illusion. I stocked up on methadone and drove over to her apartment to pick her up.

I had no idea how deeply troubled Veronica was at that point in her life. She never told me exactly what happened, but apparently she'd lost her job at the *New Yorker* when her relationship with the new editor in chief went sour. Tina Brown and Veronica had bonded at first. Ron had been really excited and *every*thing Tina did was in Ron's view *the best*. My sister was being paid, I think, an hourly freelance kind of thing, doing a ton of work, and at a certain point she demanded to be put on contract. Tina Brown was throwing around a lot of money in those days, and Ron came up with some inflated notion, I think partly abetted by her agent, of what she was going to be worth—never any half measures for Veronica. Then she and Tina fought. The next thing my sister knew, she was out of a job at the age of fifty-three with no severance pay, no pension, not even health insurance. I think they bought one piece of hers after Tina Brown arrived.

When I showed up at her apartment that day to drive her upstate, she told me she'd had a big fight with the new editor in chief, but that she wasn't going to worry about it. She felt that she'd been quite right to stick up for herself, and that for the time being she'd just have to get along without the *New Yorker*.

I was much more shaken about this news than my sister apparently was. I mean, what were the implications for *me*? Ron was my ballast. What would happen to me now that she was out here drifting too?

"Yeah, but Ron," I said with wheedling insistence. "I thought you loved working there. I mean, what do you want—do you want to be happy, or do you want to be right?"

She bent over laughing at that one. "Steve, that sounds like a line from a Mamet play. Look, I'll work this out. My friends have always been telling me I should write a novel, so now I'll have plenty of time to do it."

Well, she survived before when she'd drifted away from the *New Yorker*. But there was a subtle terseness in her voice that I'd never heard before. She showed me several chapters of the manuscript she was working on, and while I sat there in her apartment reading it, I could tell that her attention was riveted on my reactions. It was a familiar dilemma. I remembered her watching me when I'd read some of her stories, and whenever I'd laugh she'd brighten and say, "Wait. What was so funny?"

This time, though, the mood was heavier. I tried my best to focus because I knew how important it was to her, but that fact alone made it difficult, not to mention my concentration being further hampered by drugs and my need to hide that from her. The few pages I read seemed excessively wordy and overwritten, a total departure from her short stories where there was not a wasted word. This was like trying to read Henry James or some elaborate drawing room comedy. My heart broke as I sat there, wanting desperately to be a source of encouragement, but all I managed to say was how inept I felt trying to read something so brilliant.

I could tell that she didn't buy it. Snatching the manuscript from me, she tossed it on her coffee table and said, "Never mind. It's unfair to lay this on you all of a sudden. I should never have listened to these idiots who told me to write a goddamn novel and I should stick to what I do best. Let's just get going."

Relieved of this terrible responsibility, I quickly dismissed it from my mind. These were writing problems and none of my concern. She was the expert in that area and I was confident she'd work it out.

Poor Ron—she was wound up tight inside about something, perhaps job worries, but she was reluctant to talk. As we drove up the highway toward her house, she became increasingly irritated, nagging at me with outbursts of backseat driving that were highly unusual for her. It all piled up on my own frayed nerves and culminated on the second day at her house.

The only bathroom in the place was on the second floor where the bedrooms were, although she preferred to sleep on the couch downstairs next to the fireplace where it was cozy on those chilly autumn nights. One day, maybe a half hour after she'd come down from using the bathroom, I started up the stairs to do the same thing.

"Hey, Steve," she said. "Are you going to use the bathroom?"

"Yeah."

"Well, don't flush it, alright?"

"What? The hell you mean, don't flush it?"

"I'm trying to conserve the water now that I'm turning it off, and I don't want the toilet flushed anymore."

I couldn't believe I was hearing this, standing there on the steps with my bladder bursting. Besides, I could've sworn I just heard *her* flush the damned thing. At first I thought she was joking, but there was a weird tension in her voice, and it sounded completely irrational.

"Jesus Christ, Ron. What am I supposed to do? Can I fill a bucket from the kitchen to flush with?"

"Look, it's my house and I'm worried about the water pressure and stuff and I don't want you flushing the toilet. Can't you just go take a leak in the woods or something?"

"But didn't I hear you just flush the toilet a little while ago?"

"You must be hearing things."

What really got me was the "Look, it's my house." I didn't know where this was coming from but the sudden tension in her voice came out of left field. My face flushed hot with anger, an old knee-jerk reaction whenever I felt chumped-off. Here I was taking time out of my terribly busy schedule to drive her up here and be as helpful as I could, and she was breaking my balls about flushing the goddamned toilet that I knew she herself had flushed only moments before. But I swallowed it and went out to the woods with a roll of toilet paper and a shovel, like out on maneuvers in old army days.

The second day we were there, a huge orange and white, longhaired feral cat came by to visit us. At first I thought he was a mountain lion or something, but he was very friendly and let me know in no uncertain terms that he wanted a free meal. When my sister came back into the house and caught me feeding the cat a dish of milk she started in on me.

"Steve, you can't be bringing this wild cat in here and start feeding it."

"I thought you liked cats."

"I love cats, and that's why I don't want you to ruin this creature's instincts for hunting and surviving by bringing him in the house and feeding him."

"Yeah, that's great, but . . ."

She scooped up the cat who, to my mind, didn't put up much of a protest, after all I was trying to do for him. Maybe he was so starved for affection he enjoyed any kind of manhandling, but he also seemed well acquainted with my sister and this kind of treatment. She deposited him outside the screen door to the pantry where all the rakes, shovels, muddy galoshes, and wood for the fire were stored.

"Let me make it simple for you," Ronnie said when she came back to the kitchen and put a pot of water on the stove. "This is my house and I don't want you feeding wild animals in here. Period, end of story."

The cat went around the house, stood by the kitchen window, and spent a few minutes serenading us with howls, which tore at my heart, before he went off to catch a muskrat or a field mouse for his dinner.

Later that day I went out to gather some kindling wood for the evening's fire. Ronnie was out in the backyard with work gloves on, pruning a tree or some damned thing, and when she saw me heading out toward the woods she called to me.

"Hey, Steve. Where are you going with that basket?"

"I'm gonna get some wood for the fire."

"I really wish you wouldn't use that basket to carry wood in."

She said it with that strange tension in her voice. It was one of those generic baskets with woven wooden slats like you see fruit or string beans in on a roadside stand. I mean, it wasn't like it was irreplaceable. They were all over the place.

"The hell are you talking about? I always use this."

"Well, I wish you wouldn't."

"Christ, Ron—relax, willya? I'm only getting kindling to start the fire, not logs and shit."

"Well, find something else to carry it in. I don't want you messing that basket around."

My sister had always been the solid rock in my life, and this seeming crack in her rational and resourceful presence was deeply disturbing. Anger welled up in me, not so much at her, but at whatever was troubling her, at my inability to fathom it, and at her reluctance to confide in me. I found myself in the kitchen at some point yelling at her.

"I don't know what the devil is wrong with you but you've been busting my chops all day for the last two days and it's driving me fucking nuts."

She could not stand to be yelled at. "Don't you ever get violent with me!"

"*Violent?* Who's getting violent? You want to see violent? I'll show you goddamned violent." I went over and stomped on the wooden basket.

At first there'd only been something deeply troubled in her eyes, but now they turned ice cold. I knew that I'd crossed some invisible line with her, but it was too late to take it back. The basket was in splinters and so was our relationship.

"Get out. Get out of my house. Nobody threatens me in my own house."

"Christ, Ron. You're ordering me around and don't do this and don't flush the toilet and don't feed the goddamned cat and if you can't spit out what's bothering you then I'm out of here. You can ride back with me if you want, but I'm not staying in this nuthouse another hour. If you don't want to get stuck up here, do whatever you have to do to lock this place up for the winter and get your goddamned coat and meet me in the car."

Maybe it was her house, but it was my car.

She did just that, and we drove back toward the city in icy silence. A few miles down the highway I caught sight of her rigid profile and my heart broke. What was I doing? She was the only loved one I had left. Regret swept away my anger and I pulled the car over to the side of the road.

"Hey, Ron. Look, I'm sorry. I've been having a rough time myself recently and I just blew it. You know I'd never get violent with you. Have I ever raised a hand to you?"

She kept staring straight ahead down the dark highway.

"If you want to go back and do some more stuff with your house I don't mind. I'll go back with you and I know where to get you another one of those baskets."

"No, it's okay," she said without looking at me. "Let's just get back to New York."

I'm sure that everyone has situations in their life that they wish they had a chance to do over again, and this one stands out in my memory as one that I would tear my arm out of its socket if I could do it over. Maybe she sensed that I'd been using drugs but just didn't want to admit that it was happening again. It's not like I was getting ossified, though. Those days were long gone and my use was more of a steady maintenance to keep the fear at bay. Who knows? One thing I did know about my sister—she did not easily forgive or forget.

Much later I found out from her friend Ruth that Veronica had always been neurotic about that house. Although she liked the idea of owning her own getaway in the Catskills, she was totally unsuited to make it livable. First of all, she was a notorious tightwad, just like Dad, and though the house was falling apart, she was unwilling to spend the money to fix it up. It needed new gutters, electrical wiring, plumbing, and paint. Another thing was that she didn't have a car to get back and forth from the city, and was too cheap to buy one, so she was always bumming rides with the Schjeldahls or James or Ruth. Ruth laughed when she told me this, how she and her boyfriend once spent a weekend there and were terrified even to take a bath because Veronica was so stingy with the water. Veronica had cooked dinner for them one night. Lovely smells wafted out from the kitchen, but when Ronnie came in with the meal, it consisted of half a dozen steamed carrots, three potatoes, and a rather small chicken.

"Christ," Ruth's boyfriend said to her later that night, "doesn't she know that a chicken has only *two* legs?"

"Well," Ruth said, "Veronica doesn't eat much, so she probably doesn't think other people do either."

Ronnie definitely had her eccentricities. I recalled that she even recycled her paper towels, drying the dishes with them, and then carefully spreading the wet paper towels over the dishes to dry. It seems funny now, and even endearing, but during that last trip to the Catskills I lost it when she turned into an irascible Scrooge, just like the father she swore she hated. She was still my sister, though, and like Ruth I loved her even more because of her quirks.

Back in the city and reduced to making desperate moves, I got knocked walking out of a Midtown store with half a dozen compact discs. Rikers Island had once been an adventure—three-hots-and-a-cot, slam-bids with my bridge partner Freddy the Fly, singing doo-wops in the huge tiled bathrooms, and trading war stories with the other wise-guys. But I wasn't a kid anymore. My voice was gone and I'd already heard all the stories. C-76 and the rest of the buildings at Rikers were swarming with young gang members. The food really sucked, and the bus out to the island was standing room only. Since I was in my fifties and looked like seventy, the other cons took to calling me Pops.

"Yo, Blood. Move over and give Pops a seat."

"Hey, Pops. You need a cigarette?"

"What they got you up in here for, Pops?"

"Stealing CDs."

"Haw, you dig that? Pops is a booster. My man."

"Check Pops out. Got hisself some fly gabardines and an L. L. Bean. Damn, bet you was killin' 'em out there, huh, Pops?"

"Yo, Pops. Whatchoo think about this O. J. thang, huh? You think he pushed her wig back?"

I only got thirty days on that one, but I'd run out of breaks in New York and was lucky I hadn't been hit with a perpetual offender bid in prison. My last pinch came months later in Morris County, New Jersey. I had some nitwit cokehead driving me, and when he saw the cops leading me out of the store, he drove up beside them with the swag from several previous hits still in the car and asked the cops where he had to go to bail me out. The cops immediately busted him, tossed the car, and discovered my real identification with my real name on it stashed in the map compartment in the door. When the cops put my name into the computer, about twenty or thirty old arrests and aliases popped up and they started acting like they had just busted John Dillinger. An ancient warrant from Bucks County, Pennsylvania, also popped up so I couldn't make bail—not that there was anybody left out there to bail me out. I tried calling Nick but even he wasn't accepting collect calls from me anymore. The warrant was finally vacated and I got released, but not until after a month of cold turkey.

When I got back into the city I went directly to my connection's crib in the East Village to get straight, but my tolerance for drugs was unreliable and the first shot put me into seizures. The connection refused to serve me anymore and insisted that I go to see a doctor he knew. I was in pretty bad shape. I had no T cells and no platelets and was bleeding through my Jockey shorts and staining the backs of all my pants. The doctor prescribed these new drugs, the cocktail that they'd developed, and sent me to Social Security to file for disability. I started getting a monthly check, but the drugs were incredibly toxic and exhausting. I dropped weight by the pounds and could barely climb the three flights of stairs to my apartment. My old partner Smitty would look at me and shake his head.

"Yo, cuz. You look like you need a tune-up."

Stealing became increasingly difficult as my appearance continued to deteriorate. I looked like death and had little money or energy to spare for haircuts, laundry, or dry cleaning. I tried washing my clothes in the bathtub, following Smitty's example, but I'd run out of energy halfway through and the clothes would sit there for days in a wet tangle. Desperate for a shower, I'd stand on top of the clothes and tell myself that the soap and water cascading off me onto the clothes were getting two jobs done for the price of one. Smitty would go into the bathroom and find my clothes bunched up in a soggy pile at one end of the bathtub.

"Yo, hoss. This stuff on rinse cycle or what?"

Nor could I get it together to go out on the road anymore where the security was lax. That required gas money that was becoming more and more impossible to drum up. I resorted to strolling around Manhattan with Smitty, trying old hustles like art books or vintage records that still brought in a good price in those stores around St. Marks Place that catered to the vinyl-nostalgia crowd. All I wanted now was enough cash to buy off the fear for a few hours. I'd stop in front of a display window before going into a store and check myself out: *Okay, if I pull my winter cap down far enough, it hides the shaggy mop*—my hair was getting long enough to pull into a short ponytail. I turned to see a rear view, since this is how I'd be scrutinized as I walked out: *Alright, not bad. The coat is long enough to hide the stain on the back of my trousers. Actually I don't look too bad*. Amazing how powerful self-delusion is.

It was 1995 when I finally confided in my sister that I had AIDS. I needed some cash to go score, but it was a holiday or a weekend and there weren't any check-cashing joints open to cash my disability check. I went over to Ron's and asked her to give me cash for the check.

"Well," she said looking me over. "You certainly have that grunge look down pat."

I looked pretty bad, and was so weary of trying to hide it that I came out and told her that I was being treated for HIV. Why else would I be on disability anyway? I tried to make it sound clinical, like a dental problem, not a big deal. She was still wary of me after the Catskills thing, and though she tried to be sympathetic, she seemed at a total loss for what to say or do.

"Steve, listen," she said, her resourcefulness coming to the fore regardless of her own troubles. "I know this terrific writer, Jimmy McCourt. He used to be a terrible lush when I first met him, but he pulled it together and is one of the brightest guys I know. Jimmy has friends who came down with AIDS and I trust him implicitly. If I call him and set it up, will you go talk to him? Because I have no idea how to help you with this."

"Okay, Ron."

She got Jimmy on the phone and he agreed to meet me at a diner in Midtown, but Ron chatted on with him for a while. Not having any drugs in me always gave me a heightened mind state where odd things impressed themselves, and I remembered her making a remark to Jimmy about her ex–editor in chief Tina Brown.

"At first I thought she was pretty, full face, and sort of okay. But then we got into a discussion about the basic *New Yorker* writer's prerogative of writing what you'd thought up versus what some editor wants for the *theme* of the issue. And it was then, when she turned profile, that I saw the stevedore."

Whatever Jimmy McCourt said in response made Ron laugh. I sensed that he was a trusted friend, and I was a little envious that my sister couldn't confide such things in me. I had no idea of the turmoil she was going through and was incapable of being there for her anyway. Even though I was sitting right next to her, some part of my mind was already a taxi ride down the road cooking up a shot. We went over to an ATM and Ron got me the cash for my disability check. We were both relieved when I left.

I did meet Jimmy the next day, but I can't recall a word that either of us said. I vaguely remember pouring out all my misery to him while he sat there with his face full of compassion, and maybe a little horror too. He did offer one tidbit of information that my ravaged mind filed away—there was an organization called Gay Men's Health Crisis down on Twentieth Street where some of his friends with the virus had found a tremendous amount of support. The reason I didn't run right over there is because I figured you had to be gay to be a member. Plus, I felt such a relief after unburdening myself to this guy that I wanted to reward myself by getting stoned.

My disability checks didn't last long. I was past the point of going out to steal for my drugs, and so I joined a methadone clinic. In an interview with one of the counselors, I mumbled something about just wanting to die.

"When you start thinking like that," he said, "it won't be long before you sprout little wings," he flapped his hands in the air, "and off you go."

His flip attitude annoyed me, but it didn't sound too bad. I was programmed for destruction anyway. Like Dad always said, I was gonna get my tit in a wringer. He'd put the whammy on me and there was no avoiding it.

chapter 22

Something, though, kept snatching me back from the edge. Just when I thought the Devil had caught up, snapping at my heels as I groped through that terrible blizzard of '96, another little window of opportunity presented itself when I arrived on the AIDS ward of St. Luke's-Roosevelt Hospital.

After that visit by my sister, when she'd run into Smitty and then disappeared, I felt I had nobody else to turn to. I called my doctor and told him about the seizures and the complications I was having with those meds he'd prescribed. He was affiliated with St. Luke's in some capacity and said he'd see me the next day. This is the same doctor, mind you, I'd been sent to by my heroin connection who'd been only too happy to take my money for stuff that was killing me; and then suddenly, bafflingly, he'd refused my business, referred me to a doctor, and put me on another path.

This doctor was a specialist in hematology and one of the forerunners in the fight against AIDS. When he came to visit me in the hospital he listened patiently to all my complaints—until I veered into speculations of gloom and doom.

"I've been hearing, Doc, that this virus is the most cunning and deceptive virus that man has encountered since—"

"*Cun*ning? De*cep*tive?" He snorted in derision, stood up out of his chair, and banged his clipboard down on a table. "I don't have time to listen to some bullshit about what you've been *hear*ing. I've known some *really* cunning viruses in my day, viruses that you couldn't even pronounce, and the only thing cunning and deceptive about any of them is the hysteria they produce in people. Do yourself a favor and stay away from street drugs. You're better off with methadone, which actually works fairly well in combination with these new cocktails. The street drugs will do you in long before any goddamned HIV will."

He was passionate about his work, and I didn't know how fortunate I was at that moment to have found him. He reached out and squeezed my big toe.

"Don't give up the fight yet, Steve," he said. He picked absently at a nicotine patch. "I still got a whole arsenal of moves we can make on this virus and you'll probably outlive me, especially if I don't stop smoking. By the way, you want me to get you some patches? They usually slap 'em on everybody in here since you can't smoke on the ward."

After several weeks of being examined, interrogated, poked, prodded, x-rayed, and subjected to other more intrusive tests, I was released and went right back to using drugs again. Methadone or no, I just didn't know what else to do with myself besides spend what little money I got, from disability and an occasional score, on street drugs.

Smitty and I could no longer pay the rent on our apartment in Washington Heights, and after six months or so of nonpayment, the sheriff's department put a notice of eviction on the door. I remembered Jimmy McCourt telling me about Gay Men's Health Crisis and I started going there for free food handouts. One day I found myself in their legal department. A lawyer had come out into the lobby, taken one look at me, and said, "What happened to your hands?"

I had another case of frostbite from a day I'd carried two shopping bags full of books down to the Strand to sell, and when I found them closed I walked all over the East Village with them on the coldest day of that year. The straps on the bags had cut off circulation in my gloveless hands and the cold had done its worst.

"Come in here," the lawyer said.

He took me into his office, took the fur-lined, leather gloves that his wife had given him for a present out of his topcoat, and tossed them to me. Then he sent me over to Chelsea to apply for housing at a residence there. It was a godsend. There were caseworkers to help residents organize their benefits, a huge kitchen where the staff prepared at least one good meal a day, and I ended up with a neat little furnished room with a nice-sized bath. It was a quiet neighborhood that was slowly evolving out of a late-night gay-stroll for stragglers from places like Eagle and the Spike before they'd closed down. Residents walked their dogs unmolested. One day I spotted Debbie Harry, who lived nearby, walking her pooch past Clement Clarke Moore Park—another familiar traveler I'd glimpsed through the decades—mellowed now, but when I passed she flashed me the same brave smile she'd possessed as an up-and-comer and I wished I could've heard her story.

As a small ray of hope appeared on the horizon, I tried calling my sister to tell her that I was going to be okay, but she wouldn't answer the phone. It was frustrating because I wasn't calling for sympathy or a hand-out, and I left impatient messages on her answering machine.

"Hey Ron, it's Steve. Are you there or what? The hell is the matter with you? Just pick up the goddamn phone. I'm your brother ferchris-sakes. You can't even return a simple phone call?"

Then they became pleading. "Hello? Hey, Ron, it's Steve. Are you there? C'mon, pick up, please. I know you're probably worried about me, but I live in an okay place now. I'm on disability and I don't need any-thing. Really, I'm gonna be alright now. Aw, c'mon, Ron. I'm sorry if I scared you before. C'mon, pick up the phone."

I tried calling a few of her friends, but either they said they hadn't seen her or they didn't return my calls. That went on until that Christmas Eve 1997, over a year since I'd seen Ron in the hospital, when I was sitting around the residence reminiscing about the holidays and my family and about where my sister had gone. One of the guys from the front desk came up and tapped me on the shoulder. Apparently I'd fallen asleep in front of the television and hadn't moved from that chair all night. It was Christmas Day.

"Hey, Steve. Some people to see you out front."

Might be the cops, I thought, and cops don't care if it's Christmas. When I got to the lobby, I found James Hamilton and Brooke. I was happy to see them. They signaled me to come outside. My sister was the only con-nection I had with these people, so as I followed them out into that freezing, sunny December afternoon, my hopes soared, delighted at the prospect of news about the one family member I still had left on the planet.

"Steve," James said as we walked along Twenty-second Street. "Veronica died last night."

We all stopped walking.

"She was hospitalized on and off all year," said Brooke. "They tried everything, surgery, chemotherapy . . ."

On Christmas Eve of 1997, at the age of fifty-six, Veronica died of a brain tumor. New York lost one of its funniest writers and I lost my big sister, the last living member of my immediate family. Last of the Mohicans. It came as a total shock to learn of my sister's death. I had no idea she was sick. It hit me like a ton of bricks—when I'd snapped at her that time we went to her house in the Catskills, and all those days I was leaving impatient messages on her answering machine, she'd been dying of a brain tumor. That's probably what was troubling her that day she'd visited me in the hospital—it turned out to be the last time I saw Ron alive.

A few days later, as I stepped out of a taxi in front of a funeral parlor in SoHo, a woman emerged from a side street and walked over to me. It was someone I knew from the fringes of the magazine crowd. We'd become friends over the years, but my sister detested her and I could scarcely believe that she'd shown up at Veronica's wake. I was too miserable, though, to summon the energy required to elude her with any kind of aplomb, and so she accompanied me inside. Besides, I doubted if anyone in there cared a whit about seeing me or gave a damn about who I might turn up with.

Ron's wake was a closed-casket affair because of the way they'd shaved her hair to do brain surgery. I couldn't believe she was gone, so I told them to show me her casket, open it, and prove to me it wasn't all some monstrous scam. It didn't help. Shaved head and all, Veronica looked as beautiful as she'd ever looked. There still hovered about her a kind of force that struck me the moment they pulled back the top of her coffin, the features of her face now terribly serene but still possessed of that uncompromising power that had sustained her in life. It was unsettling and I leaned forward, not trusting my senses. Then I saw what was missing—her great vulnerability. She couldn't be hurt anymore.

The woman who'd accompanied me inside kept pulling on my coat, asking me to introduce her to this one or that one. She then sat next to me for about an hour, by a huge photograph taken by Hamilton of my sister that had been set up in lieu of an open coffin. I couldn't resist thinking that the event was focused on his photography rather than my sister's demise. Finally my friend got uncomfortable enough to leave. I sat there shit-faced and endured listening to several people get up and address the assembly with a few words about Veronica. Nobody came up to say hello.

After the wake I was invited to an Italian restaurant across the street from the funeral parlor where some of Ronnie's closer friends had gathered to remember her. I sat and stared at my pasta, harboring black thoughts about all her friends. They knew where to find me when she was dead. Why the hell didn't they come find me when they knew she was dying? Memories of our past made a forlorn noise in my head, like the fading wail of a distant train whistle. Coupled with my resentment, it blocked out any notion of the compassion and care that a few of these people had shown my sister during her last year.

One thing did get through to me. Someone, I think Mimi Kramer, a theater critic and one of my sister's buddies, turned to me in the restaurant at one point and asked me where it was that Veronica got such a sense of humor, and did it run in some part of our family?

Everyone present, James Hamilton, Jamaica Kincaid, Cathleen Schine, Philip Roth, Roy Blount, and the rest of my sister's literary friends, looked at me. I thought it was a good question, one that maybe only I knew the answer to, if anybody. But as I glanced around that table and made eye contact with each one of them in turn, I noticed a common texture, something predatory that I'd seen before in my sister's eyes. Several people from the wake who'd been sitting at other tables picked up on the question and moved over to our table, one woman elbowing me in the ear as she clambered for a seat. Ron, like a great actress, had touched them all deeply and left them hungering for more.

My response to the question was flip, a wisecrack about Veronica stealing all her best gags from me, but it lingered in the back of my mind—another little gift that I wouldn't appreciate until much later.

The funeral was worse. It was a bitter-cold day and the beautiful grounds of Greenwood Cemetery looked gray and desolate. I spotted Dita and her husband, and though she was the first person I felt like saying hello to, underneath her grief was a tight-lipped fury that cut short conversation. I remember nothing about the services as my head seethed with resentment and remorse, but someone had brought flowers, and Roy Blount began a procession of mourners stepping over to the grave, picking up one of the roses and tossing it onto the coffin. I waited until they'd all filed off so I could savor the moment alone.

After the wake and the funeral I spent months indulging my sorrow by staying stoned. I was incapable of grieving for her (that would come later in a delayed reaction). That long, silent, and mysterious separation from her, and then suddenly being told "Veronica died last night"—it didn't compute. I'd been completely blindsided, and I couldn't get my head around the unexplained circumstances of her death. The feeling of irreparable loss stretched out in front of me like an unremitting landscape of loneliness and pain—but it was all about me. Ron had meant so much to me—perhaps too much. She was my closest friend, my jazz buddy, movie goombah, writing mentor, confessor, and my female ideal. Whatever I did as an actor, it was her praise I hoped for. She'd shown up, no matter what was going on in her own life, at times when I found myself at death's doorstep. She'd understood me like no one else, always disdaining my junky-criminal pursuits but always the first to urge me on with all the vast resources at her disposal whenever I attempted something worthwhile. Her's was the only opinion I valued and, finally, the only person left whose love I longed for. Who would care what happened to me now?

With nobody left, I stumbled around in numbness, punctuated by occasional fits of despair and self-loathing. I'd be walking down the street and suddenly start smacking myself in the forehead and yelling out loud, "You dumb sonofabitch. She was dying and all you could do is whine into her answering machine!" I felt a sudden kinship with the bag ladies and lost souls who mumbled and railed aloud on street corners.

That deep sense of loss, though, prevented me from understanding my own part in my predicament or appreciating just how much Ron had suffered.

Although the facility where I lived offered a certain amount of security, all the residents were on a monthly "digit"—disability, SSI, a veteran's pension, or simply welfare—so once a month was like Christmas. Hallelujah. At noon on check day a small crowd would gather by ones and twos in the street outside, shooting looks up the block for a glimpse of the mailman, followed by a concerted rush to the check-cashing place on Tenth Avenue.

Then we'd all splurge on heroin, bottles of Thunderbird, forty-ounce jugs of beer, and of course the ever-present crack cocaine. A few days later we were all bumming cigarettes. Well, maybe it wasn't everybody, but the only people who showed up on my radar screen were the ones getting stoned.

I didn't even like crack and could not relate to the trifling, stressed-out knuckleheads who chased it, but I was so lonely that I'd go hang out and do whatever they were doing just to have a few moments of companionship. My health began to plummet again. I'd developed some exotic strain of pneumonia that I couldn't shake and the street drugs made it worse. I might as well have flushed those miracle meds down the toilet for all the good they were doing me.

Smitty was living in a shelter now and occasionally he'd come visit me at the residence, smoke my cigarettes, get a free meal in the cafeteria, and fall out on the floor in my room. I was glad for his company, but my conversation circled around like a demented old man who keeps repeating the same stories over and over.

"Hey, Smitty. You remember the time Dee Christian shot Boston John in Stanley Turtle's?"

"Why don't you lighten up, cuz?" Smitty said. "Talking with you is like being stuck on a one-way ride down memory lane."

I was really losing it. I was always going out and locking my keys in my room. I'd lay my glasses down on a table, turn to do something, and when I turned back around the glasses were gone. I'd walk into a room and stand there baffled, unable to remember why I'd gone there. I got letters saying that I had to recertify for my medical assistance, and the next thing I knew I'd get a letter telling me that my medical assistance was shut off because I hadn't recertified. It's a kind of dementia that AIDS victims and cancer patients are prone to. Every cell in the body is diverted to combating the sickness and toxic drugs. The mind, overtaxed and undernourished, reels and retreats. This wasn't happening because I was stoned. In fact, it was only when I was zooted-out that I could perform the simplest task, like brushing my teeth or buying toilet paper. I needed a forty-ounce Bud or a couple of Xanax to send me out the door and across town to my methadone program. My wallet mysteriously disappeared. God was playing tricks on me, punishing me for the life I'd led. No wonder. The God of Mischief always turns on you, like Loki always turned on Thor and Odin. Underneath was the terror of losing my mind. The end was near.

chapter 23

One morning I was standing near Union Square with my latest running partner, Airborne Bobby. I don't know if Bobby had ever been in the army, but he wore a field jacket with an airborne patch on the shoulder, hence the street moniker. We'd just scored a half-pint of blackberry brandy from an early morning liquor store that we dumped into our Dunkin' Donuts coffee—So here's lookin' at you, kid, and down the hatch. We were both dying, and the remorse of what I'd done to myself, and the fear of what was going to happen to me, made a buzz in my head like the static in between radio stations. But as I stood there on the street that day I knew that the volume would be reduced to a bearable level as soon as I got that brandy down. After all the horror that drinking and drugging had caused me and everyone who'd loved me, it was still the best solution I could come up with—have a drink, hit the mute button.

Bobby downed his, looked over at me, and goes, "Hey, Steve. Let's go over to Fourteenth Street. I know this place got all these anonymous meetings."

"The hell you want to do that for?"

"C'mon, man. At least we can bum a cigarette. Everybody in those meetings smokes."

I looked around. It was a rainy day and few people were on the street this early. There weren't even any dry butts in the gutter.

"Yeah, but we just had a drink."

"Fuck you think those meetings are for? It's for people who drink. Besides, they got free coffee and doughnuts at Fourteenth Street. C'mon, man. Bet there's a few good-lookin' broads too. C'mon. We still got another hour before the food pantry opens."

"Yeah, alright," I said, just to shut up his whining.

The clatter in my head drowned out what anybody said at that meeting, but the coffee was hot, people were generous with their cigarettes, and they all smelled better than Airborne Bobby. Some impulse prompted me to pick up a meeting list. The next time I was sitting in my residence dying of loneliness, I looked up the nearest meeting and went over there. I didn't hold out any hope of ever getting sober again—I just went for the cigarettes, hot coffee, and conversation.

Once again, the simple warmth of twelve-step groups provided an hour of solace during days and months of grim, hand-to-mouth survival. Crawling out of bed in the morning drenched in sweat, I'd drag my aching carcass into the shower and out to the earliest meeting that met on any given day. The meds I was taking, along with the virus, depleted the nutrients in my bones and I was developing something called osteonecrosis, or bone death. Walking caused so much pain that I'd have to sit down and recoup after a block or two. But I needed the human contact in those meetings like I needed air to breathe. I got a bicycle and discovered that the pedaling increased circulation and took the ache out of my hips and back. I started bicycling down to a meeting that met near Washington Square Park every morning at seven thirty a.m., a real lifesaver after being up all night plagued by insomnia.

Three months later I raised my hand in that meeting and announced that I had ninety days sober. I couldn't believe it. Thing was, I wasn't stupid. There still lingered some traces of reptile reasoning beneath the wasteland of my cerebral cortex that told me if I did A, then B would follow—that none of those people would shell out cigarettes or hang out with me if I was still drinking and whacked out on drugs. Ol' snake-brain just kept on keepin' on.

There was also the factor of herd instinct—like in basic training when the DI gets everybody out of their racks at four a.m. for a five-mile run with full field packs. It seems impossible to run five miles with all that gear, but you get up and do it and the fact that everybody else is doing it makes it possible. Being in my fifties, my body no longer threw off the drugs and booze so easily, but after months of restless insomnia, I gradually weaned myself off methadone—there's no price you can put on a good night's sleep.

The morning meeting I was attending every day was very different from the ones I remembered in Florida where people celebrated their sobriety, voicing their happiness about no longer waking up with the shakes, all in aid of passing along some hope to the newcomer. This group in the Village was a more fashionable, therapy-oriented crowd who went there to "get things off their chest" or "dump their problems" and commiserate with one another.

"My wife's divorce lawyer is taking me to the goddamn cleaners."

"My pussycat has a horrible skin disease and I really need to share about it."

Or, "I hate my boss. Yesterday I wanted to strangle the sonofabitch."

It was a daily soap opera and I loved it. They weren't my problems, and I couldn't wait to get down there each morning to see how the guy's divorce proceedings were developing or what became of the woman's poor pussycat. I immediately recognized the dynamic—the struggle for sympathy and attention. I was familiar with that battle since I was a child in Philly. It was like competitive misery. Whoever was in the greatest distress on any given day, that's who they'd take to coffee. I jumped right in.

"Oh, man. Listen to what happened to *me* yesterday."

Trouble was, I was treating loneliness, not the deeper soul sickness that results from years of alcoholism, addiction, and self-indulgence. I was famished for female affection—Mom and Ron were gone, and it had been years since I'd had any kind of romantic intimacy—but after the way I'd treated women, it was no wonder. I developed obsessive crushes on girls in the meeting, stayed up nights rehearsing monologues that were cleverly calculated to endear me to them and at the same time make my competition (the other men) appear trivial and inept. If a girl I had my eye on didn't smile at me for some reason, I'd go home and agonize about it all night. I was feeding my neediness, making it worse, and lust reared its head like a monster. After eight months of attending that meeting, and miraculously staying sober and drug free, I wanted to kill myself.

And then Ron seemed to make her presence felt, even from the grave.

One day I happened on an article in *New York* magazine about Veronica, a short bio in aid of publicizing a posthumous collection of her stories, *Love Trouble*, that came out in the summer of 1999. The article was called "Humor Came Her," and the writer, Jennifer Senior, described what happened to my sister at the very end of her life, giving me my first sense of Ron's last days—how she was "as tough a cancer patient as she was a writer and editor," scorning home care attendants, sending them "screaming into the night." (Ronnie would never suffer being catered to by poor conversationalists.) Marilyn Miller, one of the original *Saturday Night Live* writers and a friend of Ron's, told the reporter about seeing Ron at Sloan-Kettering "stretched out on a gurney like a beach chair, smoking with whichever hand was working" and catching "Philip Roth at her bedside gingerly trying to feed her."

The doctor at New York Hospital told Veronica that she needed surgery to remove a malignant tumor the size of a grapefruit. Ronnie asked him if she was going to die. The doctor didn't want to deprive his patient of hope—she'd already told him how alone and terrified she was—so he told her that we all have to die sometime. Then, the article went on, Veronica did something that no one had ever seen her do during the entire time she was sick—she burst into tears. I'd been privileged with seeing those tears many times and I wept at the memory. There were a lot of funny quotes from literati friends of Ronnie's in the article, and not so funny ones about how she cut off everybody at the end. The writer said—and this was the worst blow—that Veronica even cut off her brother who was "HIV positive, having problems with substance abuse, and drifting in and out of trouble. His whereabouts today are unknown."

It was the most painful thing I've ever read. Why did Ron have to be alone and terrified when her brother was right across town? Don't people automatically notify the next of kin if someone is dying? What did that writer mean when she said my whereabouts were unknown? They knew *exactly* where to find me once my sister was dead. The list of people mentioned in that article who'd been at Veronica's funeral and wake read like a who's who in the New York literary crowd, but nowhere was it mentioned that her only living family member had been there. It was as though I'd crossed over into some shadowy dimension where my presence was not simply unnewsworthy but completely undetectable.

It was ludicrousness, of course, to think that my poor sister had died tragically and all I could think about was being dissed in a magazine article. But rage was a familiar and dependable survival tool, providing momentary respite from the terrible remorse, like at Mom's death, that I feared might've destroyed me. In my head I kept playing over and over the phone calls I'd made to Ronnie's friends, trying to find out what had happened to her. Apparently my sister had made them all swear they would not tell her brother. Terrific. They were taking directions from someone who was losing her mind from a brain tumor.

Okay, so maybe I wasn't at the top of my game. But I was still her family, and nobody knew her better than I did. She knew she couldn't bullshit me. I could've cleaned up. I'd done it before a million times. I could've pulled myself together, shown her all those healing techniques I'd learned. I could've snapped her out of it, I could've . . .

Despair only took me deeper downhill. There was no one to blame but myself. I'd been a source of worry and trouble to my sister, and her friends had good reason to avoid me. I remembered the time Ronnie visited me in the AIDS ward at St. Luke's, when the guy smuggling drugs to me had eclipsed my concern for my sister. Selfishness was rebounding on me like poetic justice. Realizing she couldn't depend on me, she'd cut me off, and her literary friends had stepped in and cared for her as best they could.

I thought back over those times when I'd glimpsed cracks in Ronnie's controlled and confident exterior, particularly during that trip to the Catskills. The dementia that plagued me from a breakdown in my immune system, coupled with the side effects of the toxic antiviral drugs, brought home to me just how intolerable it must have been for my sister to lose her ability to write and to take care of herself, she who was the most self-reliant person I'd ever known. The easy empathy we'd shared as kids in Philly came back to torment me.

I was plagued by bitterness, wondering who'd made off with everything my sister had ever collected and owned, her records, her paintings, her house in the Catskills, and the rights to everything she'd written. I burned with resentment thinking about Hamilton moving some girlfriend of his into Ron's beloved apartment while she was lying helpless in a hospital bed, and all those people who never returned my phone calls when I tried to find out what happened to her. I'd line them up in my mind's eye and snipe them with an M-16. I no longer wanted to die—now I wanted revenge. I'd stay sober, by God, just to spite everybody.

One day I ran into Smitty on Twenty-third Street. He had a little gig at some Jewish Temple near where I lived, sweeping up, running errands, and doing light maintenance. He'd get a free meal and enough scratch to go cop before he checked back in at the men's shelter. I felt sorry for him.

"Yo, cuz," he said, taking out a half-pint of whiskey from his back pocket as we strolled up the block. "This is your lucky day. They got a smoker over in Ridgewood. Everybody in Knickerbocker park is bent. Had to climb over three Puerto Ricans all dead from an OD in the hallway to score. Want to go take a ride?"

"I cleaned up, kid. I'll pass."

"You on that kick again? I thought you'd figured out you're wasting your time with that bullshit." He shook his head sadly, took a nip from his half-pint, and screwed the top back on. I watched to make sure he had it on tight, didn't want him to spill any. "I just seen BJ, Tony, and Gerard. They're all asking about you."

Somewhere in the back of my mind I remembered the relief that a shot of whiskey always brought, burning as it went down and warming my belly, the soothing rush of a shot of heroin, the adventure and camaraderie of going to score, and how getting strung out always boiled all my problems down to the next drink or the next fix. I was already imagining the ride on the L train out to Ridgewood, Queens, then riding back with a few bags of junk burning holes in our pockets.

Smitty had seen me through some of my worst times, but suddenly he sounded wheedling and down at the mouth with his tired old rap. I wasn't all *that* damned lonely anymore. The twelve-step crowd had embraced me again, and I knew that if I were going to get even with all the people who'd chumped me off, I'd need my wits about me. There wasn't time for Smitty and the junk scene. I was on my way over to GMHC for a good meal, and the thought of getting stoned again actually made me queasy.

"Smitty, listen. If you ever feel like going to a meeting, you know where to find me."

I didn't have to say any more than that. He turned on his heel and split. So long old partner.

There was another reason I didn't have time for Smitty—I was excited and in a hurry. Several weeks ago, just for kicks, I'd put my name into a lottery that jumped off every semester over at Gay Men's Health Crisis. If your name came up, you got to take a class, up to a thousand dollars per semester, at NYU or The New School or a number of other schools that participate. I'd won for NYU, and another little window had opened.

I was sitting in the cafeteria at GMHC that day, looking through the NYU bulletin, when one of my friends there, Richard, came up and sat down. He knew of my interest in writing, and he leaned over and pointed to a course titled, "Make Your Novel Happen."

"That's the one you should take, Steve."

"Yeah, but it says you got to have a novel in progress."

"So what? Just go have fun with it. What are they gonna do if you lie—lock you up?"

The first day in my novel-writing workshop, everybody introduced him- or herself and said how far along they were in their stories. When it got around to me, Meredith, the woman running the workshop, asked how far along I was.

"I got about a hundred pages." It was bullshit. I had nothing.

"That's great," she said. "Bring in a scene next week and we'll take a look."

I went home and whipped up a scene on my little typewriter, something I remembered from walking around Pigalle with Wilfred. Most of my classmates at NYU were women, so I wrote the most sexually explicit scene I remembered, wanting to see their reactions. This was a familiar texture, like English class back in Orléans with Miss Rich and the cheerleaders.

I brought it in and Meredith read it out loud. They wanted to see more. By the end of that semester, after bringing in a scene every other week, I found myself a third of the way into *Bop City*, a jazz novel that took place in Paris during the Algerian crisis and a story that Ron had once encouraged me to write.

As writing began to consume me the way acting had back in the eighties, it became clear that I needed to let go of all the anger and guilt, especially surrounding my sister's death. I won that lottery at GMHC twice more, but everything I tried as a writer reminded me of Ron. When I plunged into this book about the two of us, those resentments became increasingly raw because I needed details from Ron's friends about her social and professional life. I could no longer dodge the pain, and if I didn't make some fundamental change, forget about the book—I'd surely head back to the dark side when things got tough. Writing could no more effect that change in me than acting had.

Deeply troubled, I went over to meet with Bill, a friend and mentor who worked as a banker in Midtown. Bill had been sober for some twenty years, had a good marriage, and his own business. At the end of his drinking career, he'd been a quart-a-day, fall-down public drunk with no friends, family, or visible resources, but his enthusiasm for his new life was infectious.

On the ground floor of the building on Forty-fourth Street, where Bill's office was, I stopped to admire an old-fashioned shoe-repair shop and picked up a roll of Lifesavers at the newsstand next door. Competent-looking urbanites strode by in the lobby, and a vague feeling of déjà vu persisted as I rode up in the elevator.

For the next hour or so I sat in my friend's office and told him the long litany of my woes—the stealing, jails, family I'd disappointed, women I'd treated badly, fears of dying alone, my burning resentments toward certain people—right up to and including my obsession with a girl in the meeting (where I'd recently made a complete jackass of myself).

When I finished, Bill leaned back in his chair and looked at me. It felt like the look the Baptist pastor in Clearwater shot me when I told him I wanted to join his church—Bill's eyes twinkled with a similar mixture of humor and compassion.

"Steve," he said, "I know *exactly* what's wrong with you. It's spiritual neglect. And there's a simple technique that'll address that problem. I mean, why do you think they're called twelve-step meetings? Now, I can show you that method, it's no big deal, but not so you can get the girl, or win an Academy Award, or make a million bucks. What I can do for you is show you how to sponsor other guys."

"Yeah, but Bill," I whined, "I'm a wreck. How the hell am I gonna sponsor other guys? I'm lucky I can crawl outta bed and get the laundry done."

"Ferchrissake," he said, sounding suspiciously like my father. "You've been coming to meetings since 1983 and you're what—fifty-some years old? Don't you think it's about time to pull your head out of your ass and grow up?"

Here again, I was graced with a tiny window of opportunity—I was in so much pain that I had little choice but to follow his lead. Besides, he was buying lunch.

Bill was as good as his word. Though overworked and rarely able to spend time with the wife he so obviously adored (they'd been married only a year), he put his own troubles aside to meet me several hours a week and show me the day-to-day technique he'd learned from his sponsor—basically, clean house, trust God, and help others. It required some work and practice on my part, but in a few months I was already taking some new guy through the same process. And I've never stopped passing it along since.

It's been over eight years now. My attempts to help other guys, some crazier than I had been, were not always successful and would take another book to describe, but the rewards were irrefutable—the noise in my head slowly vanished along with the black hole in my gut, and those things I'd been so ashamed of became a gold mine of information for helping guys who'd done the same. One of the few times I'd been truly happy was when I'd tried, albeit ineptly, to help Dad in his last days. The simple formula of substituting my insatiable neediness with helpfulness had been right under my nose all along, and so obvious—why the hell had I never learned or tried it? A favorite line from Hemingway's *Death in the Afternoon* came to mind: "There are some things which cannot be learned quickly and time, which is all we have, must be paid heavily for their acquiring. They are the very simplest things."

When I left Bill's office that first day, I stopped at the exit onto Forty-fourth Street and noticed the plaque riveted to the brick wall just outside the door.

LITERARY LANDMARK

The New Yorker magazine, a leading weekly journal of humor, commentary, and reviews founded in 1925 two blocks north of this site, occupied several floors of this building from 1935 to 1991. Often present on the premises were writers E. B. White, James Thurber, John

Cheever, John Updike, Geoffrey Hellman, Brendan Gill, Joseph Mitchell, A. J. Liebling, and Calvin Trillin; cartoonists Charles Addams, Peter Arno, Sam Cobean, Whitney Darrow, Jr., Robert Day, Helen Hokinson, Henry Martin, Frank Modell, William Steig, Mary Petty, George Price, Saul Steinberg, Jim Stevenson, and R. Taylor; the magazine's founding editor, Harold Ross, and his successor William Shawn. Characteristic of the magazine was a suspicion of advanced technology; its lease required that at least one manually operated elevator be kept in service at all times.

It was the very same building where Veronica had worked. I remembered stopping to get Lifesavers at that same newsstand in the lobby the day the feds brought me there from Manhattan Correctional Center and how Ron's suggestion to go stay with Dad in Florida had sent my life in another direction. I'd come around full cycle and stood in the exact same building, only now it was my sponsor's workplace.

For the next few weeks I put aside the monologues for the girl at the morning meeting and vengeful sniping scenarios. Instead, I tuned in WBGO, stretched out in bed, and went back over my life with a slightly new perspective.

I thought of that day in Philly when Ronnie and I first heard about moving to Europe: I was going around saying good-bye to old friends along Nedro Avenue, and I recalled how lush the trees were along our block, and how cool and sheltered I felt in their shade; neighbors walked their dogs, sipped tea on front porches, and girls passing by gave me the glad-eye. I remembered the spiffy cars parked along our street, Chevy Bel Airs with forward-tilting noses, new blue and white Ford Fairlanes like Uncle Bill's, jazzy Oldsmobile 88s with low, oval mouthlike grilles hungering to eat up the road (I was pretty good with cars), their owners washing them with garden hoses and as I passed they sprayed me good-naturedly. Behind the facade of every place in our neighborhood dwelt mysterious people I wanted to get to know, and I regretted that I wouldn't have the chance. I was walking around Philly thinking, Whoa, what a great town!

Parallel to my memories of a worrisome childhood—the fights between Ron and Dad, and my attraction to trouble—ran a texture of sweetness I hadn't noticed, as though another dimension now peeked through a rent in the fabric of the "real" one.

Allowing myself to slip back into those old scenes, I realized how much love there'd been in our house in Olney, all those Christmas mornings when Ron and I came down to see our tree all lit up in the exact same place, next to the stairs between the living and dining rooms, a rumpled white sheet spread underneath, like snow sparkling with gaily wrapped packages. Mom and Dad, if nothing else, had been completely reliable. We were never lacking for presents, and every holiday our house was filled with the aroma of Mom cooking a big roast in the oven.

I was lying in my room one night and an oldies show came on WBGO. Immediately I pictured our old phonograph in Philly, balanced precariously on top of the new television in the living room, a reminder of the days when we used to listen to music together as a family. A thick cylinder stood up from the turntable, reflecting Ronnie's and my obsession with current 45s and the impact of *American Bandstand*. But Mom and Dad had their favorites too, like Mario Lanza singing songs from *The Student Prince*. We all loved the soundtrack from the movie version of *Guys and Dolls* with Brando and Sinatra, and I never lost my infatuation with the characters in those great Damon Runyon stories.

There'd been early evenings before Dad came home when I'd wander into the kitchen and catch Mom engrossed at the table, cutting up string beans while she hummed along softly to Nat King Cole on the radio, cigarette smoke curling up from an ashtray and a Manhattan with a cherry, her favorite drink, sitting on a napkin by her elbow. At those times Mom had a younger, slightly melancholy look on her face, and I'd glimpse the romantic soul in her, dreaming perhaps of a more glamorous life, like the one she might've had with her first husband. But she was never stingy with her love for us. There were times when we were home from school with the flu, the aroma of Vicks VapoRub hanging in the air like incense, and Mom would sit on our beds and read to us from a book called *When We Were Very Young*, her face soft in the bedroom shadows and her carefully modulated voice filling me with warmth as it rose and fell with the nuances of the story.

As my hard-boiled veneer began to crack, I felt like I was going nuts, lying in bed, mumbling into the dark: "Mom, I'm sorry for all the trouble I caused you and Dad."

And the images kept swirling back, of weekend afternoons when we played Scrabble. Ron always won and flaunted it, so I used to get a kick out of Dad's bluffs.

"Aw, whatta you mean *fazoot* isn't a word? Of course it's a word. Where the hell did you kids learn English anyway?"

"Let's hear it in a sentence."

"I give-a you fifty cents—fazoot!"

And Dad, who'd been so irascible when we were kids, I could see him hunched over his ancient Underwood typewriter for hours peering through spectacles as he typed up forms in triplicate, seated in the chair at his scarred old desk. He used to spend hours there polishing his belt buckles and insignias with Brasso and an old T-shirt, his moodiness somehow deepened by all those years of inspections on ships' decks and parade grounds across the globe. Sometimes he'd spread out newspapers and shine his shoes, falling into a hypnotic rhythm while I sat at the dining room table watching him, impressed with his dedication to the tiniest details of his job. Mom, probably influenced again by her Spock reading, had made Dad at one point get "more involved" in my life, so he became, very briefly, a Cub Scout leader and even took me fishing at Tookany Creek. We never caught anything, and his attempts to teach me how to throw a knuckleball were equally uninformed and awkward, but I had to admit—he gave it a shot.

You only get one family in a lifetime, and if you don't make an effort to know and love them, the legacy of their stories vanishes with them. I'd never told my family how sorry I was that I hadn't been a better son and brother, especially my mother who rarely saw me have a sober day once I got beyond my teens.

Eventually, my take on Veronica's literary friends shifted, although when I tried to get in touch with them, few called back, certainly none of the men she'd had affairs with. They probably sensed the crosshairs zeroing in as they listened to my voice on their answering machines. I could hardly blame the writers, who had their own books to write, and I appreciated that the men she'd known were at least of the "kiss but don't tell" school. I remembered the wake and funeral that James Hamilton and Philip Roth had put together, something I certainly couldn't have done, much less afforded, and what an amazing demonstration it was of the love and respect that my sister had engendered in all those people. Who knows how lonely Ron would've been without them? Sure, I was pissed that, among other things, they hadn't told me she was sick, but I didn't care about inheriting my sister's money, and life was too damned short to waste on sniping and strangling people in my sleep.

When I got in touch with my sister's women friends, like Dita and Ruth, they made me understand how mightily Ron suffered at the end, being at the mercy of others after a lifetime of fierce independence. Dita told me that Ron's writer friends weren't returning my calls because Veronica had treated them so horribly. My sister, she went on, compartmentalized people, and always had the ability to cut people out of her life if they didn't meet her notion of how things worked.

"Veronica," Dita said, "was a monster!" This from a woman who'd loved my sister and who'd been reluctant to talk to me, not wanting to speak unkindly of the dead. I wasn't sure whether to laugh at that one or cry. Good old Dita. She sure didn't mince words, and that's exactly what my sister had loved about her. But hey, it's not like Ronnie was clocking people over the head with claw hammers or torching them with lighter fluid. She was definitely no saint, and as far as I'm concerned we're all driven at times by a terrible lust for fame, fortune, and romance, harboring envy and betrayal in our fierce little monster hearts. Who knows how many years my sister had been affected by that crippling brain tumor? To cut her brother and others out of her life under that kind of duress was no more indicative of who she was than my contracting AIDS defines who I am today.

Unfortunately, that shift in perception was no magic wand that lifted my sorrow. It was a cross I'd just have to bear, and for all I know it may never go away. But I did notice that it lightened with time, and with my commitment to another way of living. That year or two when Ronnie cut off all communication with me was no longer a raw wound but her parting gift, an unresolved longing that could not be mended, except perhaps through the labor and love of writing.

Which brings me to this final, favorite memory of Veronica at her best, a moment when, infused with the love of her craft, she thanked me for my humble contribution to a piece she was working on (suggesting a name for the trombone player) by cooking me dinner and taking me to a movie. I was sober at the time, which was just before Tina Brown showed up at the *New Yorker*.

She stood up from her typewriter, happy with the character's name (Curtis, after the beloved Curtis Fuller), and said to me, "I've been dying to see this movie about Monk that Clint Eastwood did. It's playing down at the Greenwich, Steve. What do you say?"

It was a no-brainer. I could hardly get enough of Monk, movies, or my sister.

Veronica was not only in good spirits, but looked more attractive than I'd ever seen her. Maybe it was the salt-and-pepper thing in her hair, but eclipsing her physical charms was a particular glow she exuded whenever she found the key to some writing problem.

After we polished off chicken cutlets and steamed veggies that she made, she took an overcoat out of a closet and pulled it on, smirking at me as she buttoned it up to the neck. It was an old Harris Tweed with raglan sleeves that I'd found in a thrift shop, and then let her wear when I caught her admiring it. At first she'd worn it with the sleeves rolled up, showing several inches of silk lining for cuffs (Veronica had a way of receiving gifts—she paraded around in that thing like I'd given her a mink coat), but when I saw her put it on for the movies I noticed that she'd shortened the sleeves and moved the buttons. So much for ever getting my coat back. I pulled on my own coat and off we went to the movies.

One thing Ronnie and I'd always shared was our fondness for Thelonious Sphere Monk. We loved everything about him—the goofy spin he put on old standards, the poignant combination of blues, quirky humor, and faultless instinct for composition. Clearly, the guy was a genius.

That night we sat watching the movie with tears rolling down our cheeks while Monk, suffering the bizarre side effects of a brain tumor, shuffled around in little circles mumbling to himself, almost a dance, as though responding to some inner rhythm that could not be repressed. All the while his wife patiently packed their bags for a road gig, helped him put on his clothes, bought the plane tickets, and ordered the food. On the soundtrack over those scenes was Monk doing a solo version of "I Should Care," slowly, tenderly, each note wobbling against your funny bone and fumbling at your heart. Someone once told me that Monk could "bend" the notes on a piano—like when you stretch the strings on a guitar—which seems an impossible feat since the keys are fixed. But you could hear him do it on a ballad, searching in between the keys until he'd coaxed the piano to some strange new place, and doing it in spite of his misfortune.

I used to think that Monk, like my other jazz heroes, was an addict and a lush, and that he behaved the way he did because he was stoned. But he wasn't. He, like my sister, had a brain tumor, and both his music and my sister's writing kept coming out of them in entirely unique ways.

Roger Angell nailed it when he later said to me: "When people as different as Veronica come along, Steve, everything changes. Veronica changed American humor because there was nobody like her. Your sister," he said, "was so passionate about the work she did here she changed all of us."

At one point in the movie, during a close-up of Monk's hands and fingers jumping around the keyboard, Ronnie leaned over and whispered: "That's what I want to do with writing, Steve." She laughed softly at the idea, her eyes still moist. "I try to, but I'm not quite that good."

I remember wanting to stroke her forehead when she'd said that, to smooth out the wrinkles of doubt, to run my hand over her hair and reassure her that she'd been writing like that all along. But now I'm glad I didn't. Otherwise she might not have then leaned her head on my shoulder and gifted me with a few trusting, blissful moments—before she slyly reached over and stole a handful of my popcorn.

acknowledgments

First thanks to George Hodgman, my editor at Holt, who encouraged me to write this brother-sister story before I even considered it myself. I owe much to Roger Angell and Chip McGrath, who, since I knew little about Veronica's life at the *New Yorker* when I began this book, let me tape an interview with them about their history with her. Next guy to step to the plate was Bob Gottlieb, who agreed to read an early draft, devoured all four hundred pages in one night, and responded with such enthusiasm that soon publishers and agents were calling *me*. Chip McGrath reacted with similar enthusiasm and sent the book to his agent friend David Mc-Cormick, who volunteered to represent me. These guys all knew Veronica, who seemed to be helping me from the grave. Ron's writer friend James McCourt encouraged me throughout and was such a fan of the project that he even let me steal a line of his own father's dialogue: "They should pour this stuff back into the horse." Roy Blount offered his sage advice early on, and much of this book was written in appreciation for, and dedicated to, everyone who ever loved my sister

Author's note: The only things fictitious in this story are the names of several characters. In order of appearance, they are Lorraine, Stella (and the name of her saloon, Stella's), Sean, Nick, and Laura. Everybody else is who I said they were, and they all did and said the things I herein described and remembered, may they forgive me. The dialogue is mostly from memory and subject to the tricks memory can play. But I have worked hard to ensure that all dialogue is true to each character's intentions and style. If some writers feel the need to exaggerate to make their stories compelling, I had to tone mine down. I mean, *I* can hardly believe I survived all this.

STEVE GENG lives in New York City.